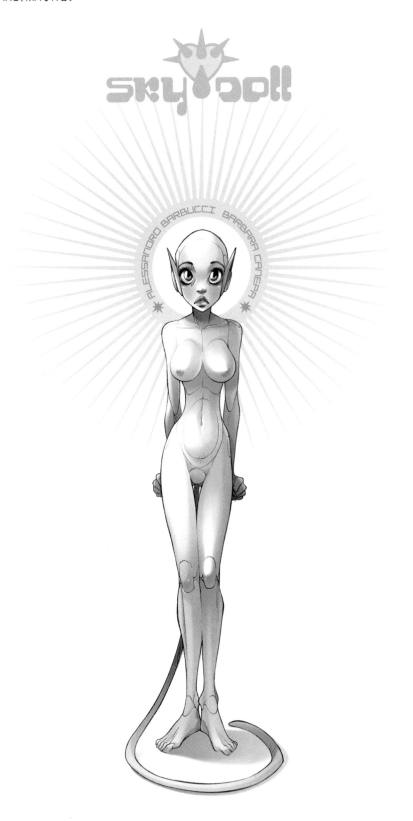

sky doll

ALESSANDRO BARBUCCI BARBARA CANEPA

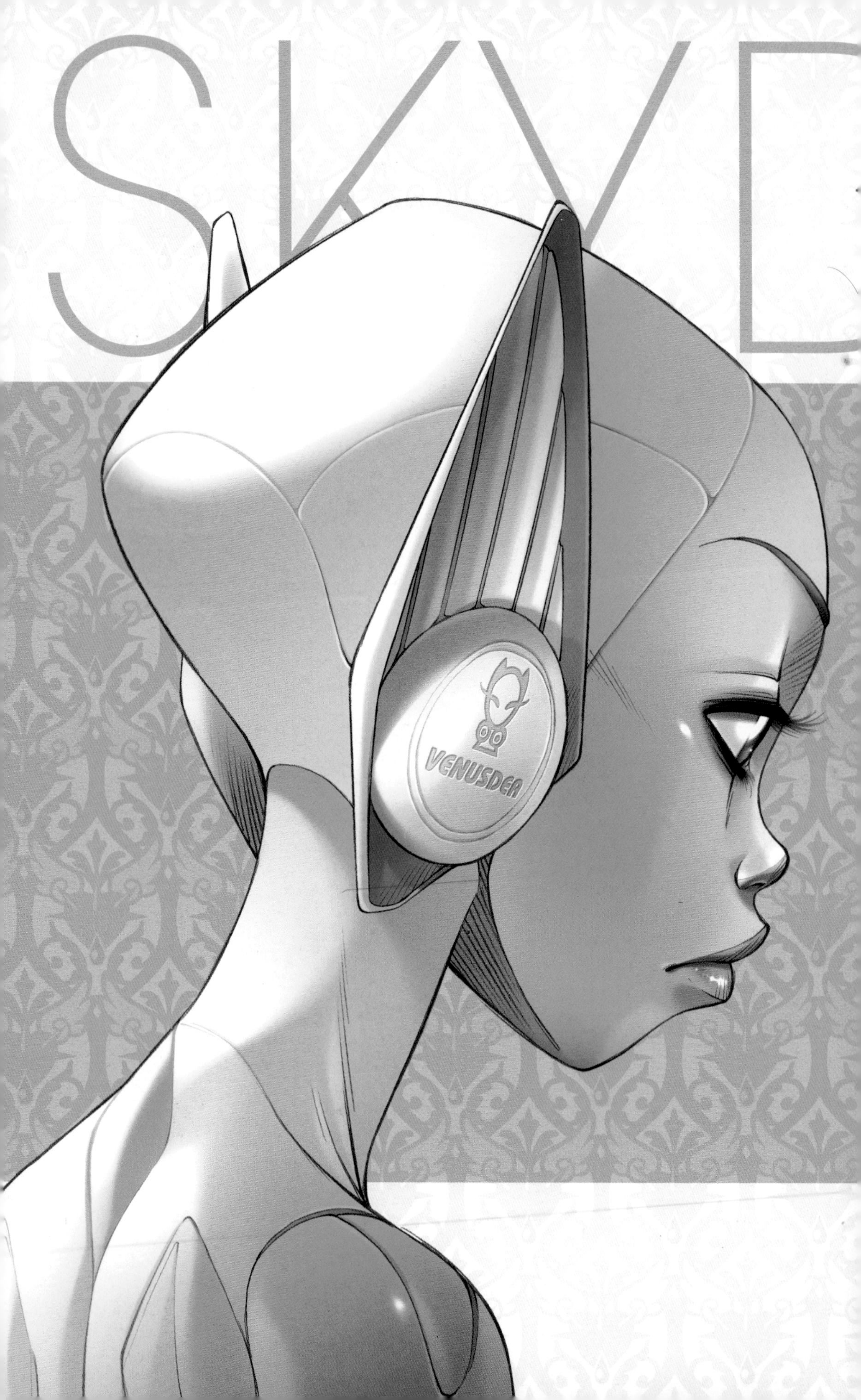
SKYD
VENUSDEA

STORY, ART AND COLORS:
ALESSANDRO BARBUCCI & BARBARA CANEPA

ADAPTATION: **C.B. CEBULSKI**
LETTERING: **JOE CARAMAGNA**
TRANSLATION: **STEPHANIE LOGAN** & **MATTEO CASALI**

SPECIAL THANKS TO **RUWAN JAYATILLEKE**

FOR SOLEIL:
MANAGING EDITOR: **OLIVIER JALABERT**
EDITOR IN CHIEF: **JEAN WACQUET**
PUBLISHER: **MOURAD BOUDJELLAL**

FOR MARVEL:
COLLECTION EDITOR: **CORY LEVINE**
EDITORIAL ASSISTANT: **ALEX STARBUCK**
ASSISTANT EDITOR: **JOHN DENNING**
EDITORS, SPECIAL PROJECTS: **JENNIFER GRÜNWALD** & **MARK D. BEAZLEY**
SENIOR EDITOR, SPECIAL PROJECTS: **JEFF YOUNGQUIST**
SENIOR VICE PRESIDENT OF SALES: **DAVID GABRIEL**
BOOK DESIGN: **RODOLFO MURAGUCHI AND MATTEO DE LONGIS**
& STUDIO SOLEIL
EDITOR IN CHIEF: **JOE QUESADA**
PUBLISHER: **DAN BUCKLEY**

SKY DOLL. Contains material originally published in magazine form as SKY DOLL #1-3. First printing 2008. ISBN# 978-0-7851-3236-3. Published by MARVEL PUBLISHING, INC., a subsidiary of MARVEL ENTERTAINMENT, INC. OFFICE OF PUBLICATION: 417 5th Avenue, New York, NY 10016. SKYDOLL and its logos are © 2008 MC PRODUCTIONS/CANEPA/BARBUCCI. Marvel and its logos are TM & © 2008 Marvel Characters, Inc. All rights reserved. $24.99 per copy in the U.S. and $26.50 in Canada (GST #R127032852); Canadian Agreement #40668537. All characters featured in this issue and the distinctive names and likenesses thereof, and all related indicia are trademarks of the respective copyright holders, listed above. No similarity between any of the names, characters, persons, and/or institutions in this magazine with those of any living or dead person or institution is intended, and any such similarity which may exist is purely coincidental. **Printed in the U.S.A.** ALAN FINE, CEO Marvel Toys & Publishing Divisions and CMO Marvel Entertainment, Inc.; DAVID GABRIEL, SVP of Publishing Sales & Circulation; DAVID BOGART, SVP of Business Affairs & Talent Management; MICHAEL PASCIULLO, VP of Merchandising & Communications; JIM O'KEEFE, VP of Operations & Logistics; DAN CARR, Executive Director of Publishing Technology; JUSTIN F. GABRIE, Director of Editorial Operations; SUSAN CRESPI, Editorial Operations Manager; OMAR OTIEKU, Production Manager; STAN LEE, Chairman Emeritus. For information regarding advertising in Marvel Comics or on Marvel.com, please contact Mitch Dane, Advertising Director, at mdane@marvel.com. For Marvel subscription inquiries, please call 800-217-9158.

10 9 8 7 6 5 4 3 2 1

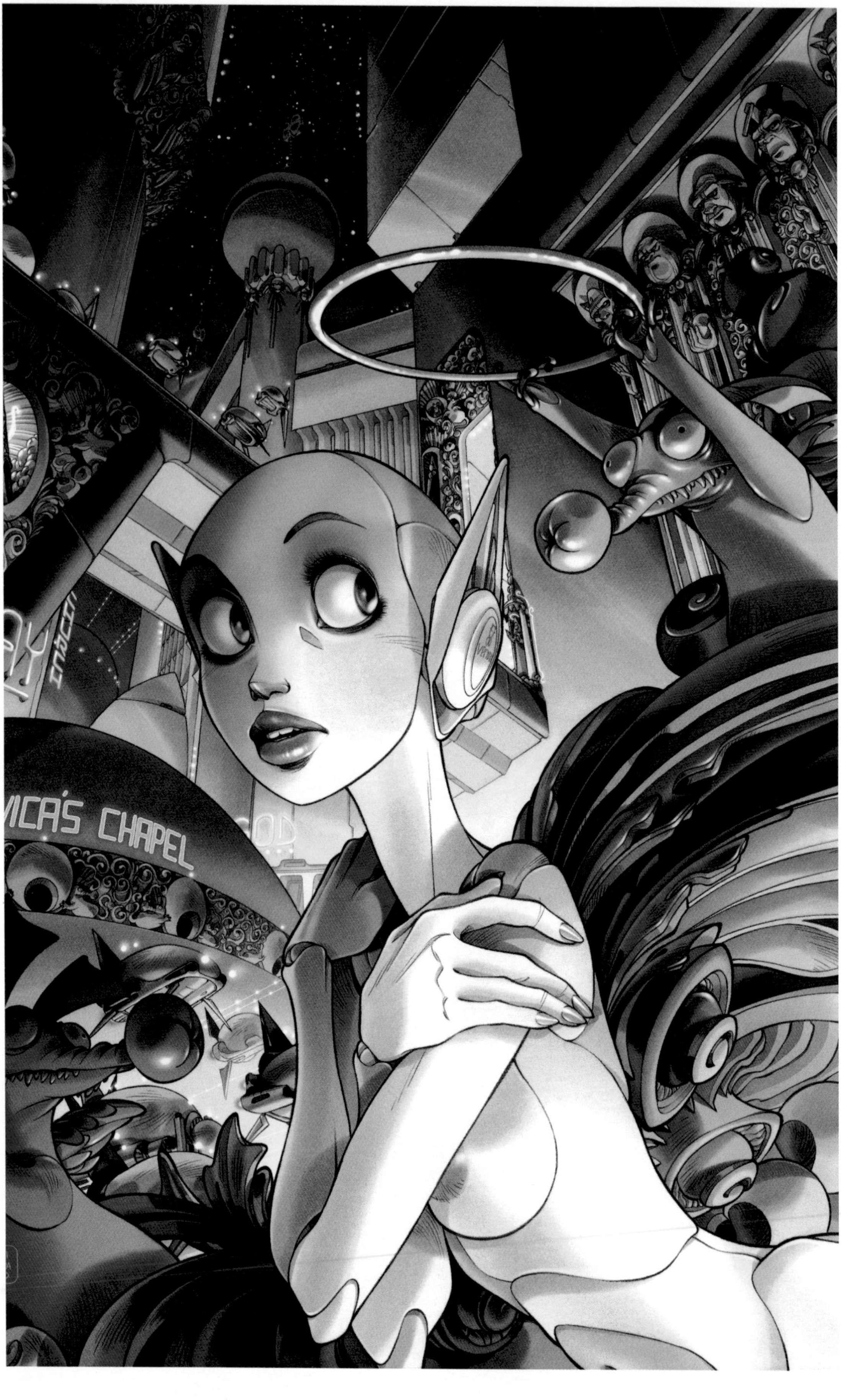
VICA'S CHAPEL

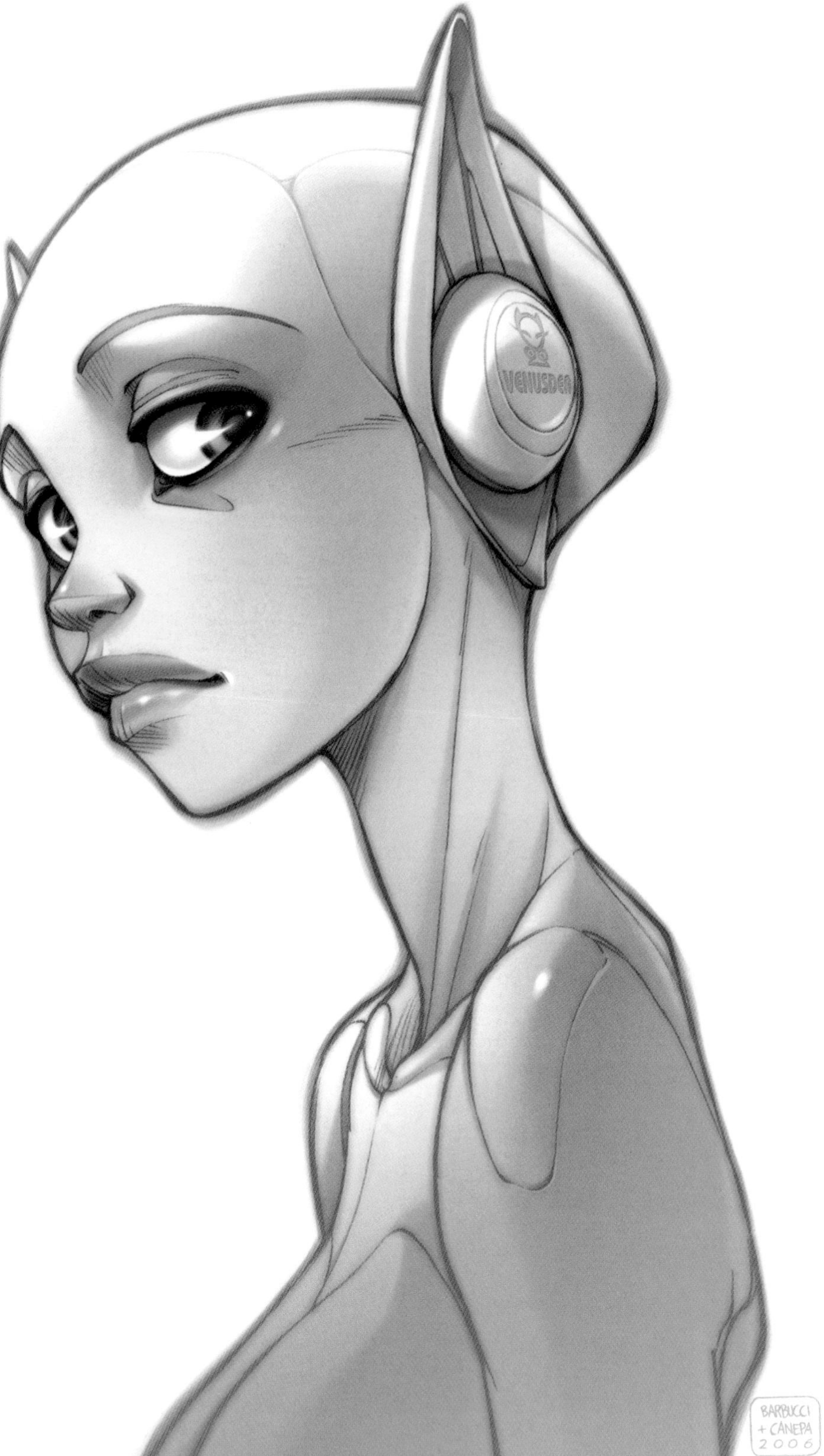
VENUSDEA
BARBUCCI
+ CANEPA
2006

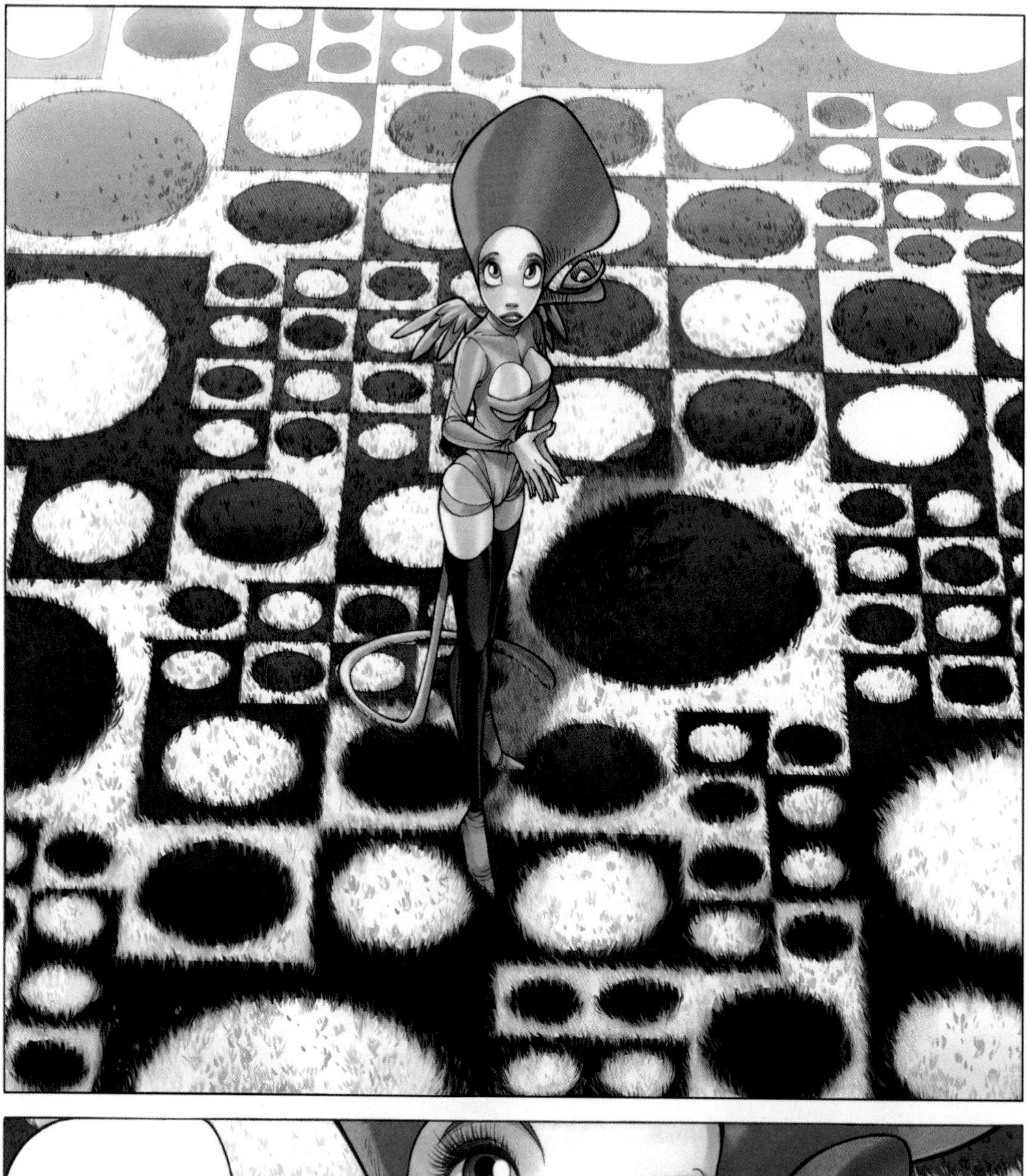

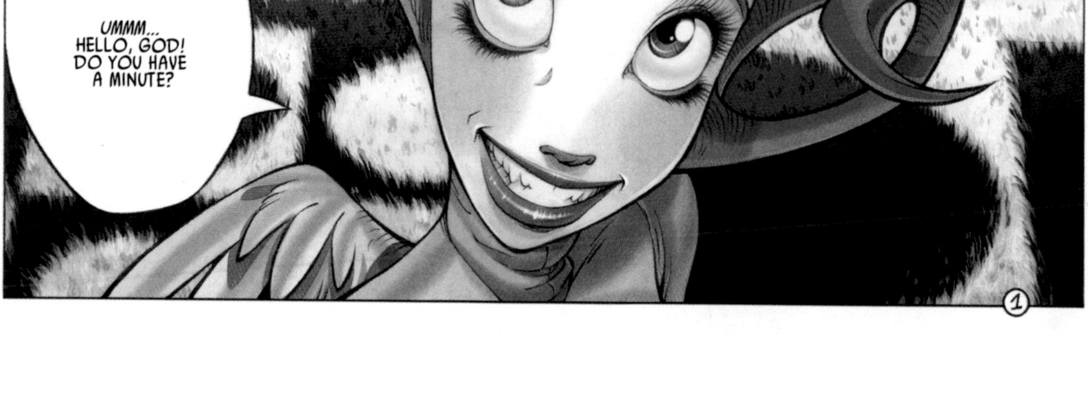
UMMM... HELLO, GOD! DO YOU HAVE A MINUTE?

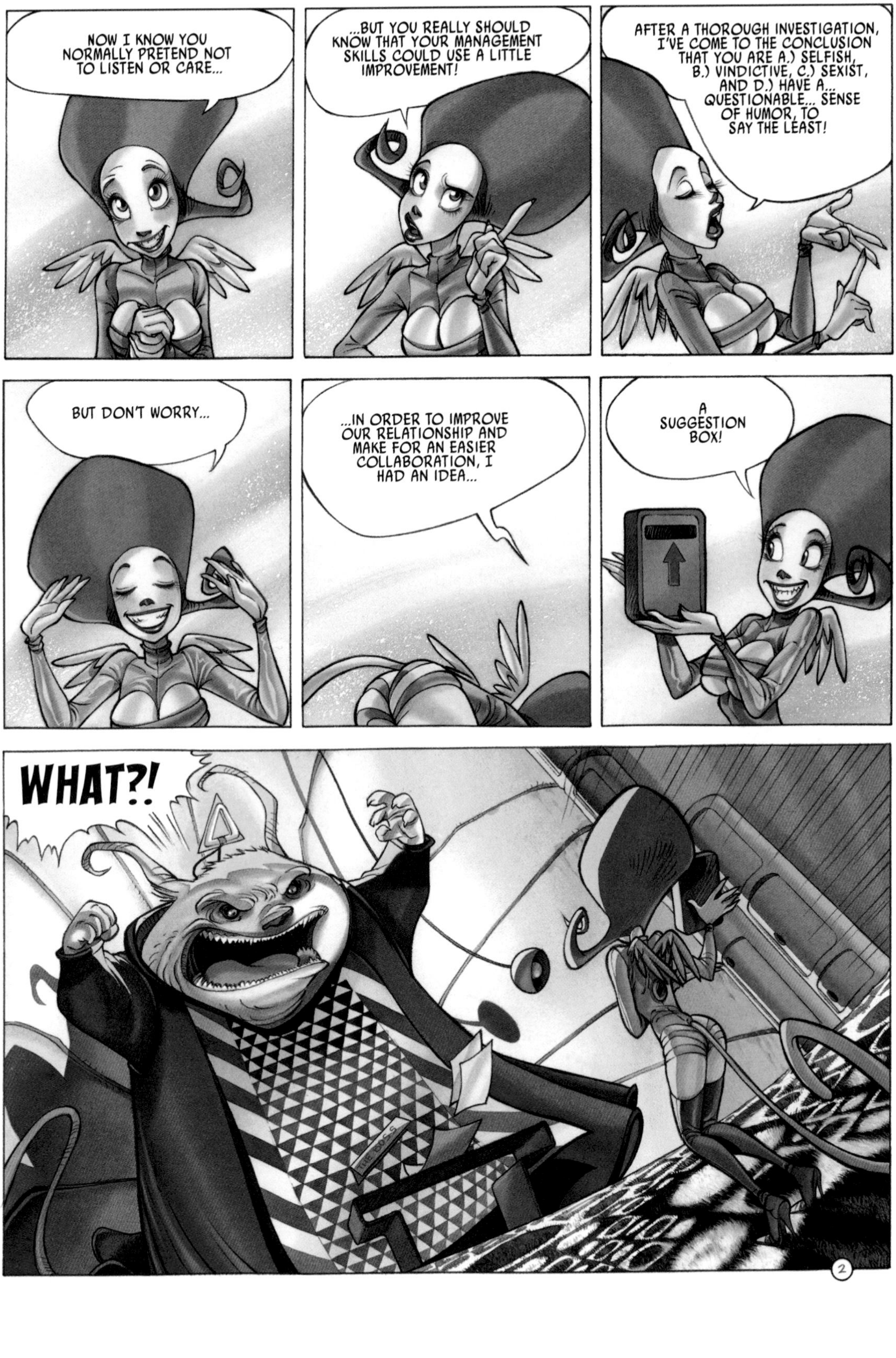
NOW I KNOW YOU NORMALLY PRETEND NOT TO LISTEN OR CARE...
...BUT YOU REALLY SHOULD KNOW THAT YOUR MANAGEMENT SKILLS COULD USE A LITTLE IMPROVEMENT!
AFTER A THOROUGH INVESTIGATION, I'VE COME TO THE CONCLUSION THAT YOU ARE A.) SELFISH, B.) VINDICTIVE, C.) SEXIST, AND D.) HAVE A... QUESTIONABLE... SENSE OF HUMOR, TO SAY THE LEAST!
BUT DON'T WORRY...
...IN ORDER TO IMPROVE OUR RELATIONSHIP AND MAKE FOR AN EASIER COLLABORATION, I HAD AN IDEA...
A SUGGESTION BOX!
WHAT?!

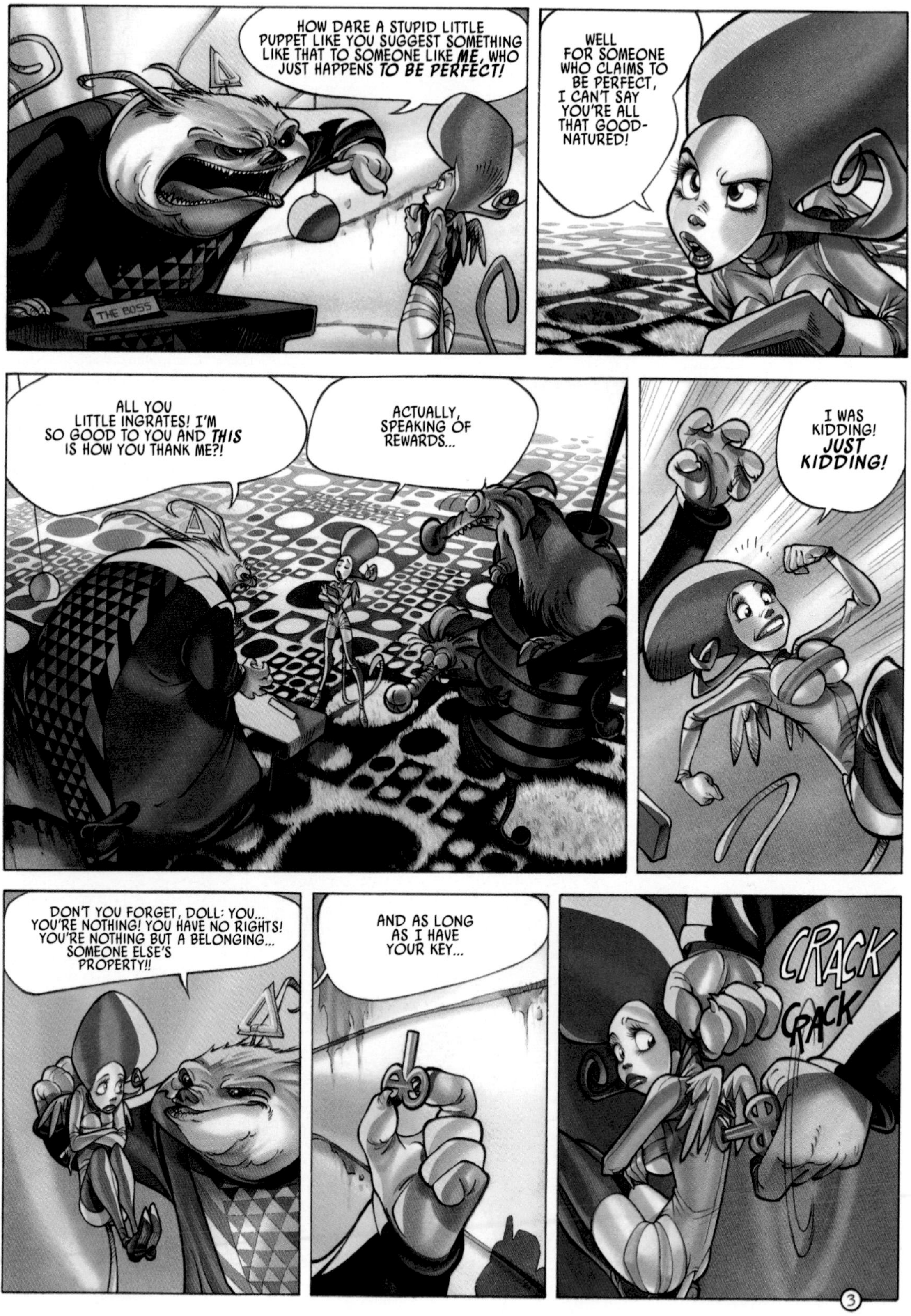
HOW DARE A STUPID LITTLE PUPPET LIKE YOU SUGGEST SOMETHING LIKE THAT TO SOMEONE LIKE ME, WHO JUST HAPPENS TO BE PERFECT!
THE BOSS
WELL FOR SOMEONE WHO CLAIMS TO BE PERFECT, I CAN'T SAY YOU'RE ALL THAT GOOD-NATURED!
ALL YOU LITTLE INGRATES! I'M SO GOOD TO YOU AND THIS IS HOW YOU THANK ME?!
ACTUALLY, SPEAKING OF REWARDS...
I WAS KIDDING! JUST KIDDING!
DON'T YOU FORGET, DOLL: YOU... YOU'RE NOTHING! YOU HAVE NO RIGHTS! YOU'RE NOTHING BUT A BELONGING... SOMEONE ELSE'S PROPERTY!!
AND AS LONG AS I HAVE YOUR KEY...
CRACK
CRACK

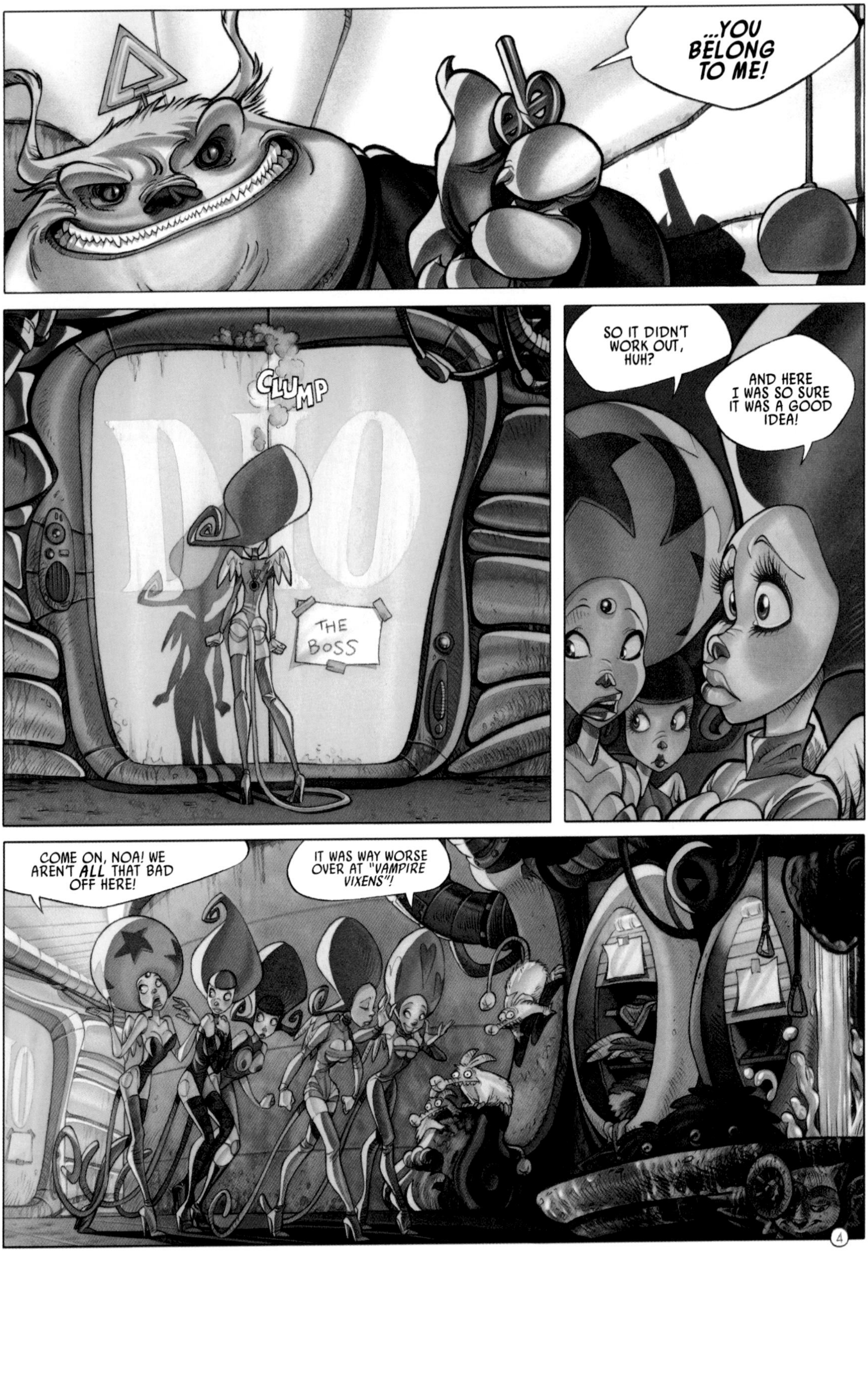
...YOU BELONG TO ME!
CLUMP
DIO
THE BOSS
SO IT DIDN'T WORK OUT, HUH?
AND HERE I WAS SO SURE IT WAS A GOOD IDEA!
COME ON, NOA! WE AREN'T ALL THAT BAD OFF HERE!
IT WAS WAY WORSE OVER AT "VAMPIRE VIXENS"!

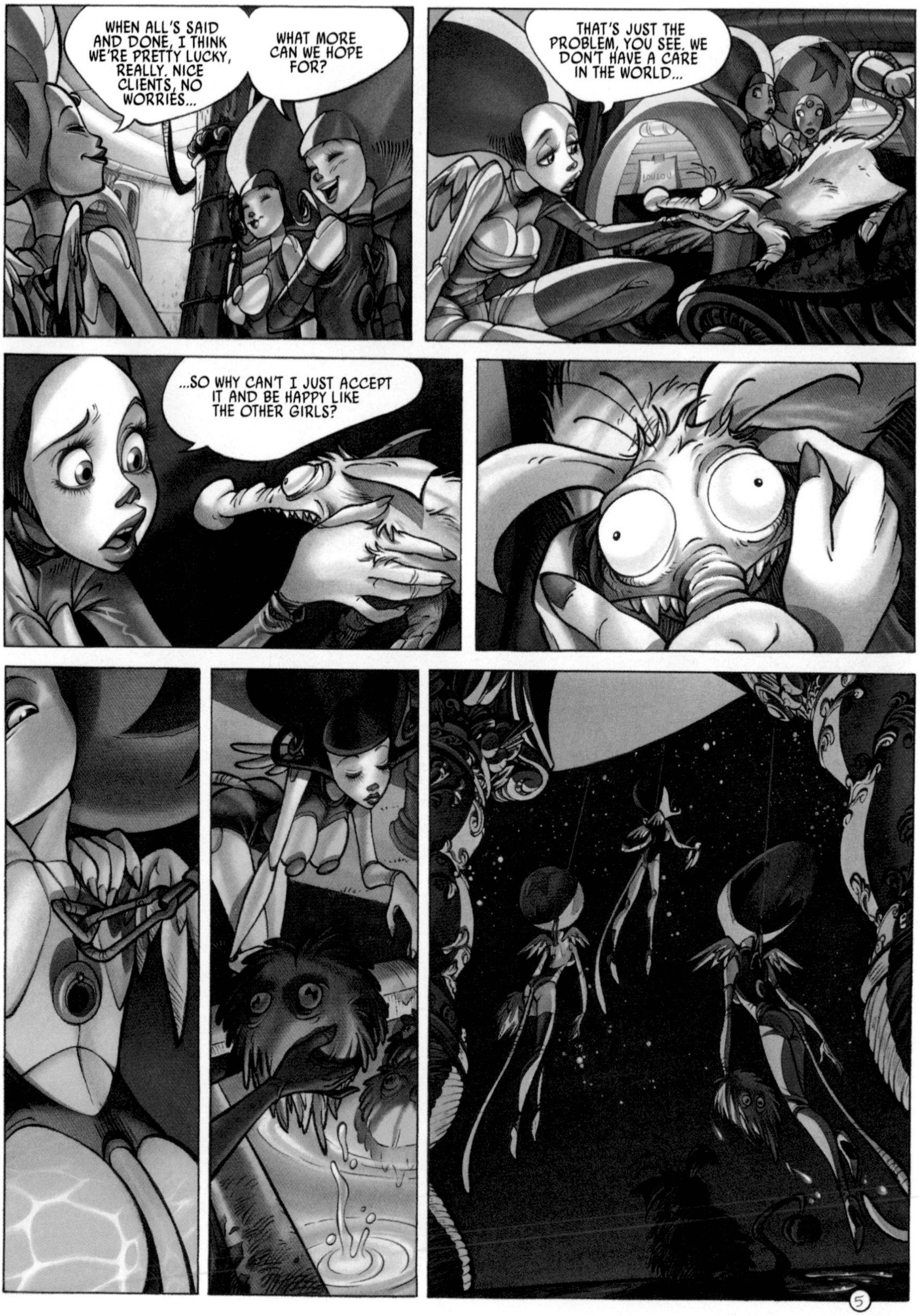

WHEN ALL'S SAID AND DONE, I THINK WE'RE PRETTY LUCKY, REALLY. NICE CLIENTS, NO WORRIES...
WHAT MORE CAN WE HOPE FOR?
THAT'S JUST THE PROBLEM, YOU SEE. WE DON'T HAVE A CARE IN THE WORLD...
...SO WHY CAN'T I JUST ACCEPT IT AND BE HAPPY LIKE THE OTHER GIRLS?

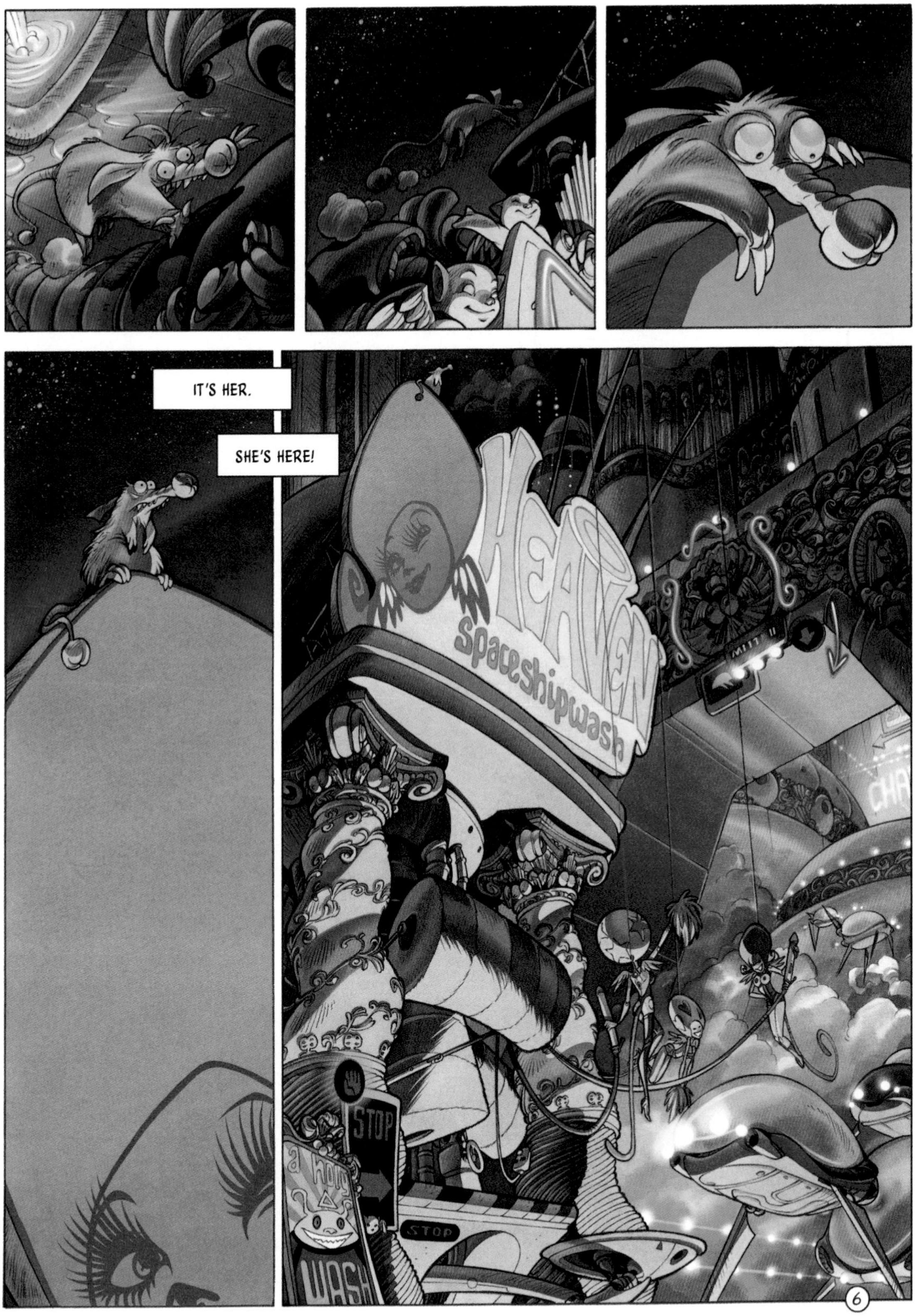
IT'S HER.
SHE'S HERE!
HEAVEN
spaceshipwash
STOP
STOP
WASH

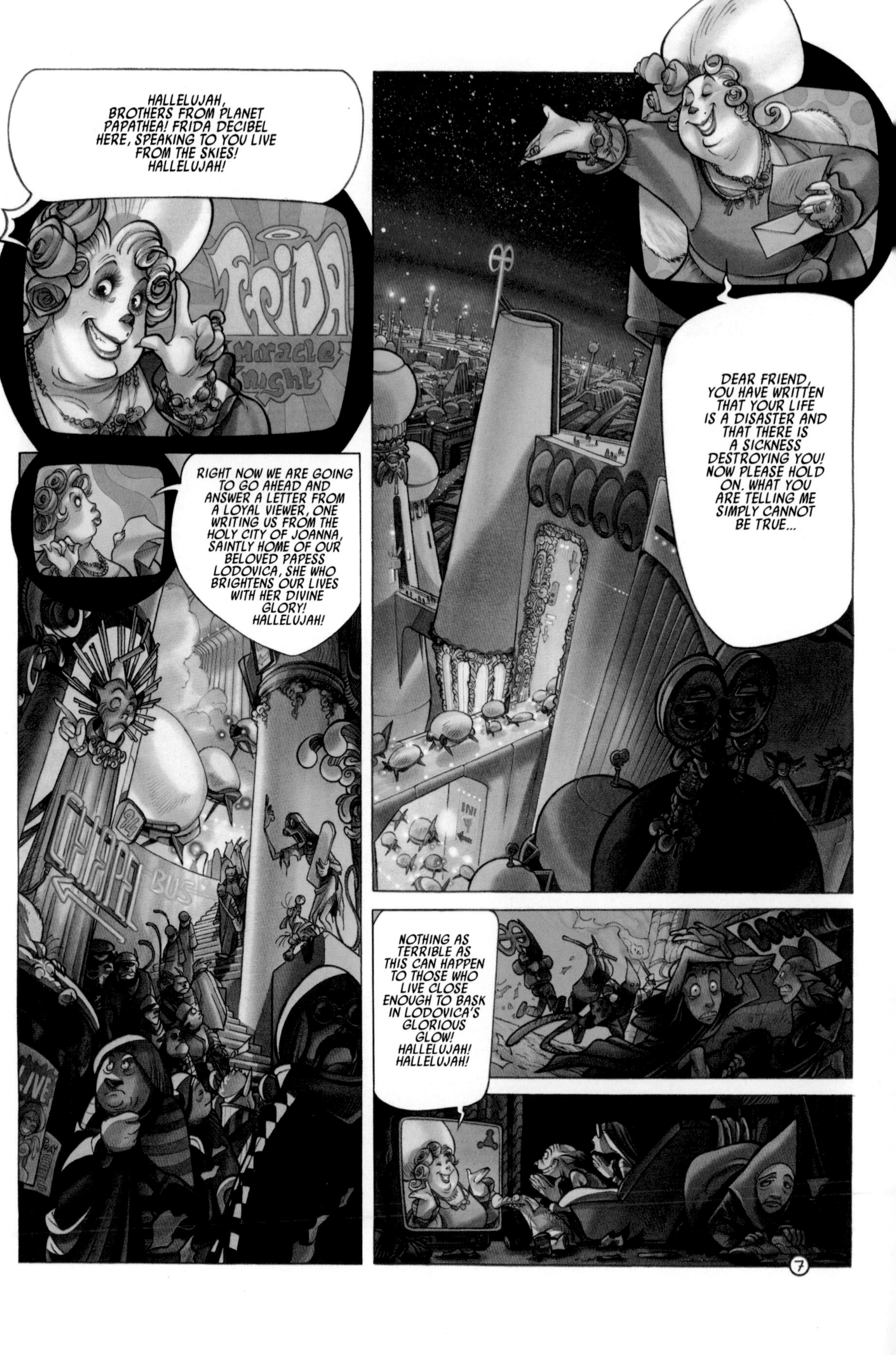
HALLELUJAH, BROTHERS FROM PLANET PAPATHEA! FRIDA DECIBEL HERE, SPEAKING TO YOU LIVE FROM THE SKIES! HALLELUJAH!
FRIDA
Miracle Night
RIGHT NOW WE ARE GOING TO GO AHEAD AND ANSWER A LETTER FROM A LOYAL VIEWER, ONE WRITING US FROM THE HOLY CITY OF JOANNA, SAINTLY HOME OF OUR BELOVED PAPESS LODOVICA, SHE WHO BRIGHTENS OUR LIVES WITH HER DIVINE GLORY! HALLELUJAH!
BUS
LIVE
DEAR FRIEND, YOU HAVE WRITTEN THAT YOUR LIFE IS A DISASTER AND THAT THERE IS A SICKNESS DESTROYING YOU! NOW PLEASE HOLD ON. WHAT YOU ARE TELLING ME SIMPLY CANNOT BE TRUE...
NOTHING AS TERRIBLE AS THIS CAN HAPPEN TO THOSE WHO LIVE CLOSE ENOUGH TO BASK IN LODOVICA'S GLORIOUS GLOW! HALLELUJAH! HALLELUJAH!

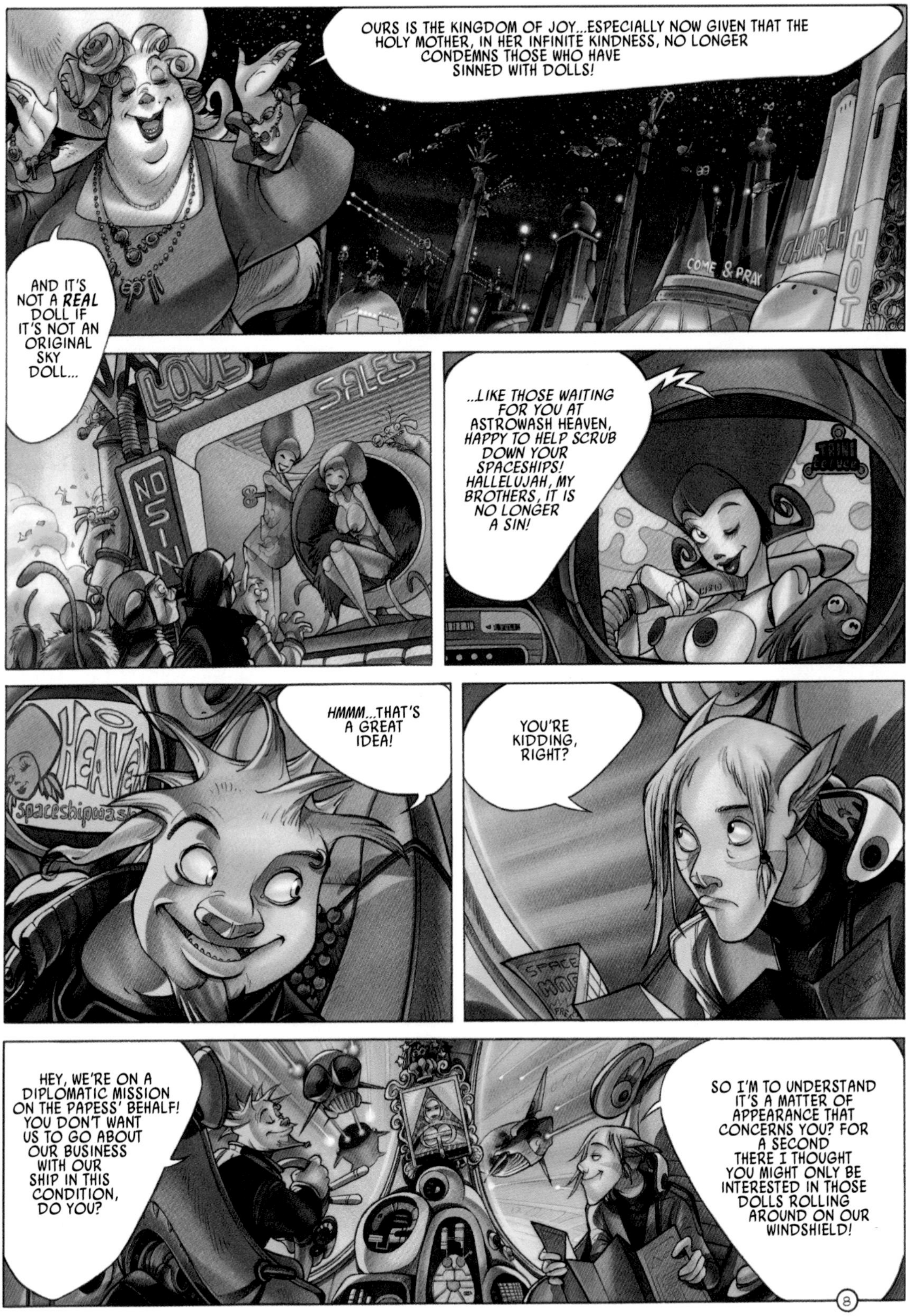
OURS IS THE KINGDOM OF JOY...ESPECIALLY NOW GIVEN THAT THE HOLY MOTHER, IN HER INFINITE KINDNESS, NO LONGER CONDEMNS THOSE WHO HAVE SINNED WITH DOLLS!
COME & PRAY
CHURCH
HOT
AND IT'S NOT A *REAL* DOLL IF IT'S NOT AN ORIGINAL SKY DOLL...
LOVE
SALES
NO SIN
...LIKE THOSE WAITING FOR YOU AT ASTROWASH HEAVEN, HAPPY TO HELP SCRUB DOWN YOUR SPACESHIPS! HALLELUJAH, MY BROTHERS, IT IS NO LONGER A SIN!
HEAVEN
spaceshipwash
HMMM...THAT'S A GREAT IDEA!
YOU'RE KIDDING, RIGHT?
HEY, WE'RE ON A DIPLOMATIC MISSION ON THE PAPESS' BEHALF! YOU DON'T WANT US TO GO ABOUT OUR BUSINESS WITH OUR SHIP IN THIS CONDITION, DO YOU?
SO I'M TO UNDERSTAND IT'S A MATTER OF APPEARANCE THAT CONCERNS YOU? FOR A SECOND THERE I THOUGHT YOU MIGHT ONLY BE INTERESTED IN THOSE DOLLS ROLLING AROUND ON OUR WINDSHIELD!

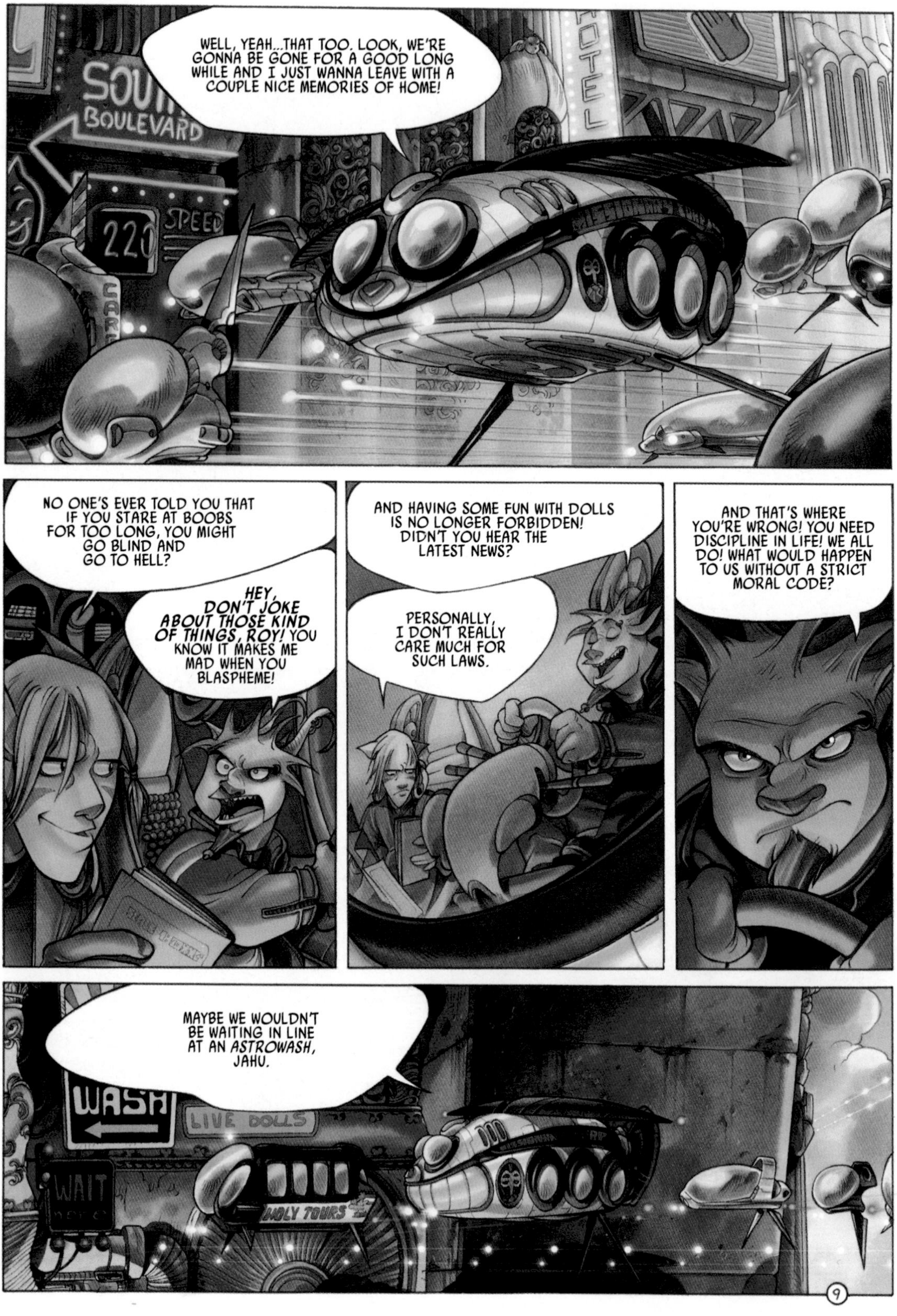
WELL, YEAH...THAT TOO. LOOK, WE'RE GONNA BE GONE FOR A GOOD LONG WHILE AND I JUST WANNA LEAVE WITH A COUPLE NICE MEMORIES OF HOME!
BOULEVARD
220
SPEED
NO ONE'S EVER TOLD YOU THAT IF YOU STARE AT BOOBS FOR TOO LONG, YOU MIGHT GO BLIND AND GO TO HELL?
HEY, DON'T JOKE ABOUT THOSE KIND OF THINGS, ROY! YOU KNOW IT MAKES ME MAD WHEN YOU BLASPHEME!
AND HAVING SOME FUN WITH DOLLS IS NO LONGER FORBIDDEN! DIDN'T YOU HEAR THE LATEST NEWS?
PERSONALLY, I DON'T REALLY CARE MUCH FOR SUCH LAWS.
AND THAT'S WHERE YOU'RE WRONG! YOU NEED DISCIPLINE IN LIFE! WE ALL DO! WHAT WOULD HAPPEN TO US WITHOUT A STRICT MORAL CODE?
MAYBE WE WOULDN'T BE WAITING IN LINE AT AN ASTROWASH, JAHU.
WASH
LIVE DOLLS
WAIT
HOLY TOURS

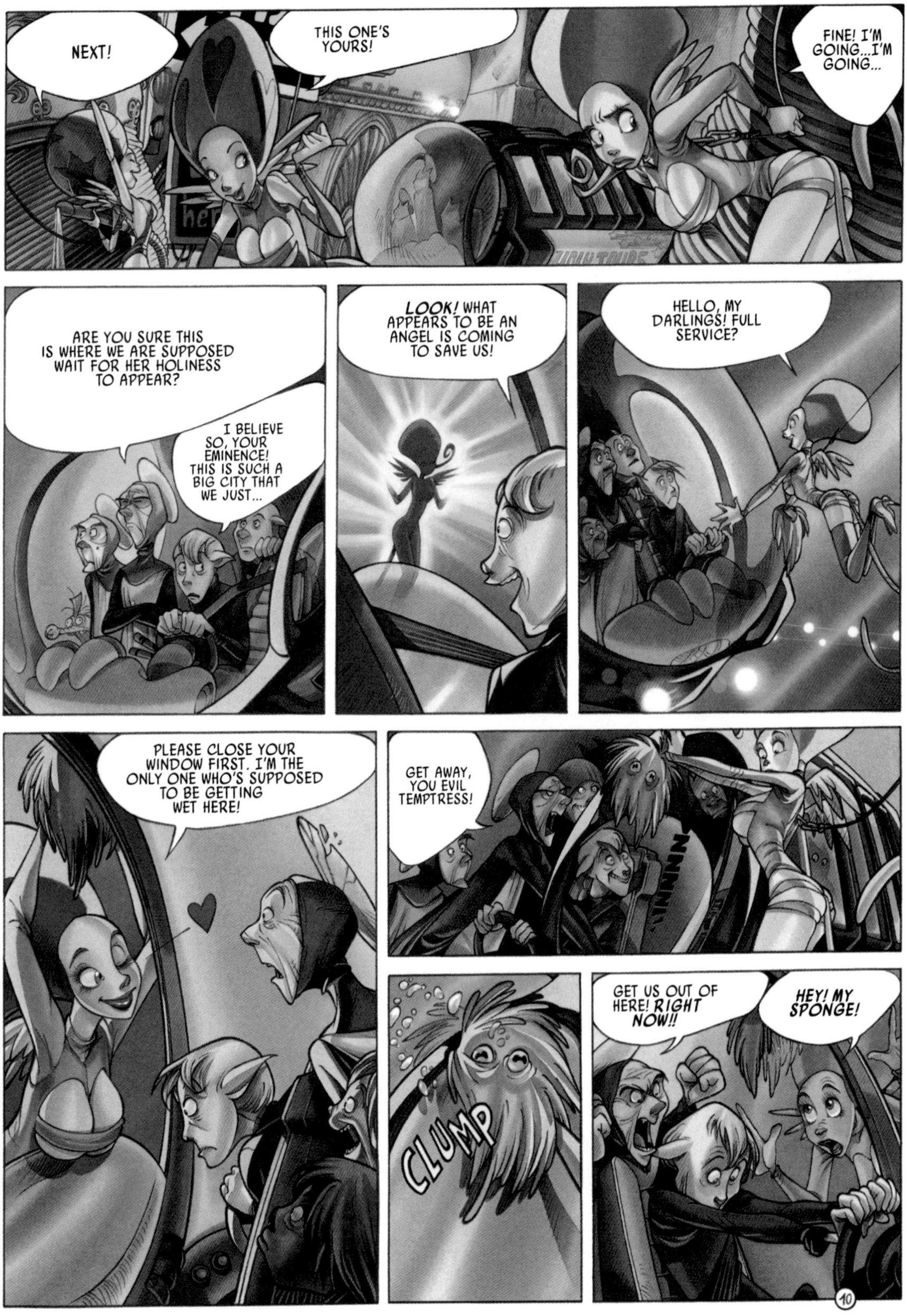
NEXT!
THIS ONE'S YOURS!
FINE! I'M GOING...I'M GOING...
ARE YOU SURE THIS IS WHERE WE ARE SUPPOSED WAIT FOR HER HOLINESS TO APPEAR?
I BELIEVE SO, YOUR EMINENCE! THIS IS SUCH A BIG CITY THAT WE JUST...
LOOK! WHAT APPEARS TO BE AN ANGEL IS COMING TO SAVE US!
HELLO, MY DARLINGS! FULL SERVICE?
PLEASE CLOSE YOUR WINDOW FIRST. I'M THE ONLY ONE WHO'S SUPPOSED TO BE GETTING WET HERE!
GET AWAY, YOU EVIL TEMPTRESS!
NNNNN!
CLUMP
GET US OUT OF HERE! RIGHT NOW!!
HEY! MY SPONGE!

C'MON... PLEASE OPEN UP! OPEN UP!

AAARGH! BEGONE!

OOOOH!

REVERSE

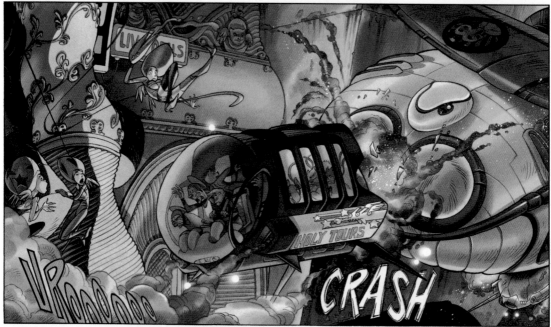

VROOOOOO

HOLY TOURS

CRASH

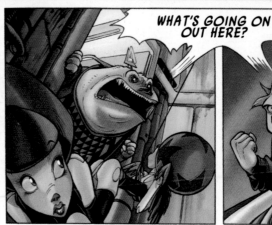

WHAT'S GOING ON OUT HERE?

11

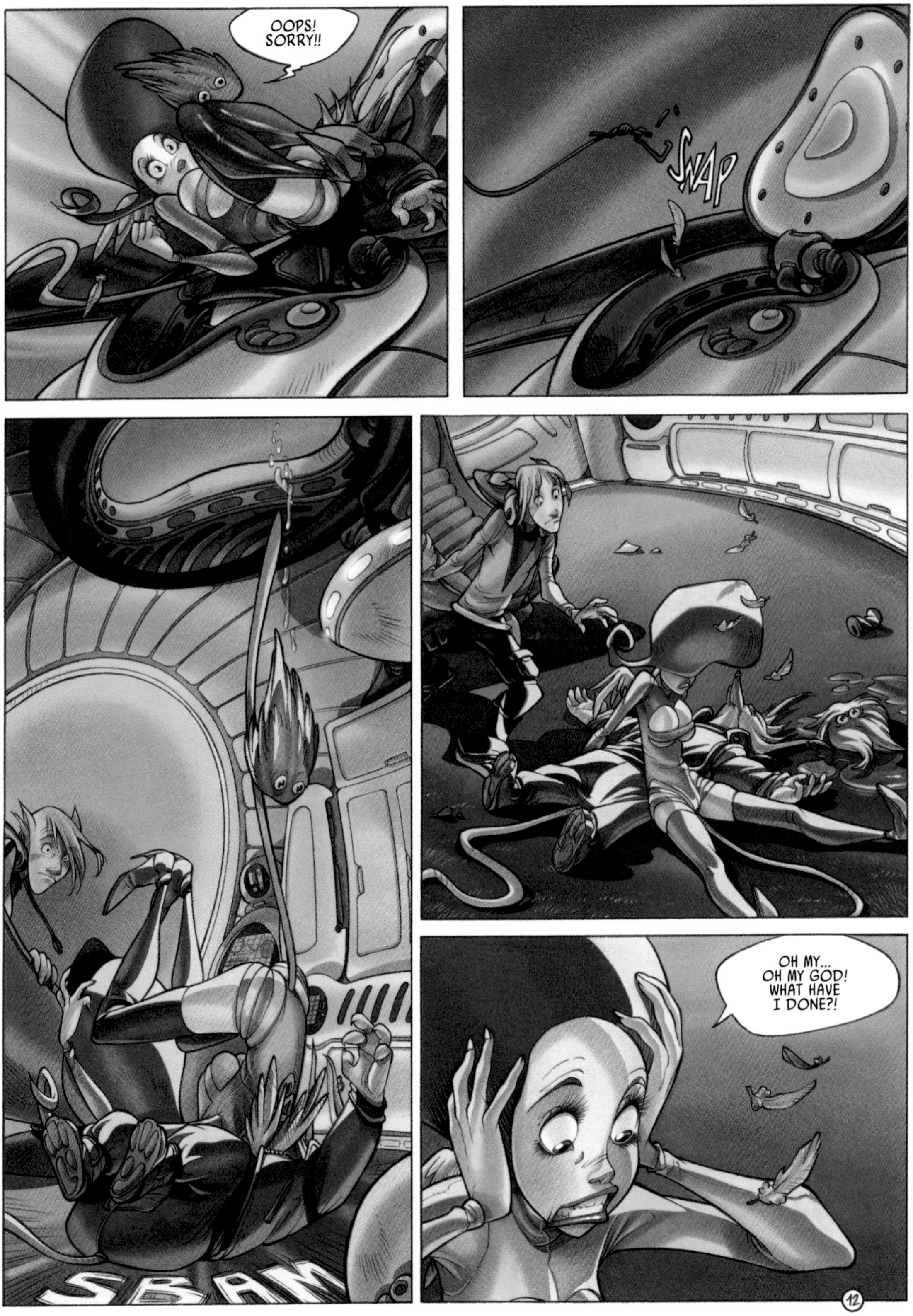
OOPS! SORRY!!
SNAP
SBAM
OH MY... OH MY GOD! WHAT HAVE I DONE?!

IT'S NOT MY FAULT! THEY STARTED YELLING AND I TRIED TO PULL BACK AND...

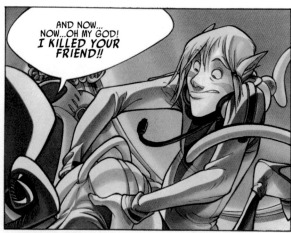

AND NOW... NOW...OH MY GOD! *I KILLED YOUR FRIEND!!*

UMM... JUST WHAT ARE YOU DOING?

AND DON'T WORRY ABOUT JAHU! HE MAY NOT BE MADE OF PLASTIC, BUT HE'S PRETTY SOLID!

OH, NO...UMMM... ACTUALLY...I WAS JUST... UHHH...YOU DIDN'T BREAK ANYTHING, DID YOU?

HMPH! I'M NOT MADE OF *ONLY* PLASTIC, YOU KNOW!

WHAT I MEANT WAS THAT YOU... YOU'RE...

I'M NOA!

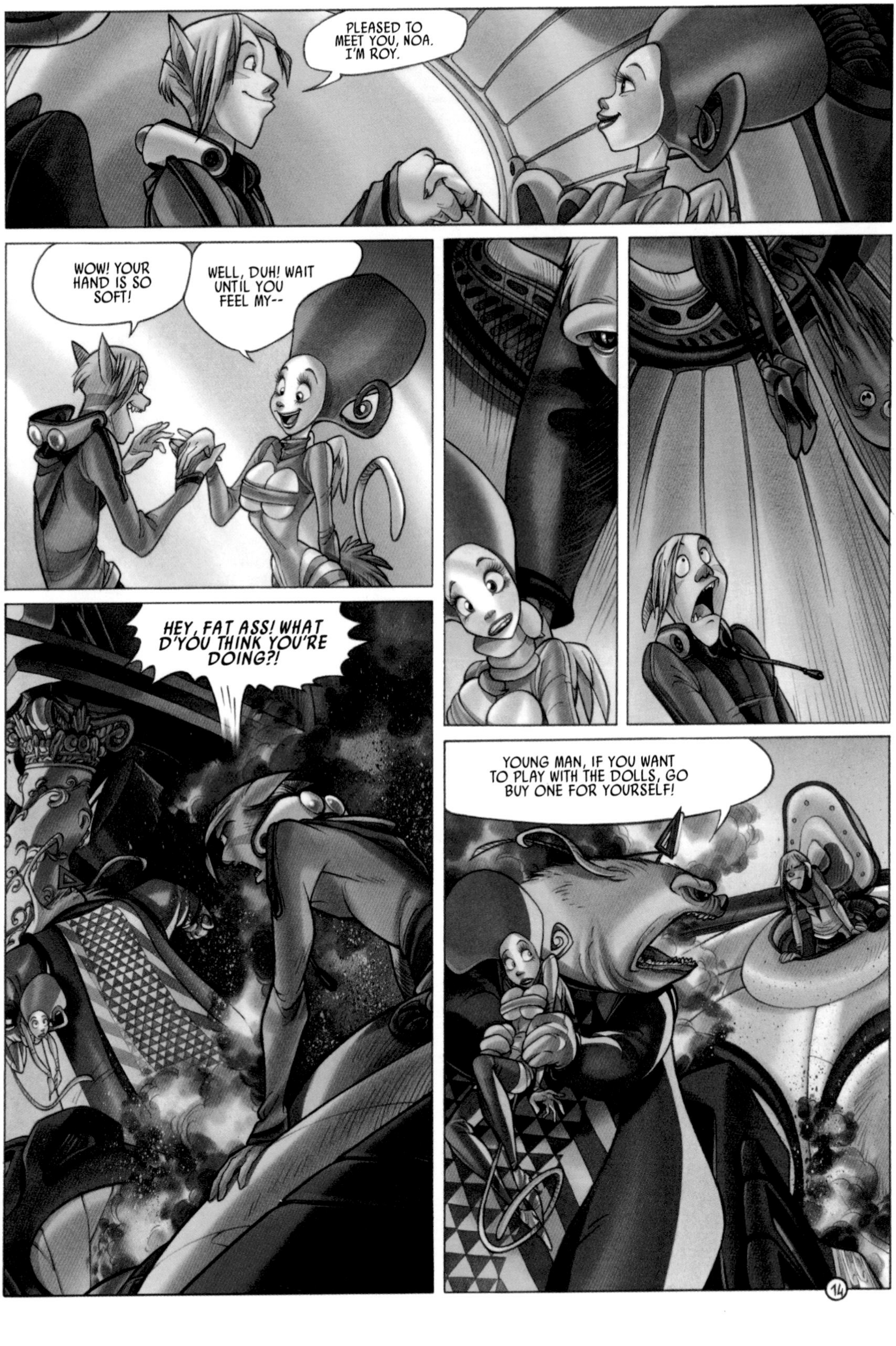
PLEASED TO MEET YOU, NOA. I'M ROY.
WOW! YOUR HAND IS SO SOFT!
WELL, DUH! WAIT UNTIL YOU FEEL MY--
HEY, FAT ASS! WHAT D'YOU THINK YOU'RE DOING?!
YOUNG MAN, IF YOU WANT TO PLAY WITH THE DOLLS, GO BUY ONE FOR YOURSELF!

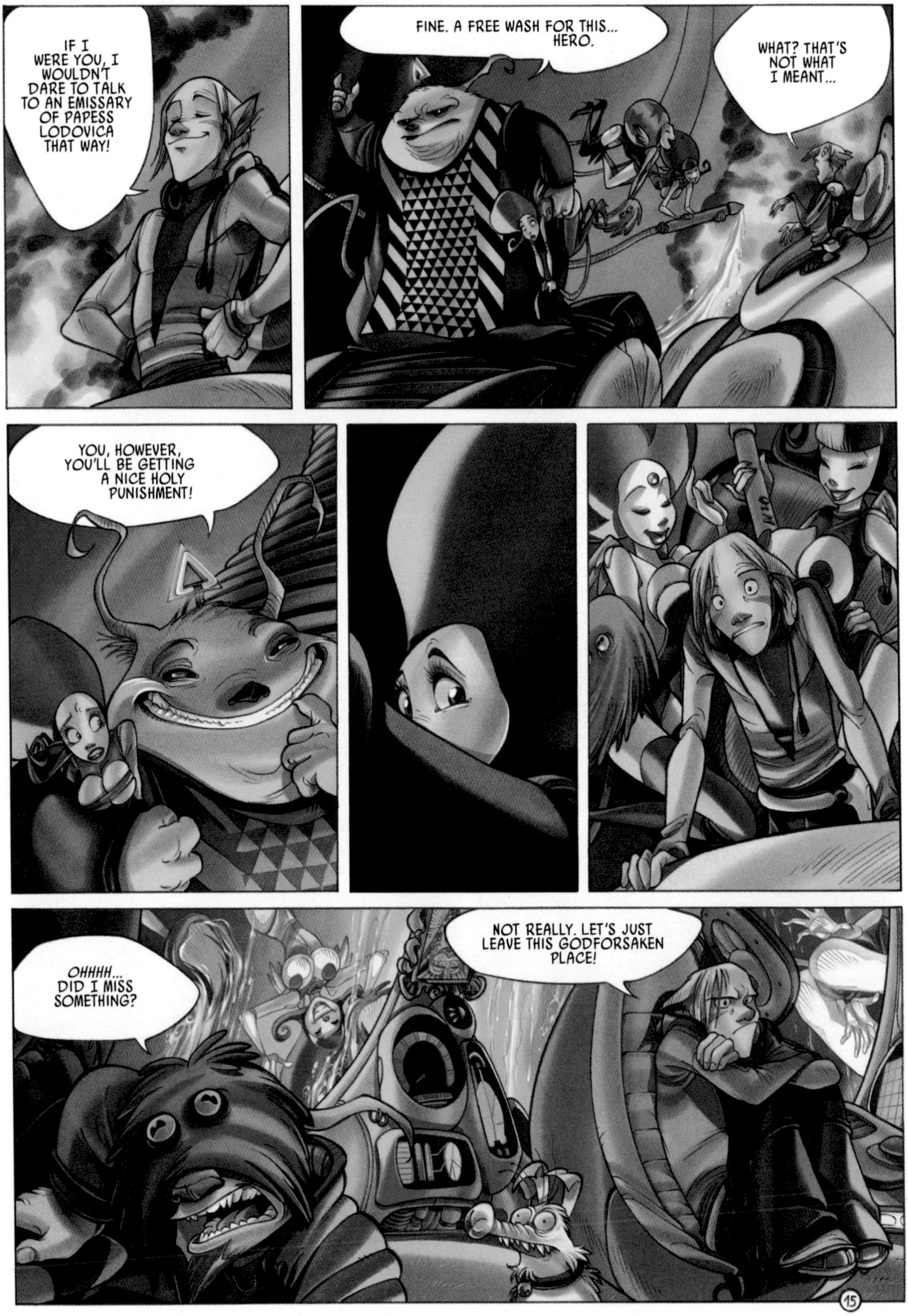
IF I WERE YOU, I WOULDN'T DARE TO TALK TO AN EMISSARY OF PAPESS LODOVICA THAT WAY!
FINE. A FREE WASH FOR THIS... HERO.
WHAT? THAT'S NOT WHAT I MEANT...
YOU, HOWEVER, YOU'LL BE GETTING A NICE HOLY PUNISHMENT!
OHHHH... DID I MISS SOMETHING?
NOT REALLY. LET'S JUST LEAVE THIS GODFORSAKEN PLACE!

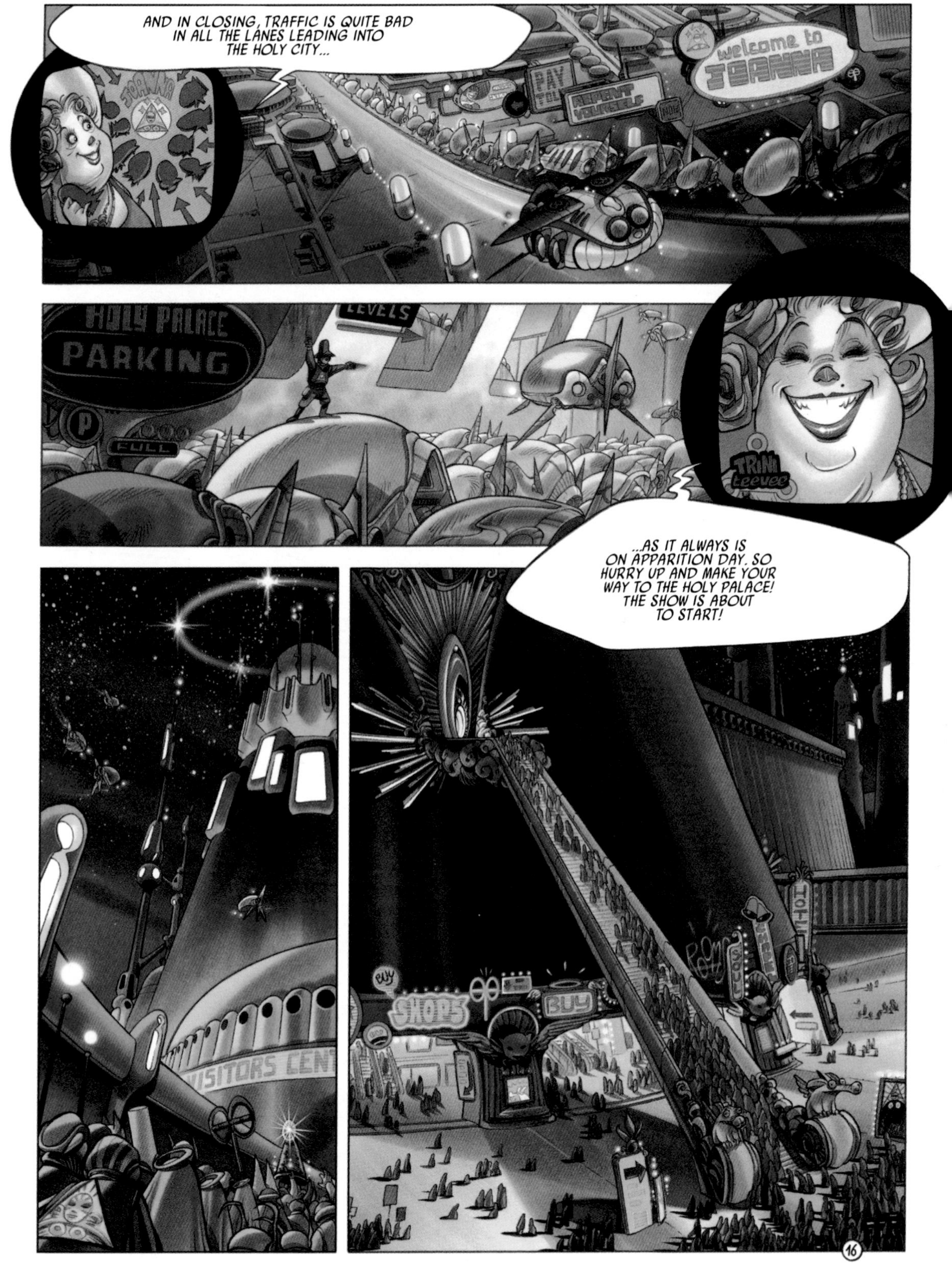
AND IN CLOSING, TRAFFIC IS QUITE BAD IN ALL THE LANES LEADING INTO THE HOLY CITY...
HOLY PALACE
PARKING
LEVELS
FULL
...AS IT ALWAYS IS ON APPARITION DAY. SO HURRY UP AND MAKE YOUR WAY TO THE HOLY PALACE! THE SHOW IS ABOUT TO START!
VISITORS CENT
SHOPS
BUY
BUY

GET BACK, YOU IDIOTS!

THE VIEWING ROOM IS PACKED BEYOND CAPACITY.

PLEASE! WE'VE TRAVELED SO FAR TO COME HERE AND SEE IT!

WE BEG OF YOU ON BENDED KNEE--

TOO BAD FOR YOU! THE APPARITION'S ALREADY STARTED!

GREETINGS TO YOU, OH LODOVICA! PLEASE REVEAL YOURSELF TO US!

17

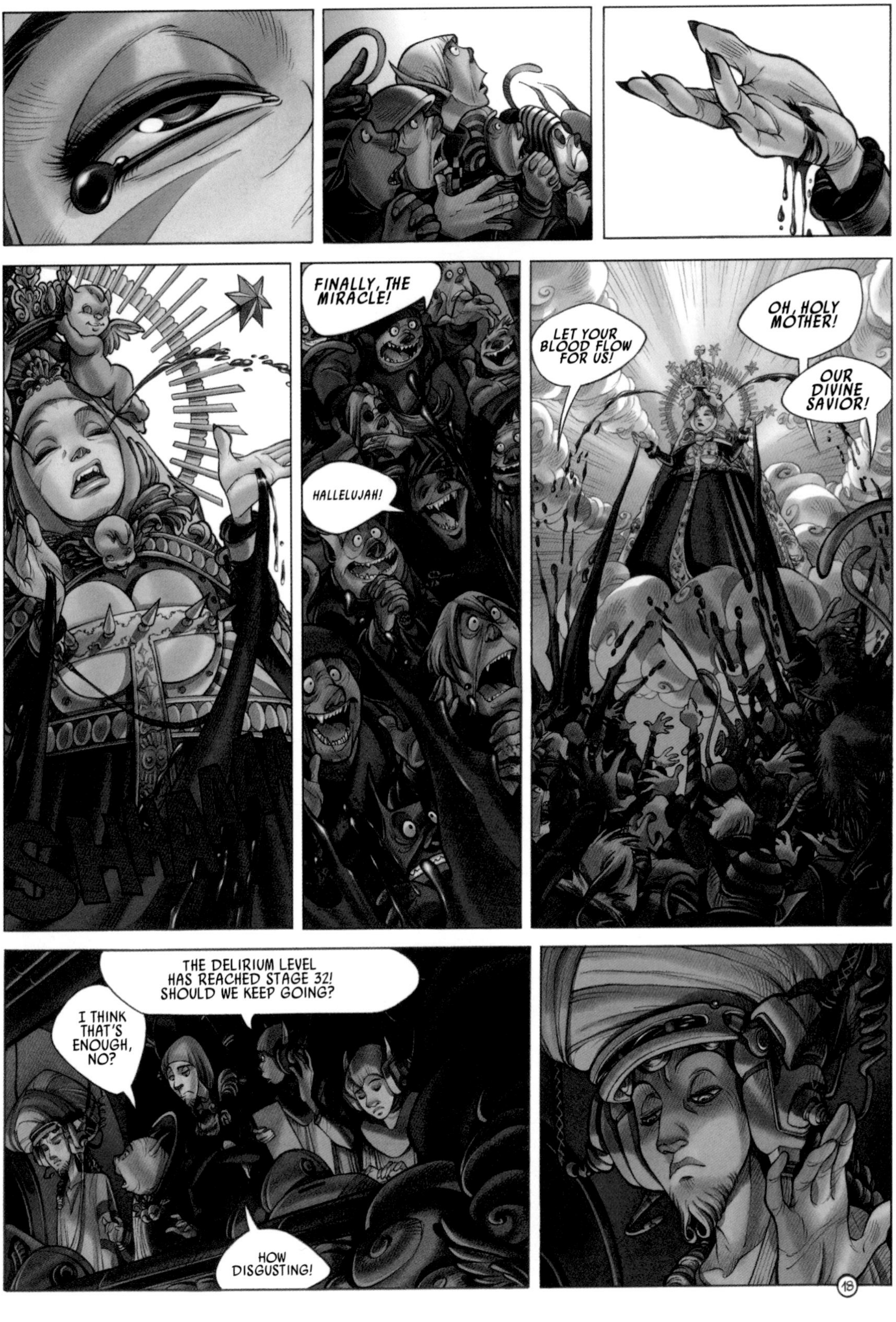
FINALLY, THE MIRACLE!
HALLELUJAH!
LET YOUR BLOOD FLOW FOR US!
OH, HOLY MOTHER!
OUR DIVINE SAVIOR!
THE DELIRIUM LEVEL HAS REACHED STAGE 32! SHOULD WE KEEP GOING?
I THINK THAT'S ENOUGH, NO?
HOW DISGUSTING!

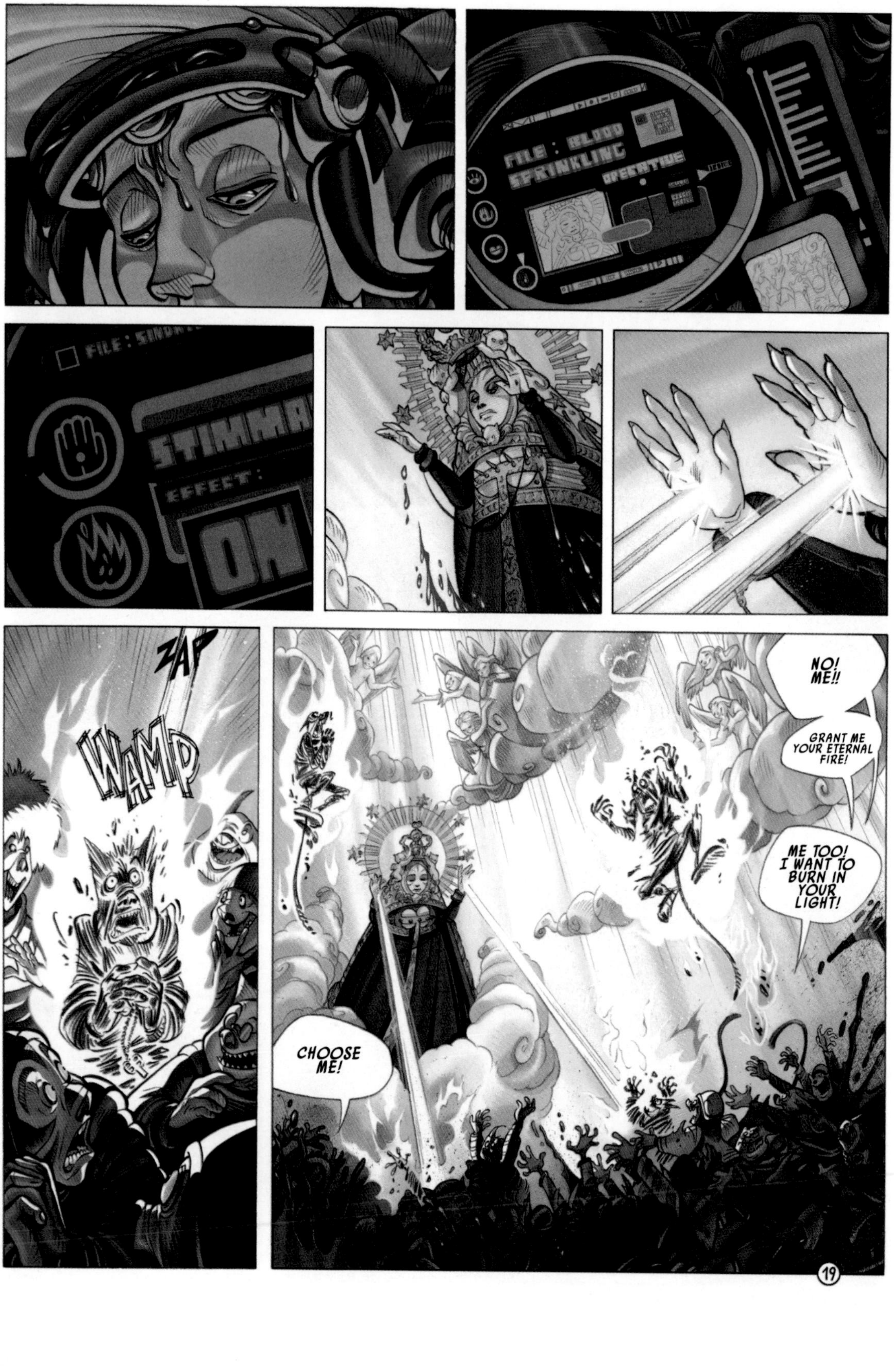
FILE : BLOOD
SPRINKLING
OPERATIVE
EFFECT :
ON
ZAP
WAMP
NO! ME!!
GRANT ME YOUR ETERNAL FIRE!
ME TOO! I WANT TO BURN IN YOUR LIGHT!
CHOOSE ME!

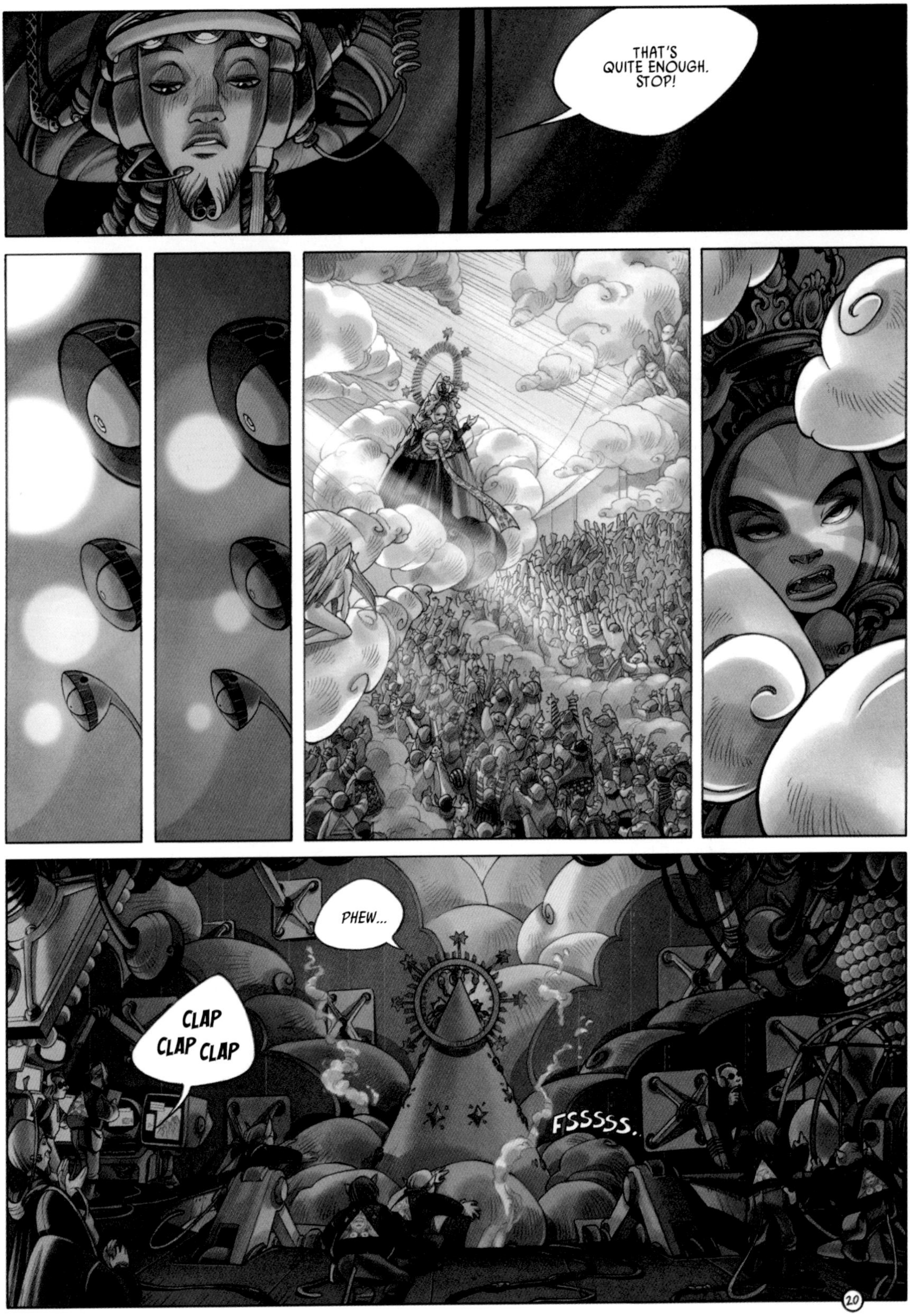
THAT'S QUITE ENOUGH. STOP!
PHEW...
CLAP CLAP CLAP
FSSSSS..

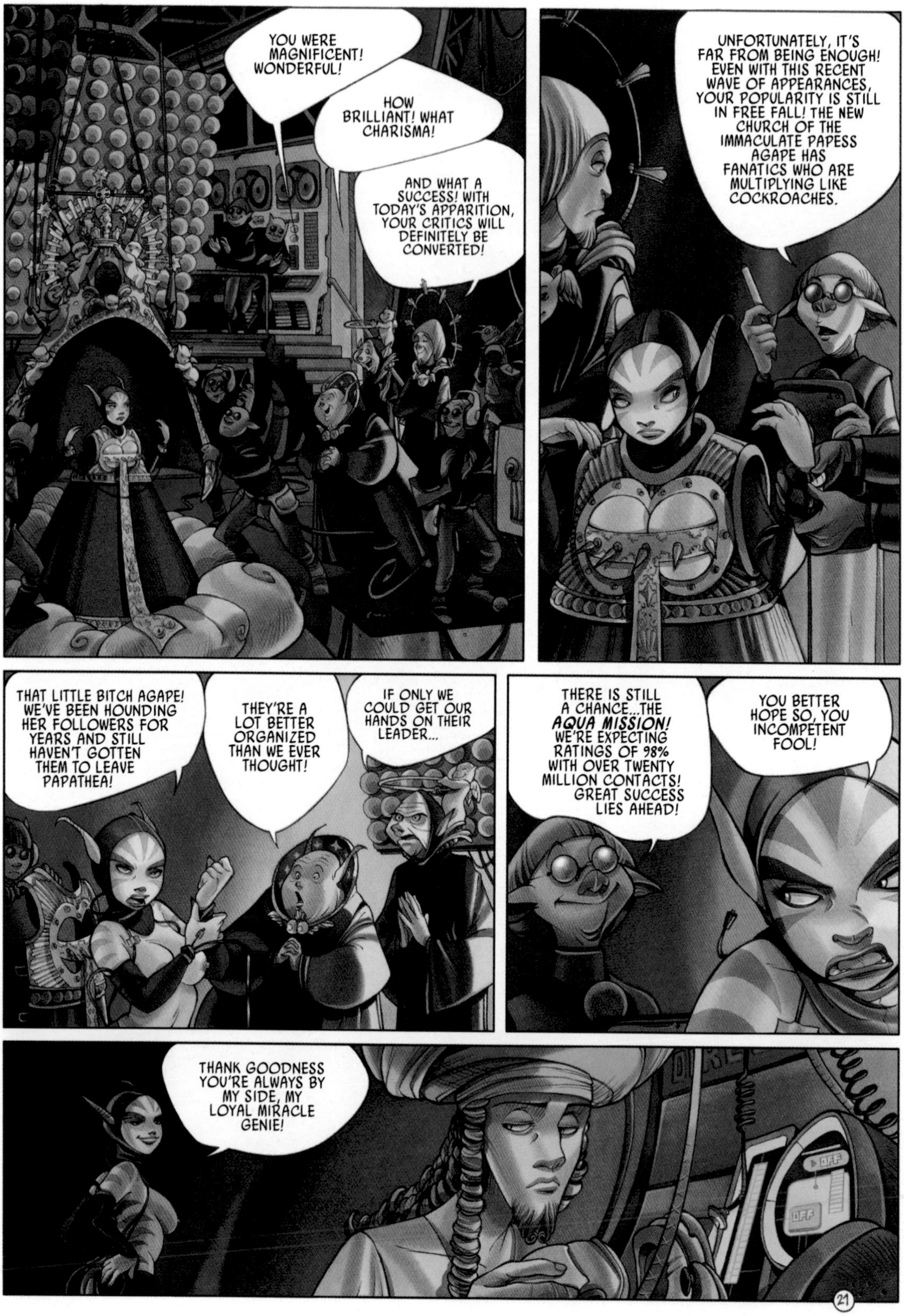
YOU WERE MAGNIFICENT! WONDERFUL!
HOW BRILLIANT! WHAT CHARISMA!
AND WHAT A SUCCESS! WITH TODAY'S APPARITION, YOUR CRITICS WILL DEFINITELY BE CONVERTED!
UNFORTUNATELY, IT'S FAR FROM BEING ENOUGH! EVEN WITH THIS RECENT WAVE OF APPEARANCES, YOUR POPULARITY IS STILL IN FREE FALL! THE NEW CHURCH OF THE IMMACULATE PAPESS AGAPE HAS FANATICS WHO ARE MULTIPLYING LIKE COCKROACHES.
THAT LITTLE BITCH AGAPE! WE'VE BEEN HOUNDING HER FOLLOWERS FOR YEARS AND STILL HAVEN'T GOTTEN THEM TO LEAVE PAPATHEA!
THEY'RE A LOT BETTER ORGANIZED THAN WE EVER THOUGHT!
IF ONLY WE COULD GET OUR HANDS ON THEIR LEADER...
THERE IS STILL A CHANCE...THE AQUA MISSION! WE'RE EXPECTING RATINGS OF 98% WITH OVER TWENTY MILLION CONTACTS! GREAT SUCCESS LIES AHEAD!
YOU BETTER HOPE SO, YOU INCOMPETENT FOOL!
THANK GOODNESS YOU'RE ALWAYS BY MY SIDE, MY LOYAL MIRACLE GENIE!

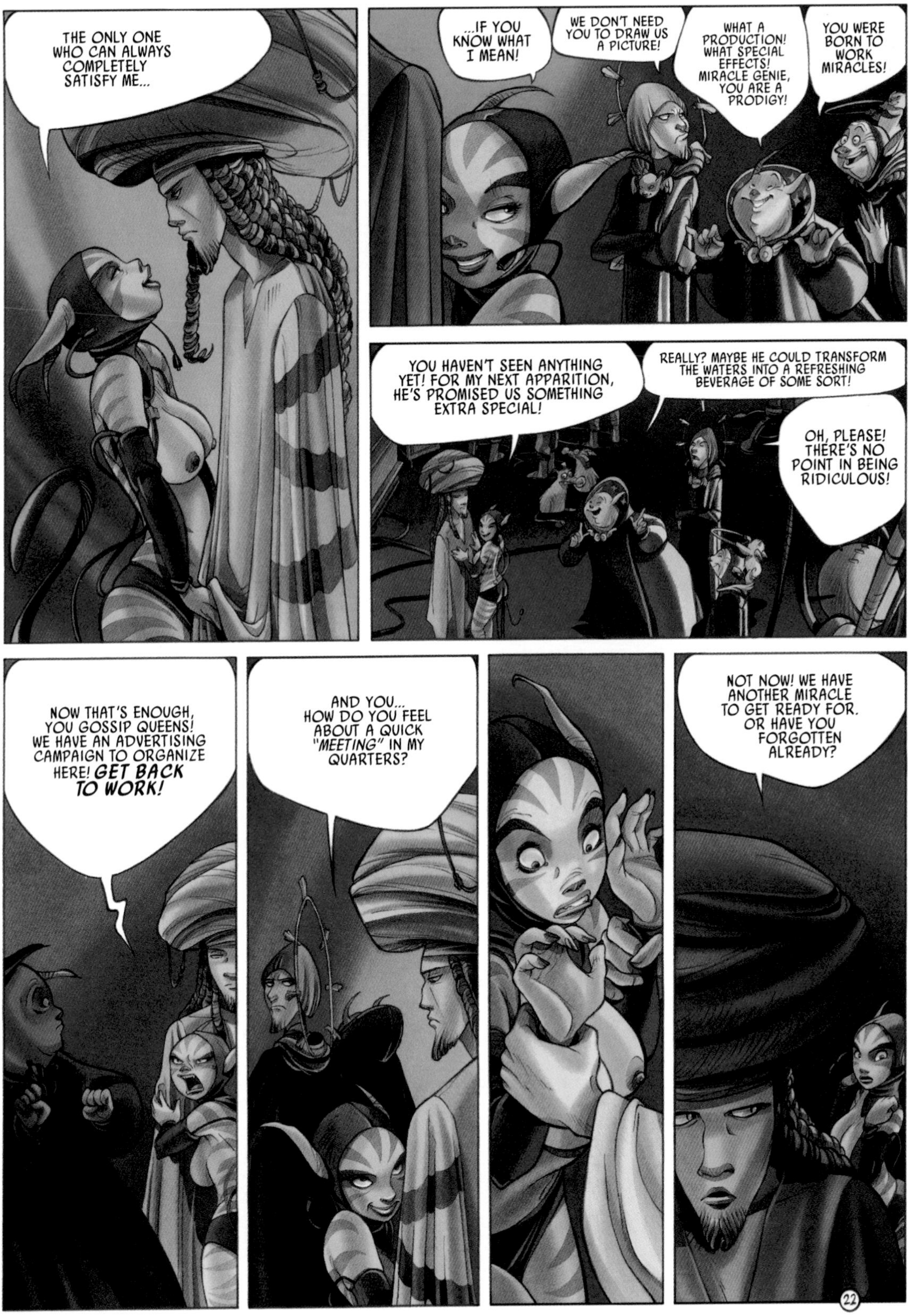
THE ONLY ONE WHO CAN ALWAYS COMPLETELY SATISFY ME...
...IF YOU KNOW WHAT I MEAN!
WE DON'T NEED YOU TO DRAW US A PICTURE!
WHAT A PRODUCTION! WHAT SPECIAL EFFECTS! MIRACLE GENIE, YOU ARE A PRODIGY!
YOU WERE BORN TO WORK MIRACLES!
YOU HAVEN'T SEEN ANYTHING YET! FOR MY NEXT APPARITION, HE'S PROMISED US SOMETHING EXTRA SPECIAL!
REALLY? MAYBE HE COULD TRANSFORM THE WATERS INTO A REFRESHING BEVERAGE OF SOME SORT!
OH, PLEASE! THERE'S NO POINT IN BEING RIDICULOUS!
NOW THAT'S ENOUGH, YOU GOSSIP QUEENS! WE HAVE AN ADVERTISING CAMPAIGN TO ORGANIZE HERE! GET BACK TO WORK!
AND YOU... HOW DO YOU FEEL ABOUT A QUICK "MEETING" IN MY QUARTERS?
NOT NOW! WE HAVE ANOTHER MIRACLE TO GET READY FOR. OR HAVE YOU FORGOTTEN ALREADY?

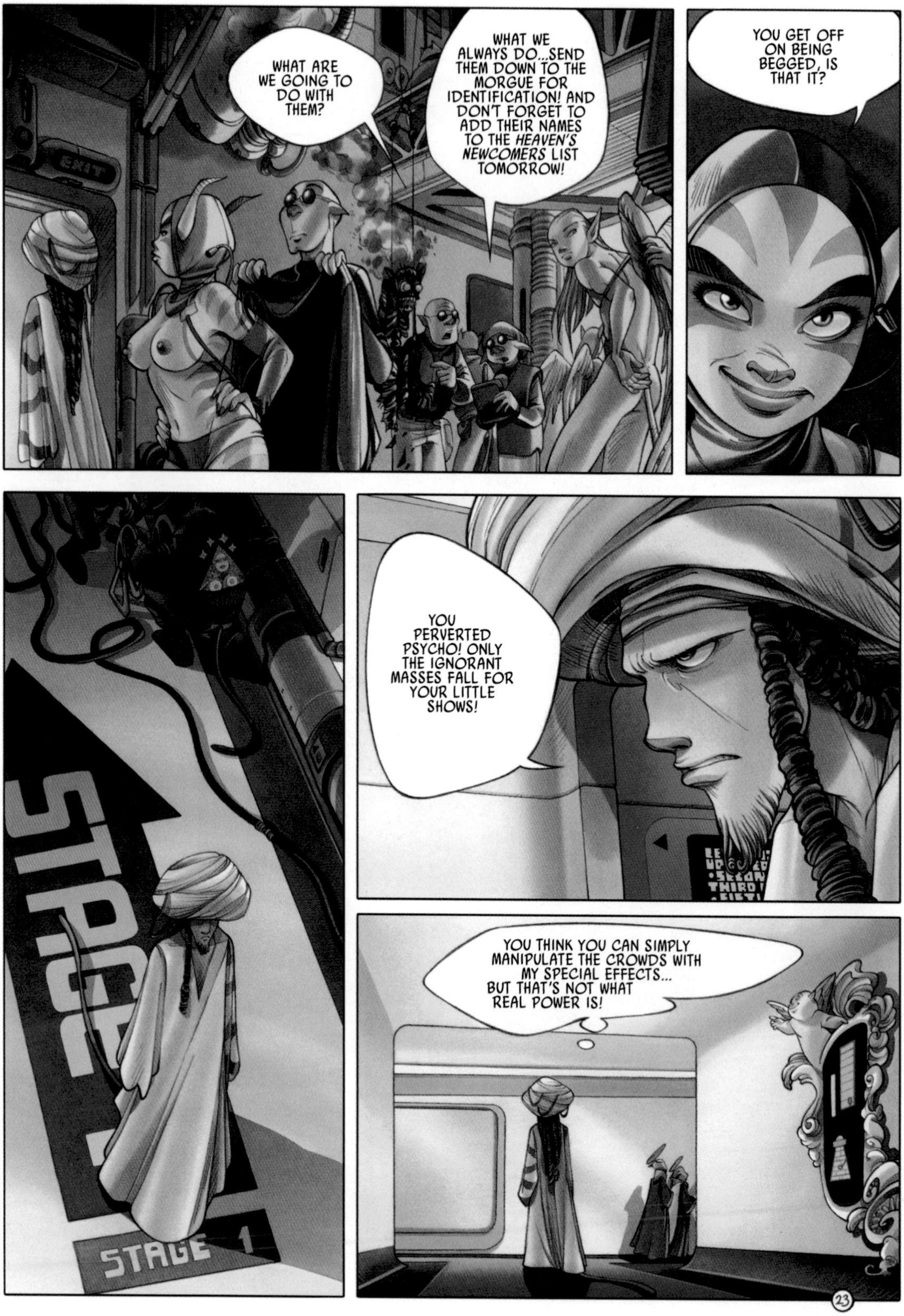
WHAT ARE WE GOING TO DO WITH THEM?
WHAT WE ALWAYS DO...SEND THEM DOWN TO THE MORGUE FOR IDENTIFICATION! AND DON'T FORGET TO ADD THEIR NAMES TO THE *HEAVEN'S NEWCOMERS* LIST TOMORROW!
EXIT
YOU GET OFF ON BEING BEGGED, IS THAT IT?
STAGE
STAGE 1
YOU PERVERTED PSYCHO! ONLY THE IGNORANT MASSES FALL FOR YOUR LITTLE SHOWS!
YOU THINK YOU CAN SIMPLY MANIPULATE THE CROWDS WITH MY SPECIAL EFFECTS... BUT THAT'S NOT WHAT REAL POWER IS!

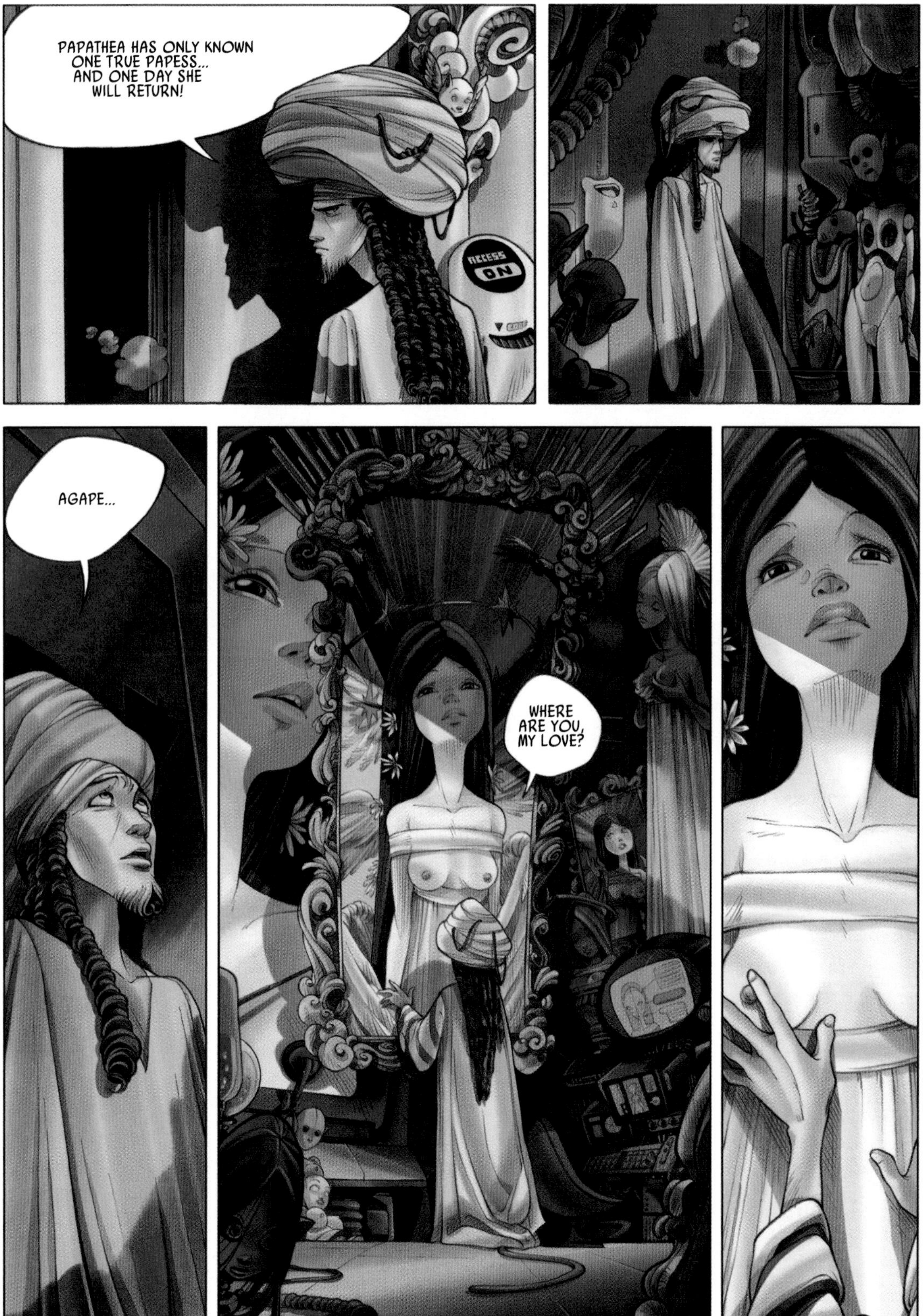
PAPATHEA HAS ONLY KNOWN ONE TRUE PAPESS... AND ONE DAY SHE WILL RETURN!
AGAPE...
WHERE ARE YOU, MY LOVE?

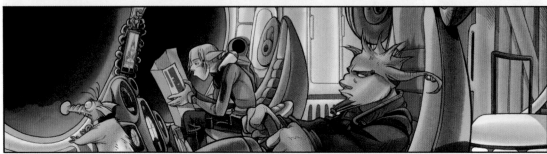

HA! THAT WAS A GOOD ONE! STILL AS DIRTY-MINDED AS EVER, AREN'T YOU?

WAIT, I'M NOT DONE YET. LISTEN TO THIS ONE... THERE'S THESE TWO PRIESTS, YOU SEE...

ﾝﾝﾝ

ZZZZ!!

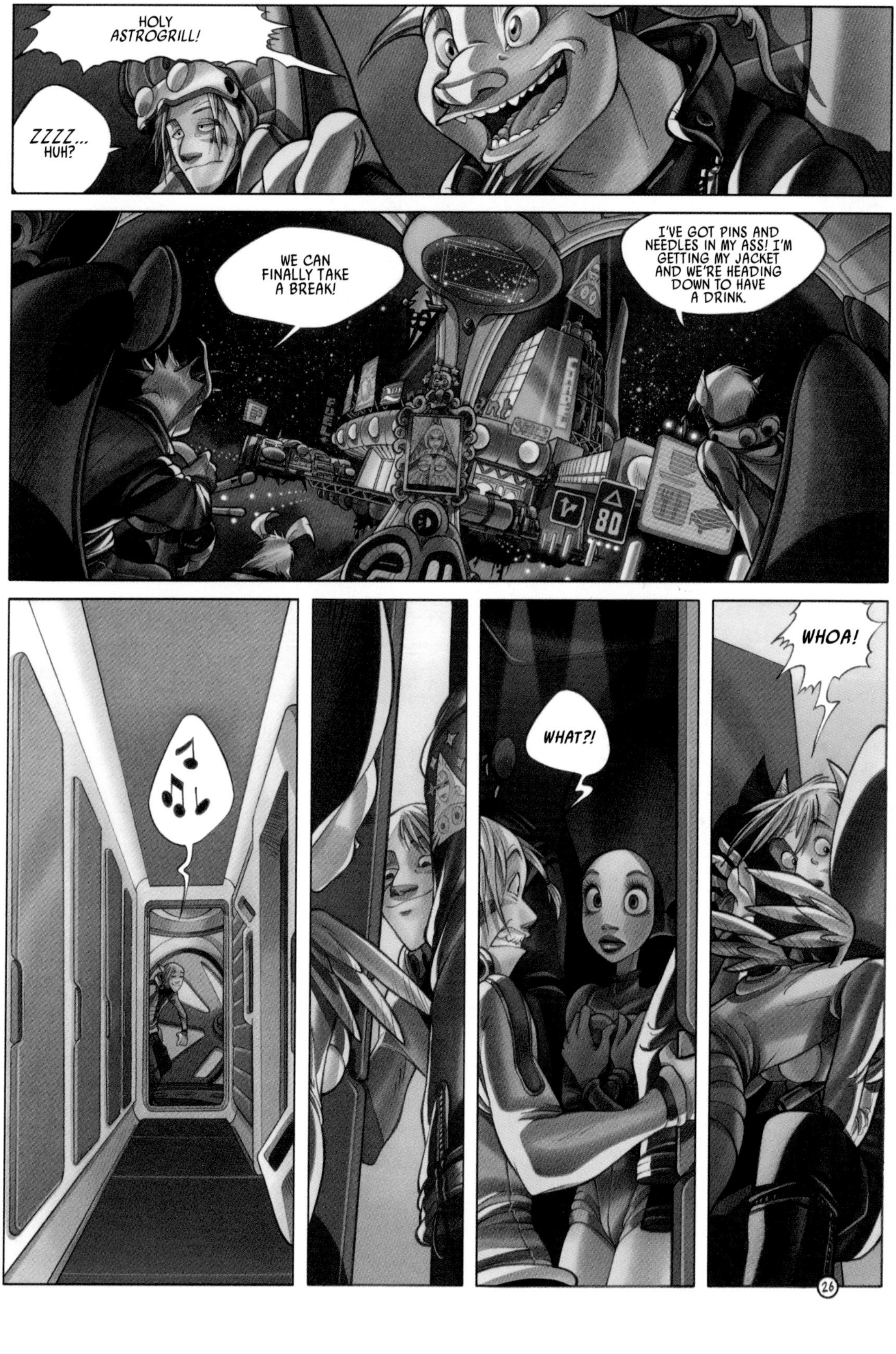
HOLY ASTROGRILL!
ZZZZ... HUH?
WE CAN FINALLY TAKE A BREAK!
I'VE GOT PINS AND NEEDLES IN MY ASS! I'M GETTING MY JACKET AND WE'RE HEADING DOWN TO HAVE A DRINK.
WHAT?!
WHOA!

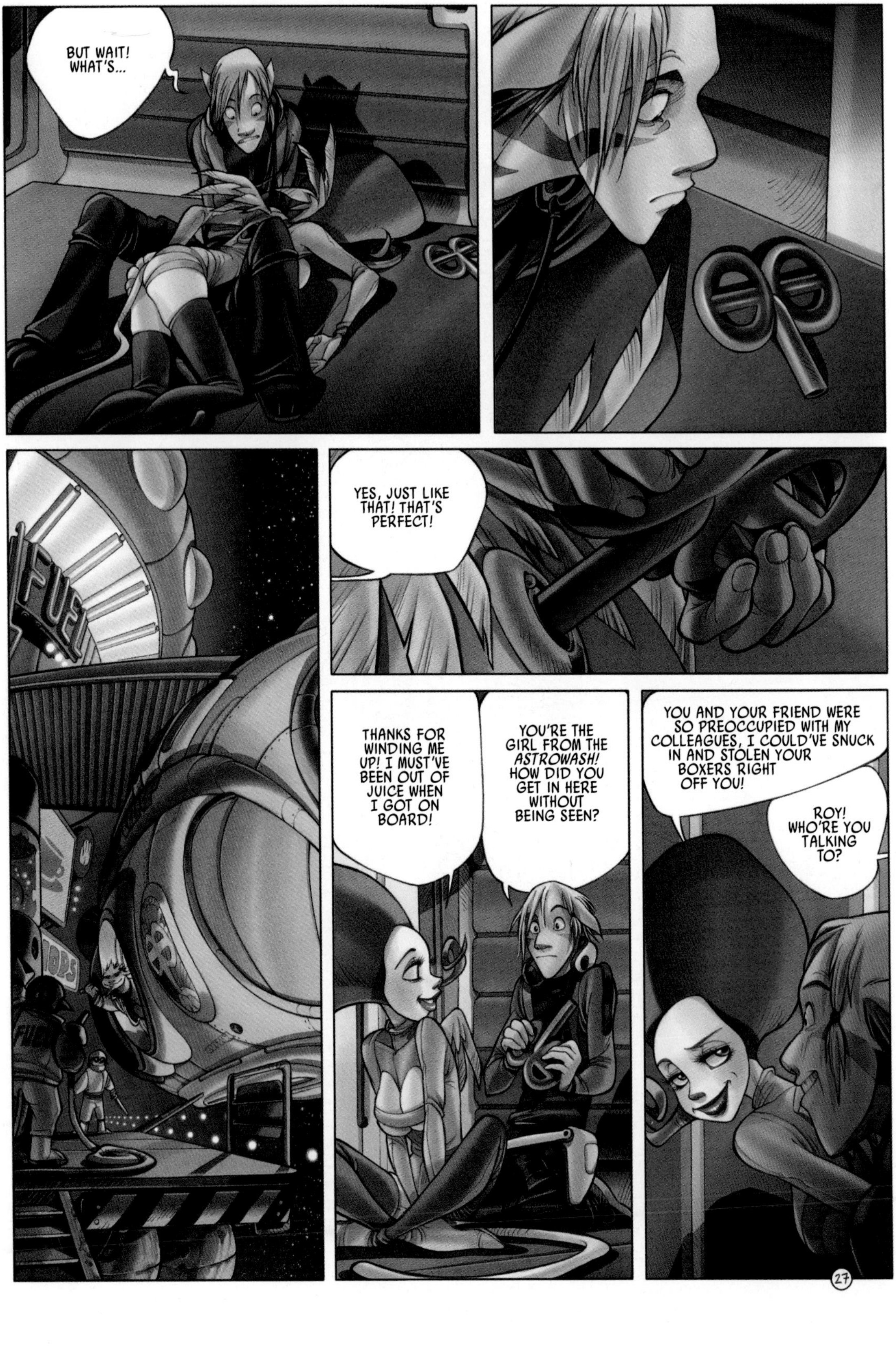
BUT WAIT! WHAT'S...
YES, JUST LIKE THAT! THAT'S PERFECT!
THANKS FOR WINDING ME UP! I MUST'VE BEEN OUT OF JUICE WHEN I GOT ON BOARD!
YOU'RE THE GIRL FROM THE *ASTROWASH!* HOW DID YOU GET IN HERE WITHOUT BEING SEEN?
YOU AND YOUR FRIEND WERE SO PREOCCUPIED WITH MY COLLEAGUES, I COULD'VE SNUCK IN AND STOLEN YOUR BOXERS RIGHT OFF YOU!
ROY! WHO'RE YOU TALKING TO?

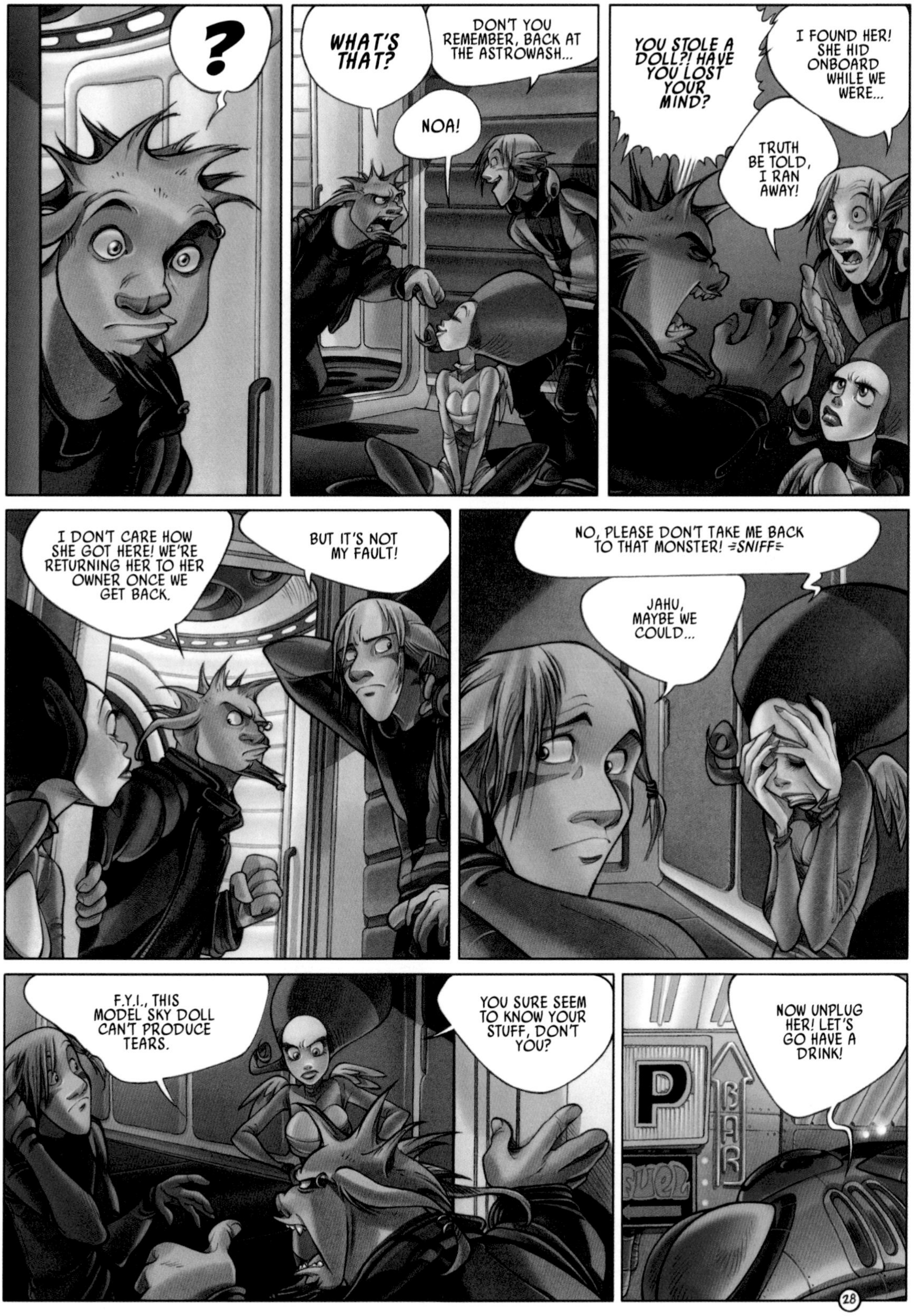
?
WHAT'S THAT?
DON'T YOU REMEMBER, BACK AT THE ASTROWASH...
NOA!
YOU STOLE A DOLL?! HAVE YOU LOST YOUR MIND?
I FOUND HER! SHE HID ONBOARD WHILE WE WERE...
TRUTH BE TOLD, I RAN AWAY!
I DON'T CARE HOW SHE GOT HERE! WE'RE RETURNING HER TO HER OWNER ONCE WE GET BACK.
BUT IT'S NOT MY FAULT!
NO, PLEASE DON'T TAKE ME BACK TO THAT MONSTER! =SNIFF=
JAHU, MAYBE WE COULD...
F.Y.I., THIS MODEL SKY DOLL CAN'T PRODUCE TEARS.
YOU SURE SEEM TO KNOW YOUR STUFF, DON'T YOU?
NOW UNPLUG HER! LET'S GO HAVE A DRINK!
P
BAR

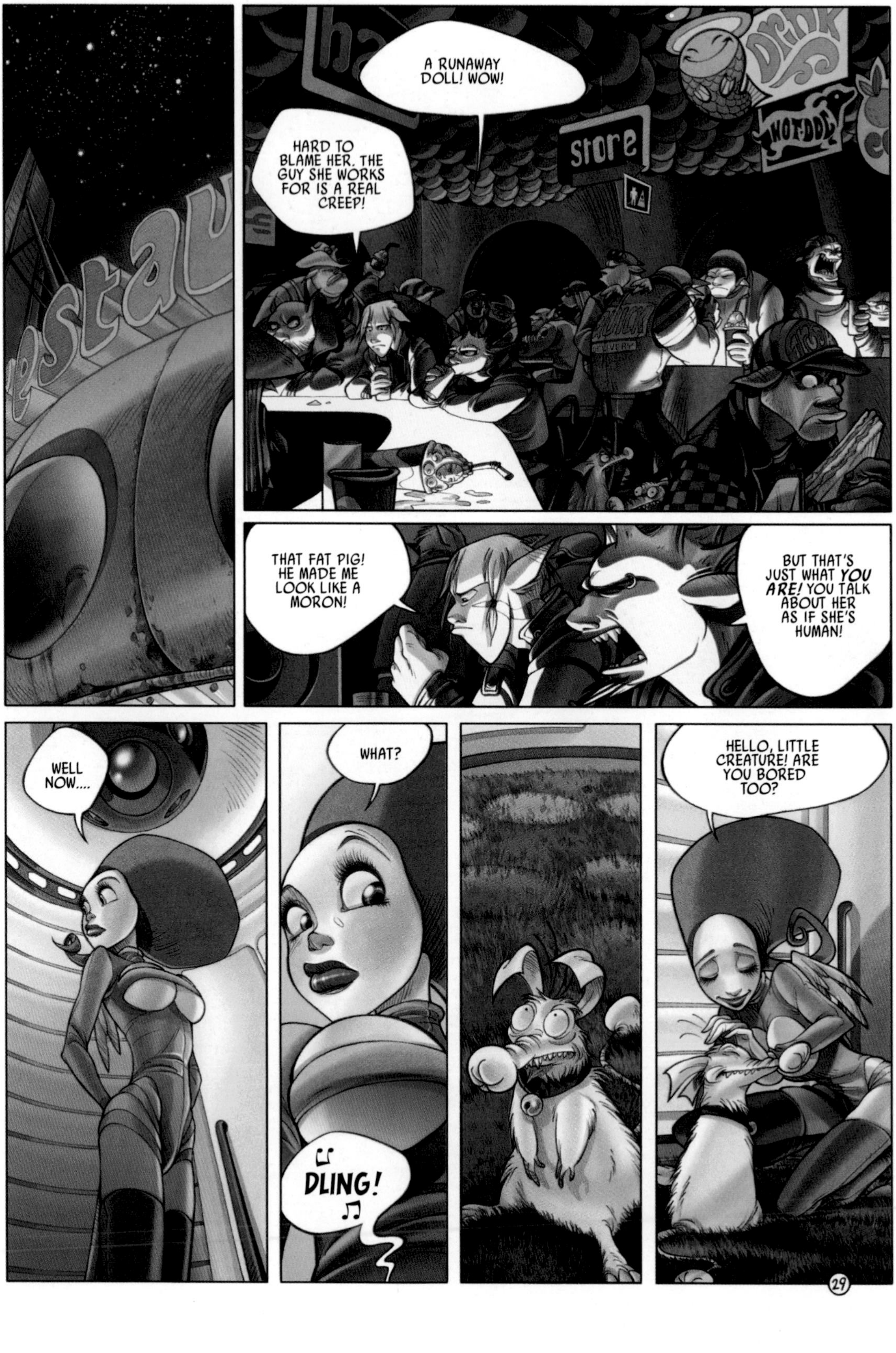
A RUNAWAY DOLL! WOW!
HARD TO BLAME HER. THE GUY SHE WORKS FOR IS A REAL CREEP!
store
HOT-DOG
THAT FAT PIG! HE MADE ME LOOK LIKE A MORON!
BUT THAT'S JUST WHAT *YOU ARE!* YOU TALK ABOUT HER AS IF SHE'S HUMAN!
WELL NOW....
WHAT?
DLING!
HELLO, LITTLE CREATURE! ARE YOU BORED TOO?

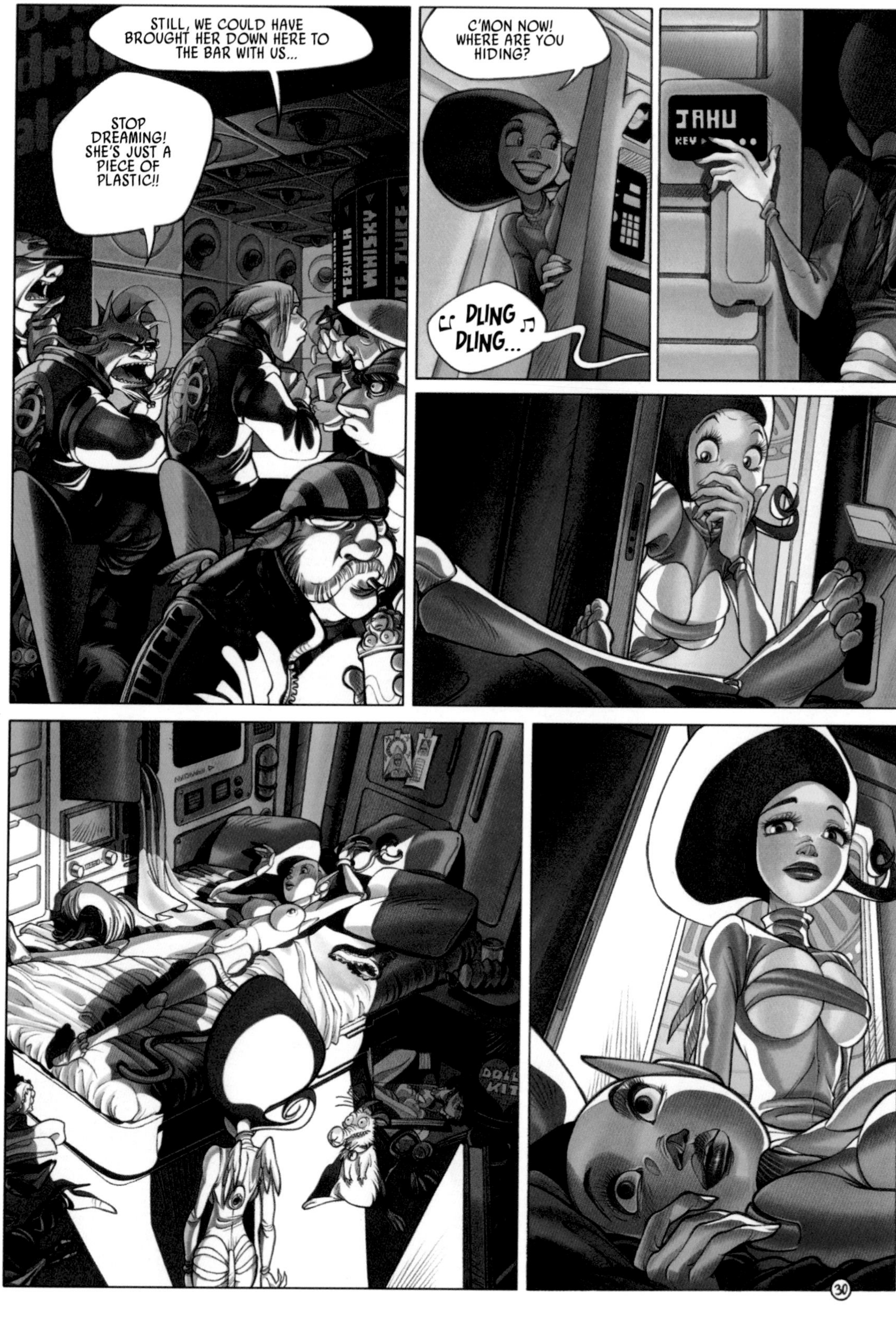
STILL, WE COULD HAVE BROUGHT HER DOWN HERE TO THE BAR WITH US...
STOP DREAMING! SHE'S JUST A PIECE OF PLASTIC!!
TEQUILA
WHISKY
C'MON NOW! WHERE ARE YOU HIDING?
DLING DLING...
JAHU
KEY

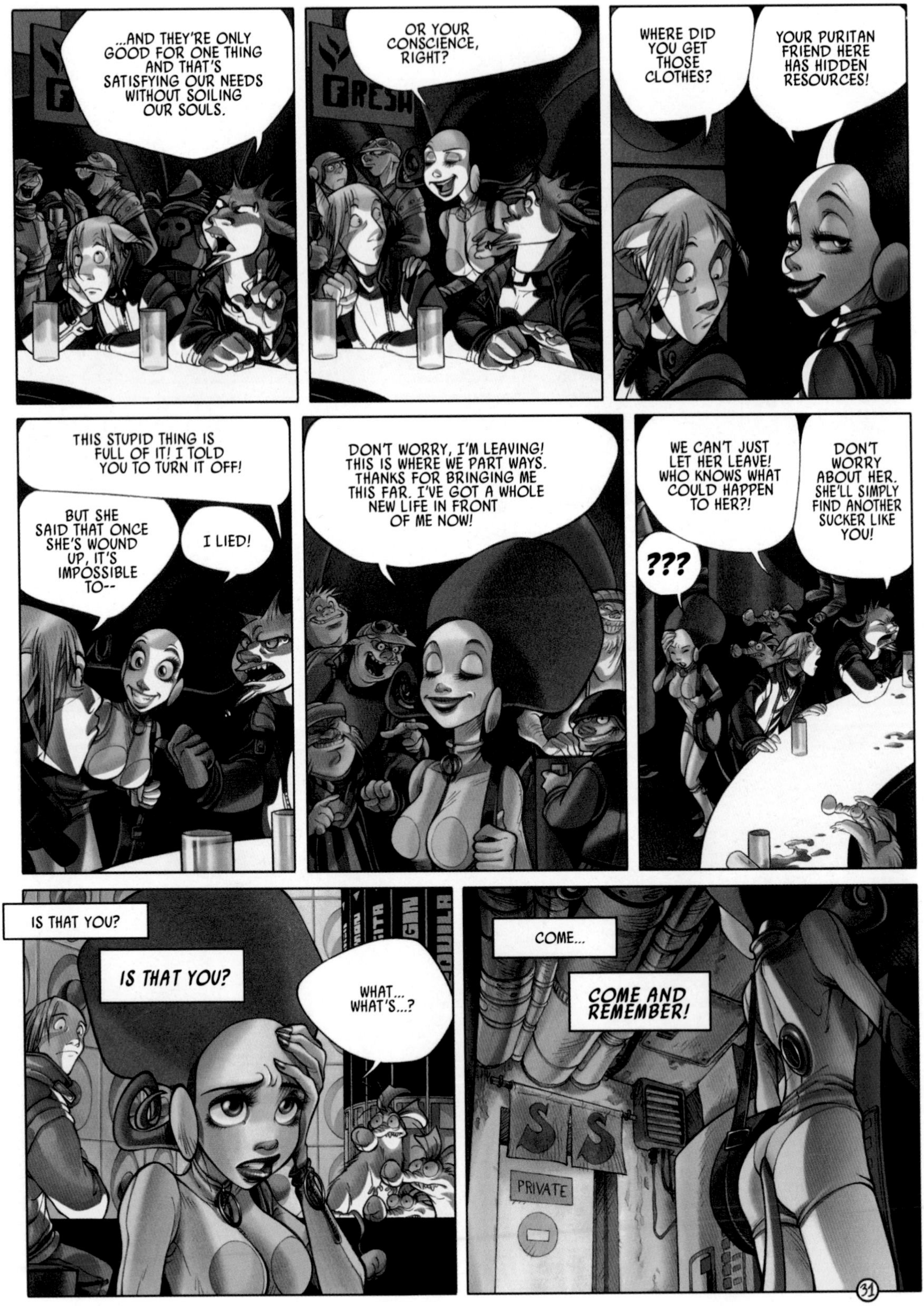
...AND THEY'RE ONLY GOOD FOR ONE THING AND THAT'S SATISFYING OUR NEEDS WITHOUT SOILING OUR SOULS.
FRESH
OR YOUR CONSCIENCE, RIGHT?
WHERE DID YOU GET THOSE CLOTHES?
YOUR PURITAN FRIEND HERE HAS HIDDEN RESOURCES!
THIS STUPID THING IS FULL OF IT! I TOLD YOU TO TURN IT OFF!
BUT SHE SAID THAT ONCE SHE'S WOUND UP, IT'S IMPOSSIBLE TO--
I LIED!
DON'T WORRY, I'M LEAVING! THIS IS WHERE WE PART WAYS. THANKS FOR BRINGING ME THIS FAR. I'VE GOT A WHOLE NEW LIFE IN FRONT OF ME NOW!
WE CAN'T JUST LET HER LEAVE! WHO KNOWS WHAT COULD HAPPEN TO HER?!
???
DON'T WORRY ABOUT HER. SHE'LL SIMPLY FIND ANOTHER SUCKER LIKE YOU!
IS THAT YOU?
IS THAT YOU?
WHAT... WHAT'S...?
COME...
COME AND REMEMBER!
PRIVATE

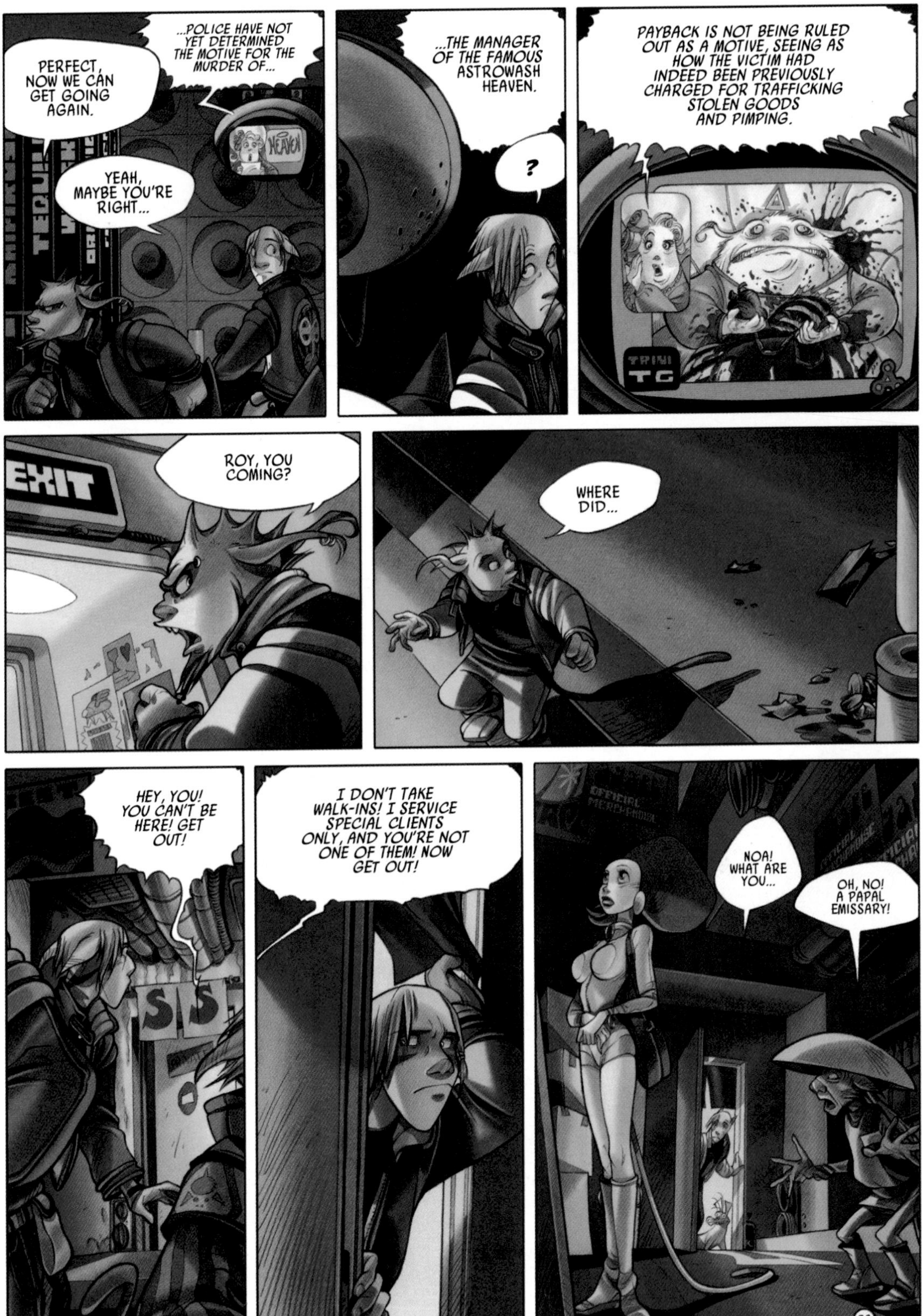
...POLICE HAVE NOT YET DETERMINED THE MOTIVE FOR THE MURDER OF...
PERFECT, NOW WE CAN GET GOING AGAIN.
YEAH, MAYBE YOU'RE RIGHT...
...THE MANAGER OF THE FAMOUS ASTROWASH HEAVEN.
?
PAYBACK IS NOT BEING RULED OUT AS A MOTIVE, SEEING AS HOW THE VICTIM HAD INDEED BEEN PREVIOUSLY CHARGED FOR TRAFFICKING STOLEN GOODS AND PIMPING.
TG
EXIT
ROY, YOU COMING?
WHERE DID...
HEY, YOU! YOU CAN'T BE HERE! GET OUT!
I DON'T TAKE WALK-INS! I SERVICE SPECIAL CLIENTS ONLY, AND YOU'RE NOT ONE OF THEM! NOW GET OUT!
NOA! WHAT ARE YOU...
OH, NO! A PAPAL EMISSARY!

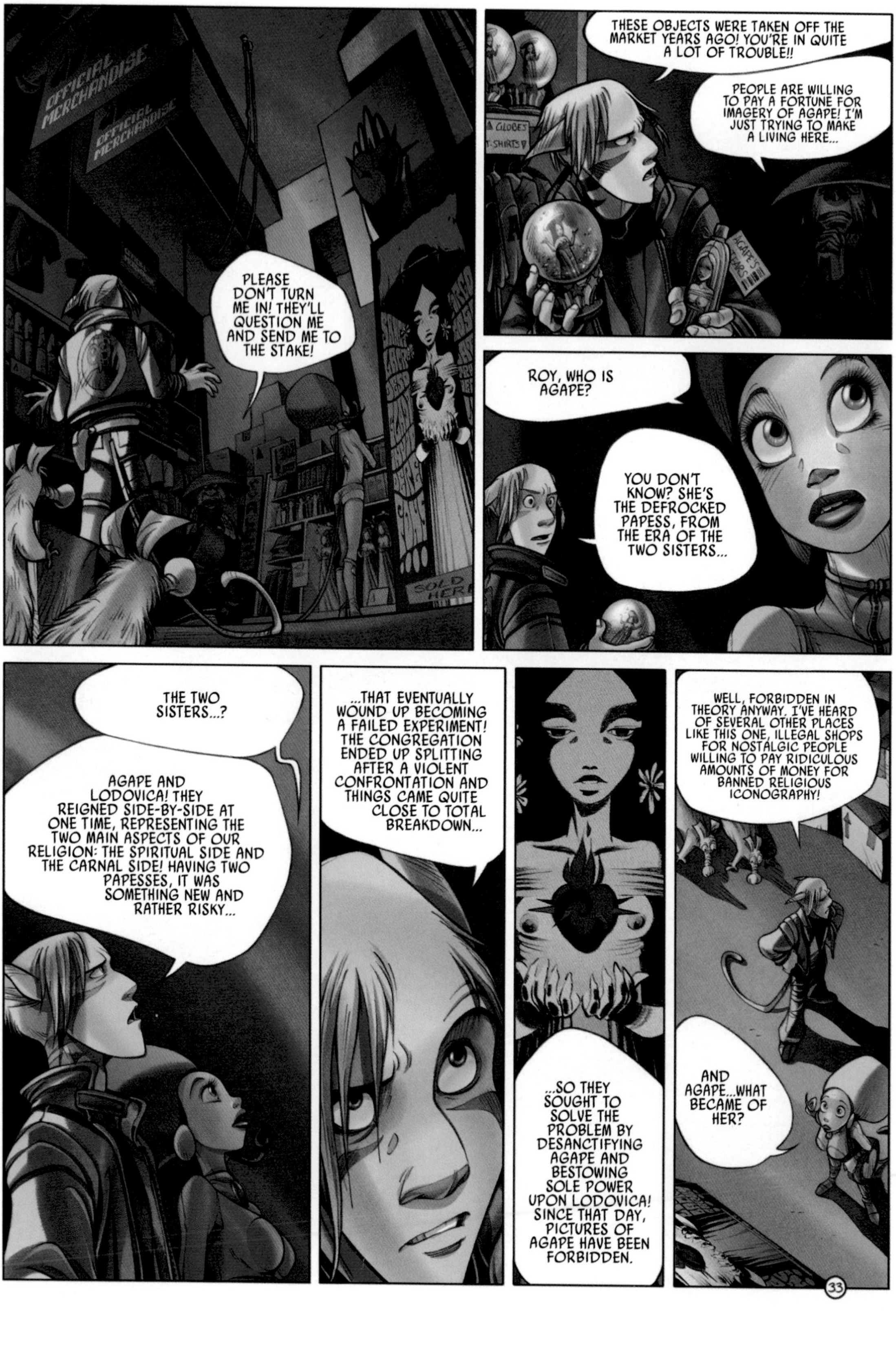
PLEASE DON'T TURN ME IN! THEY'LL QUESTION ME AND SEND ME TO THE STAKE!
OFFICIAL MERCHANDISE
THESE OBJECTS WERE TAKEN OFF THE MARKET YEARS AGO! YOU'RE IN QUITE A LOT OF TROUBLE!!
PEOPLE ARE WILLING TO PAY A FORTUNE FOR IMAGERY OF AGAPE! I'M JUST TRYING TO MAKE A LIVING HERE...
GLOBES
T-SHIRTS
ROY, WHO IS AGAPE?
YOU DON'T KNOW? SHE'S THE DEFROCKED PAPESS, FROM THE ERA OF THE TWO SISTERS...
THE TWO SISTERS...?
AGAPE AND LODOVICA! THEY REIGNED SIDE-BY-SIDE AT ONE TIME, REPRESENTING THE TWO MAIN ASPECTS OF OUR RELIGION: THE SPIRITUAL SIDE AND THE CARNAL SIDE! HAVING TWO PAPESSES, IT WAS SOMETHING NEW AND RATHER RISKY...
...THAT EVENTUALLY WOUND UP BECOMING A FAILED EXPERIMENT! THE CONGREGATION ENDED UP SPLITTING AFTER A VIOLENT CONFRONTATION AND THINGS CAME QUITE CLOSE TO TOTAL BREAKDOWN...
...SO THEY SOUGHT TO SOLVE THE PROBLEM BY DESANCTIFYING AGAPE AND BESTOWING SOLE POWER UPON LODOVICA! SINCE THAT DAY, PICTURES OF AGAPE HAVE BEEN FORBIDDEN.
WELL, FORBIDDEN IN THEORY ANYWAY. I'VE HEARD OF SEVERAL OTHER PLACES LIKE THIS ONE, ILLEGAL SHOPS FOR NOSTALGIC PEOPLE WILLING TO PAY RIDICULOUS AMOUNTS OF MONEY FOR BANNED RELIGIOUS ICONOGRAPHY!
AND AGAPE...WHAT BECAME OF HER?

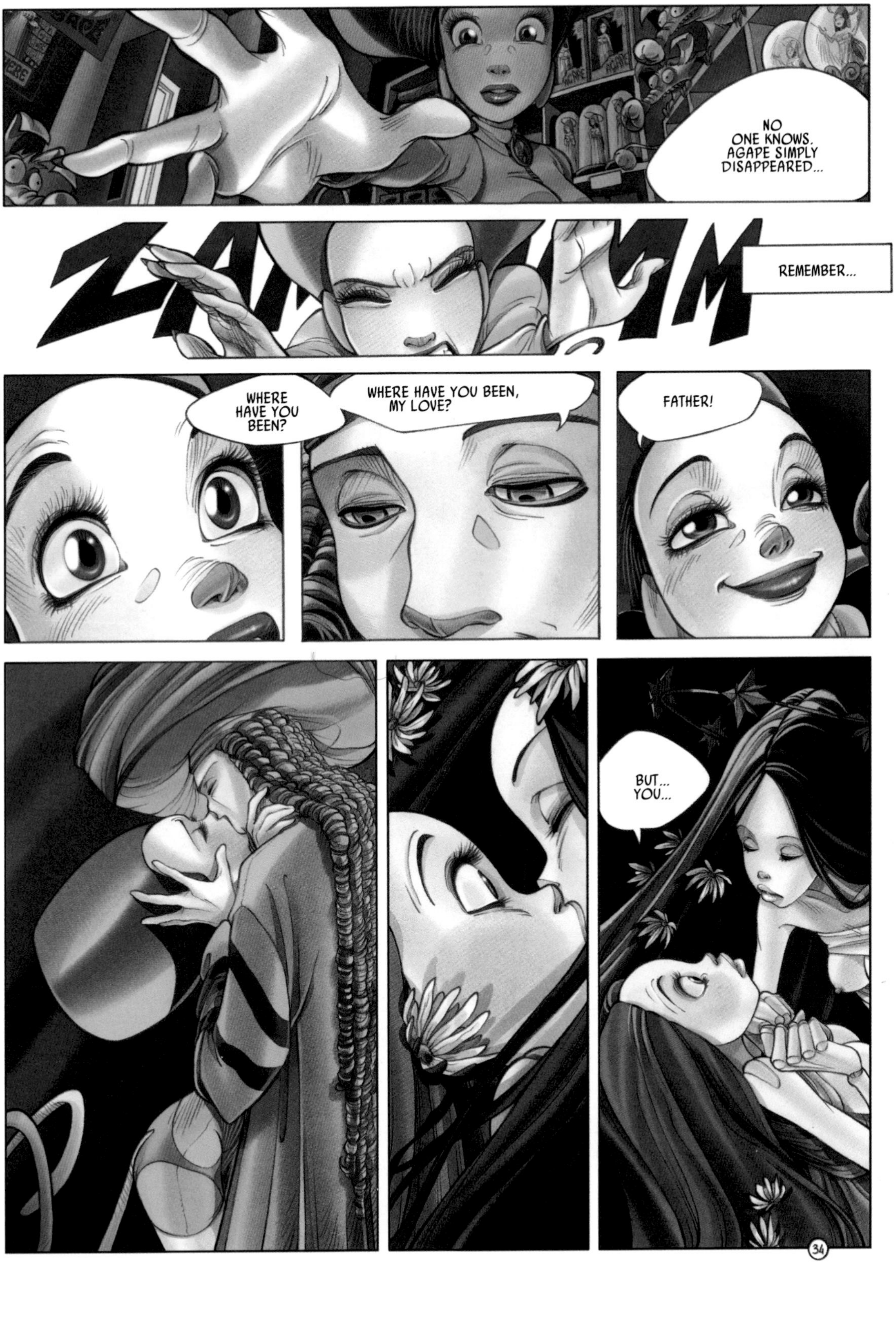
NO ONE KNOWS. AGAPE SIMPLY DISAPPEARED...
REMEMBER...
WHERE HAVE YOU BEEN?
WHERE HAVE YOU BEEN, MY LOVE?
FATHER!
BUT... YOU...

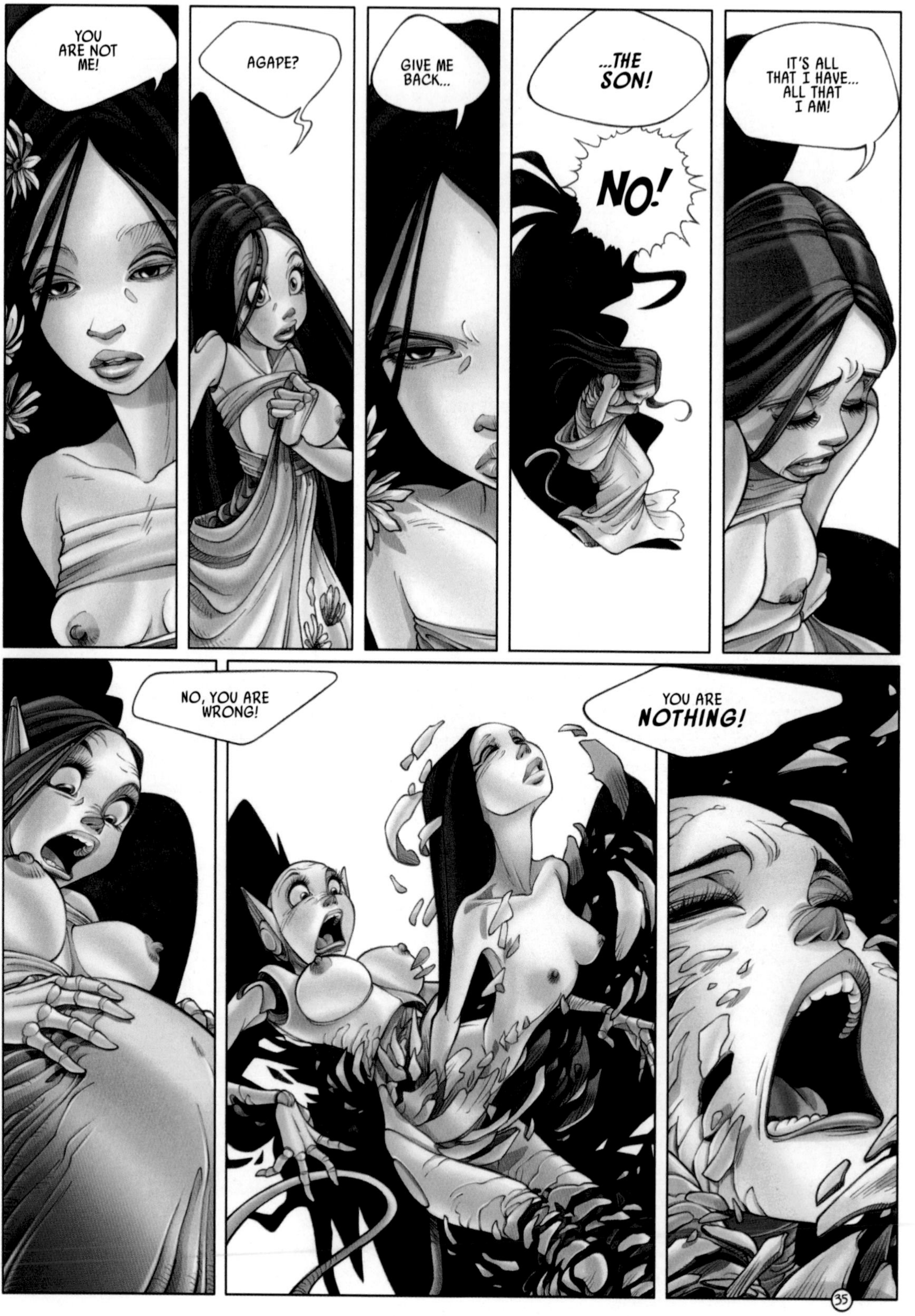

YOU ARE NOT ME!
AGAPE?
GIVE ME BACK...
...THE SON!
NO!
IT'S ALL THAT I HAVE... ALL THAT I AM!
NO, YOU ARE WRONG!
YOU ARE NOTHING!

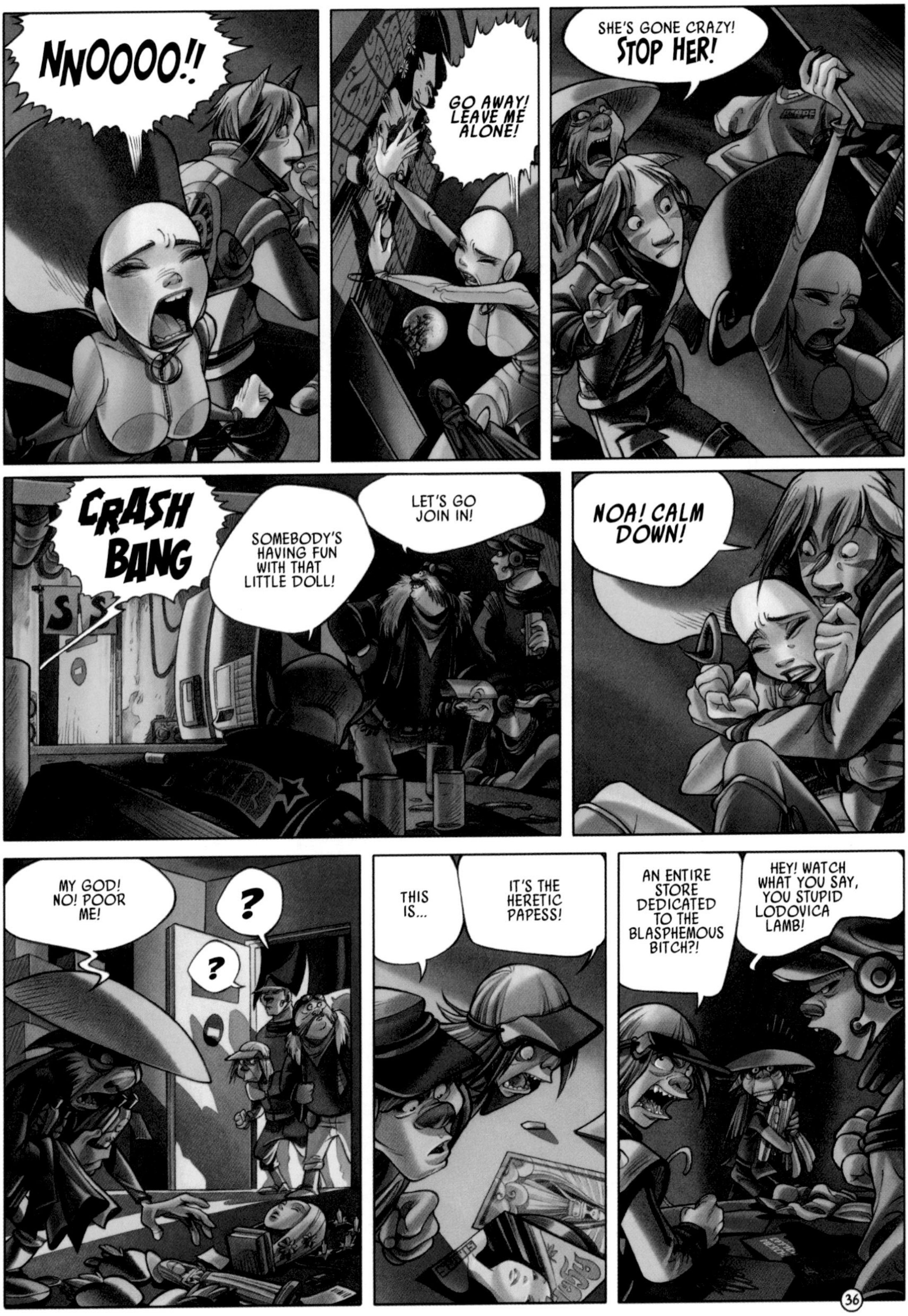
NNOOOO!!
GO AWAY! LEAVE ME ALONE!
SHE'S GONE CRAZY! STOP HER!
CRASH BANG
SOMEBODY'S HAVING FUN WITH THAT LITTLE DOLL!
LET'S GO JOIN IN!
NOA! CALM DOWN!
MY GOD! NO! POOR ME!
?
?
THIS IS...
IT'S THE HERETIC PAPESS!
AN ENTIRE STORE DEDICATED TO THE BLASPHEMOUS BITCH?!
HEY! WATCH WHAT YOU SAY, YOU STUPID LODOVICA LAMB!

AAHH! SO THERE ARE HERETICS AMONG US....
YOU FILTHY TRAITORS! GO BACK TO YOUR PIGSTY!
HOW CAN YOU SUPPORT THAT THRONE THIEF?!
THAT'S ENOUGH OUTTA YOU! WE'RE SICK OF YOU DRAGGING AGAPE'S NAME THROUGH THE MUD! WE'VE BEEN AT YOUR MERCY FOR TOO LONG!
GET UP, NOA! WE'D BETTER GET OUT OF HERE!
...IT'S ALL THAT I HAVE... DO YOU UNDERSTAND?

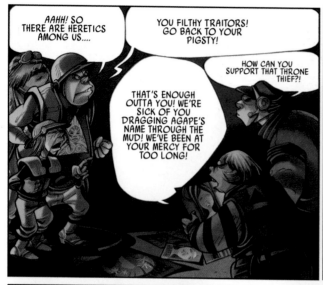

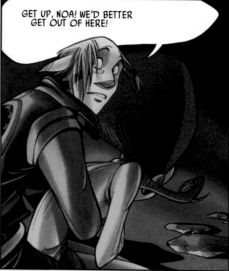

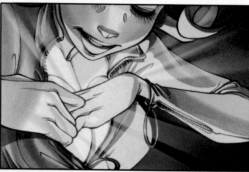

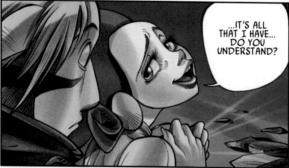

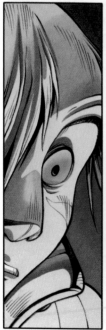

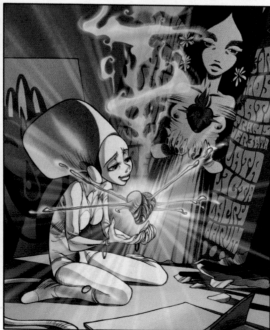

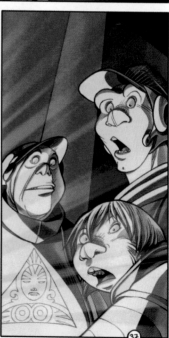

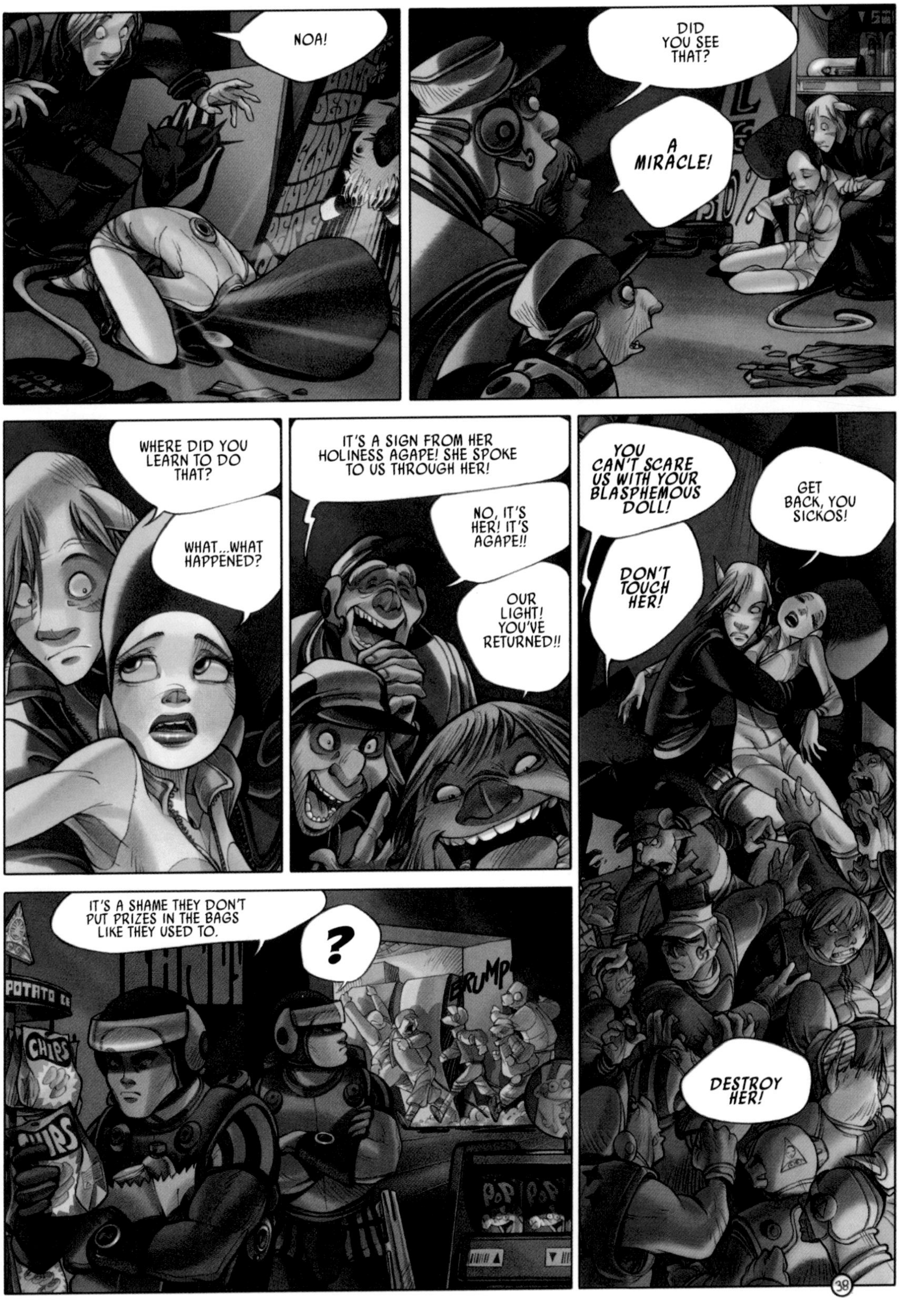
NOA!
DID YOU SEE THAT?
A MIRACLE!
WHERE DID YOU LEARN TO DO THAT?
WHAT...WHAT HAPPENED?
IT'S A SIGN FROM HER HOLINESS AGAPE! SHE SPOKE TO US THROUGH HER!
NO, IT'S HER! IT'S AGAPE!!
OUR LIGHT! YOU'VE RETURNED!!
YOU CAN'T SCARE US WITH YOUR BLASPHEMOUS DOLL!
GET BACK, YOU SICKOS!
DON'T TOUCH HER!
DESTROY HER!
IT'S A SHAME THEY DON'T PUT PRIZES IN THE BAGS LIKE THEY USED TO.
?
BRUMP
POTATO
CHIPS
CHIPS
POP
POP

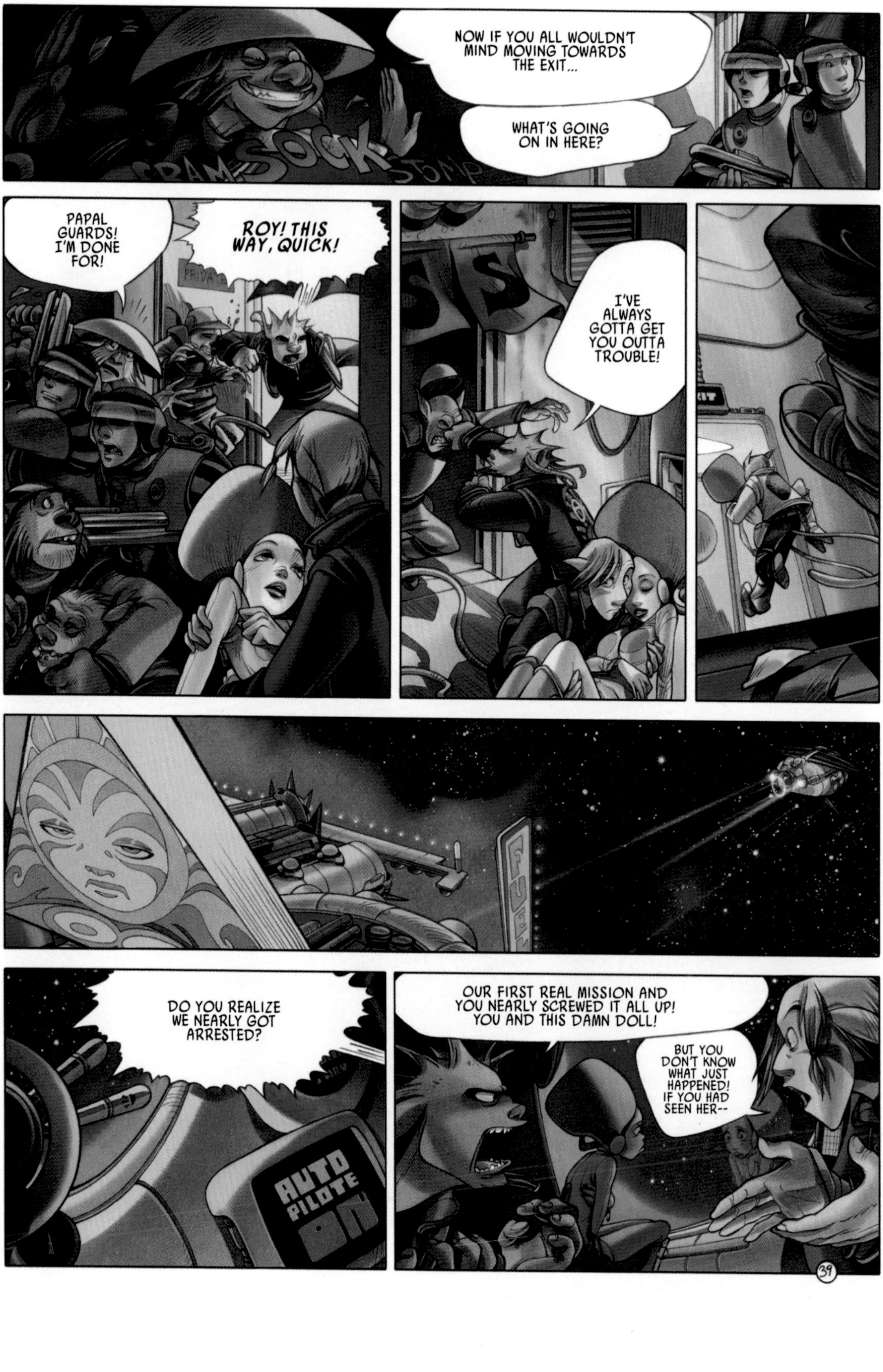
NOW IF YOU ALL WOULDN'T MIND MOVING TOWARDS THE EXIT...
SOCK
STOMP
WHAT'S GOING ON IN HERE?
PAPAL GUARDS! I'M DONE FOR!
ROY! THIS WAY, QUICK!
PRIVATE
I'VE ALWAYS GOTTA GET YOU OUTTA TROUBLE!
DO YOU REALIZE WE NEARLY GOT ARRESTED?
AUTO PILOTE ON
OUR FIRST REAL MISSION AND YOU NEARLY SCREWED IT ALL UP! YOU AND THIS DAMN DOLL!
BUT YOU DON'T KNOW WHAT JUST HAPPENED! IF YOU HAD SEEN HER--

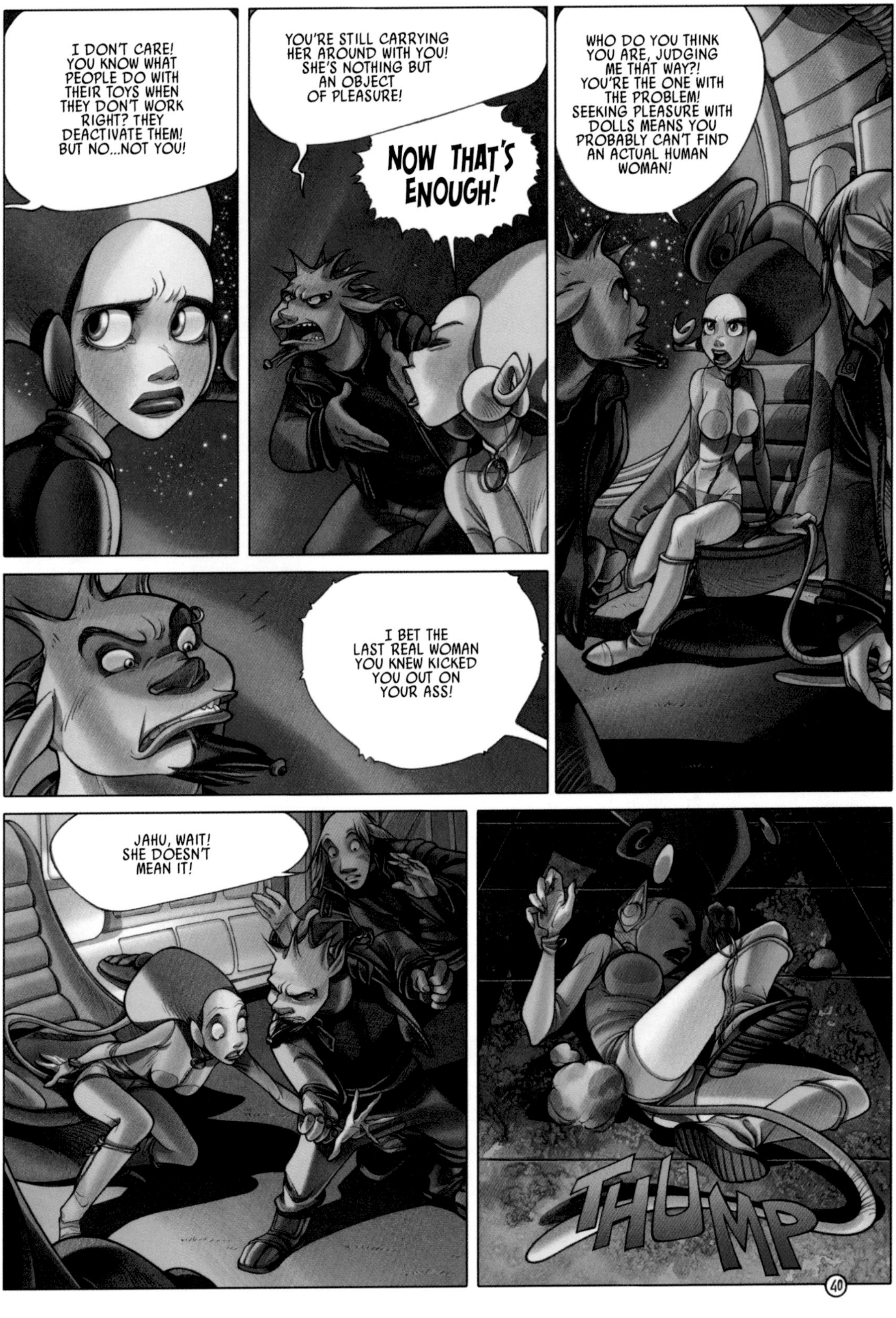
I DON'T CARE! YOU KNOW WHAT PEOPLE DO WITH THEIR TOYS WHEN THEY DON'T WORK RIGHT? THEY DEACTIVATE THEM! BUT NO...NOT YOU!
YOU'RE STILL CARRYING HER AROUND WITH YOU! SHE'S NOTHING BUT AN OBJECT OF PLEASURE!
NOW THAT'S ENOUGH!
WHO DO YOU THINK YOU ARE, JUDGING ME THAT WAY?! YOU'RE THE ONE WITH THE PROBLEM! SEEKING PLEASURE WITH DOLLS MEANS YOU PROBABLY CAN'T FIND AN ACTUAL HUMAN WOMAN!
I BET THE LAST REAL WOMAN YOU KNEW KICKED YOU OUT ON YOUR ASS!
JAHU, WAIT! SHE DOESN'T MEAN IT!
THUMP

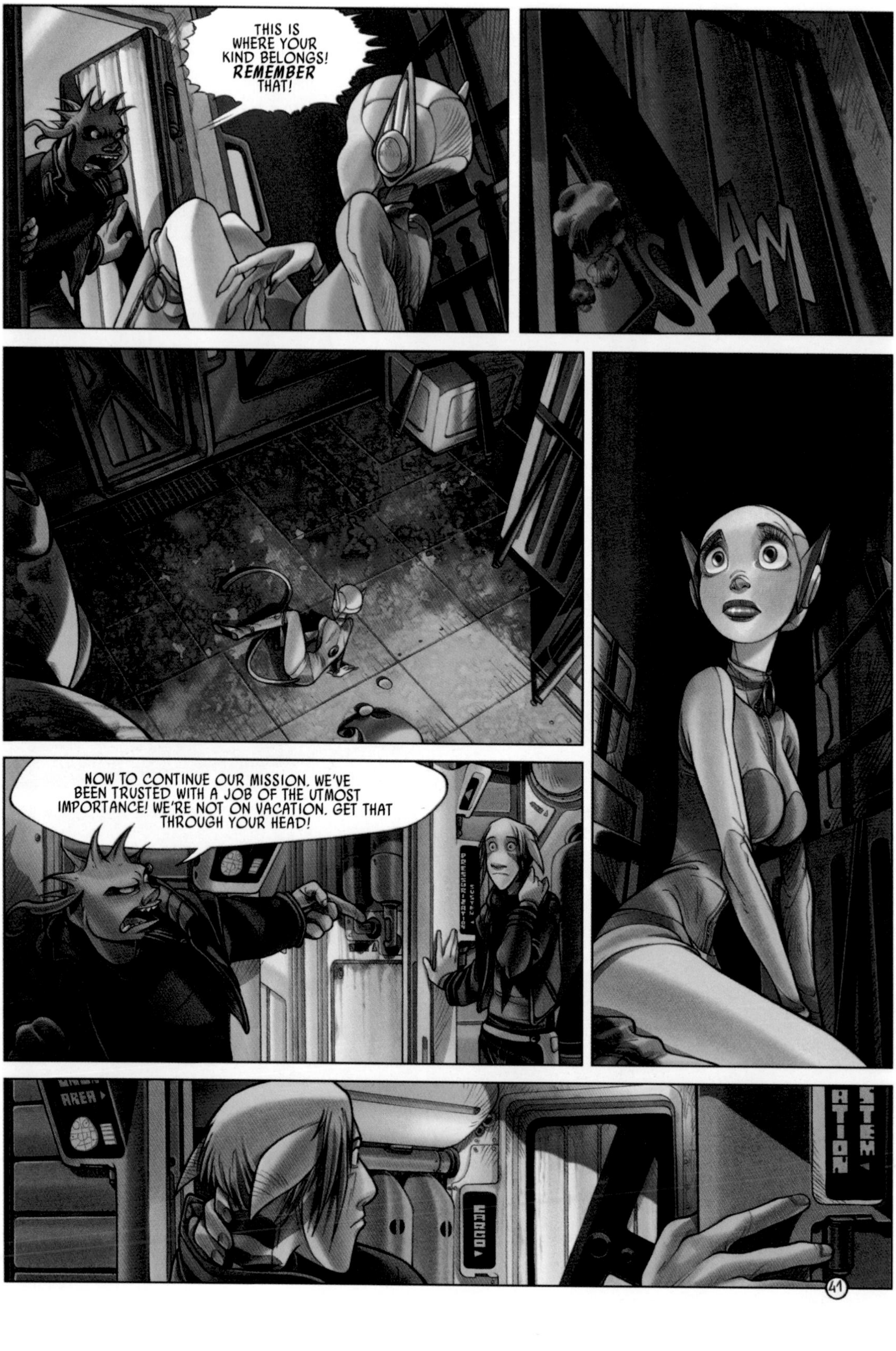
THIS IS WHERE YOUR KIND BELONGS! REMEMBER THAT!
SLAM
NOW TO CONTINUE OUR MISSION. WE'VE BEEN TRUSTED WITH A JOB OF THE UTMOST IMPORTANCE! WE'RE NOT ON VACATION. GET THAT THROUGH YOUR HEAD!
AREA

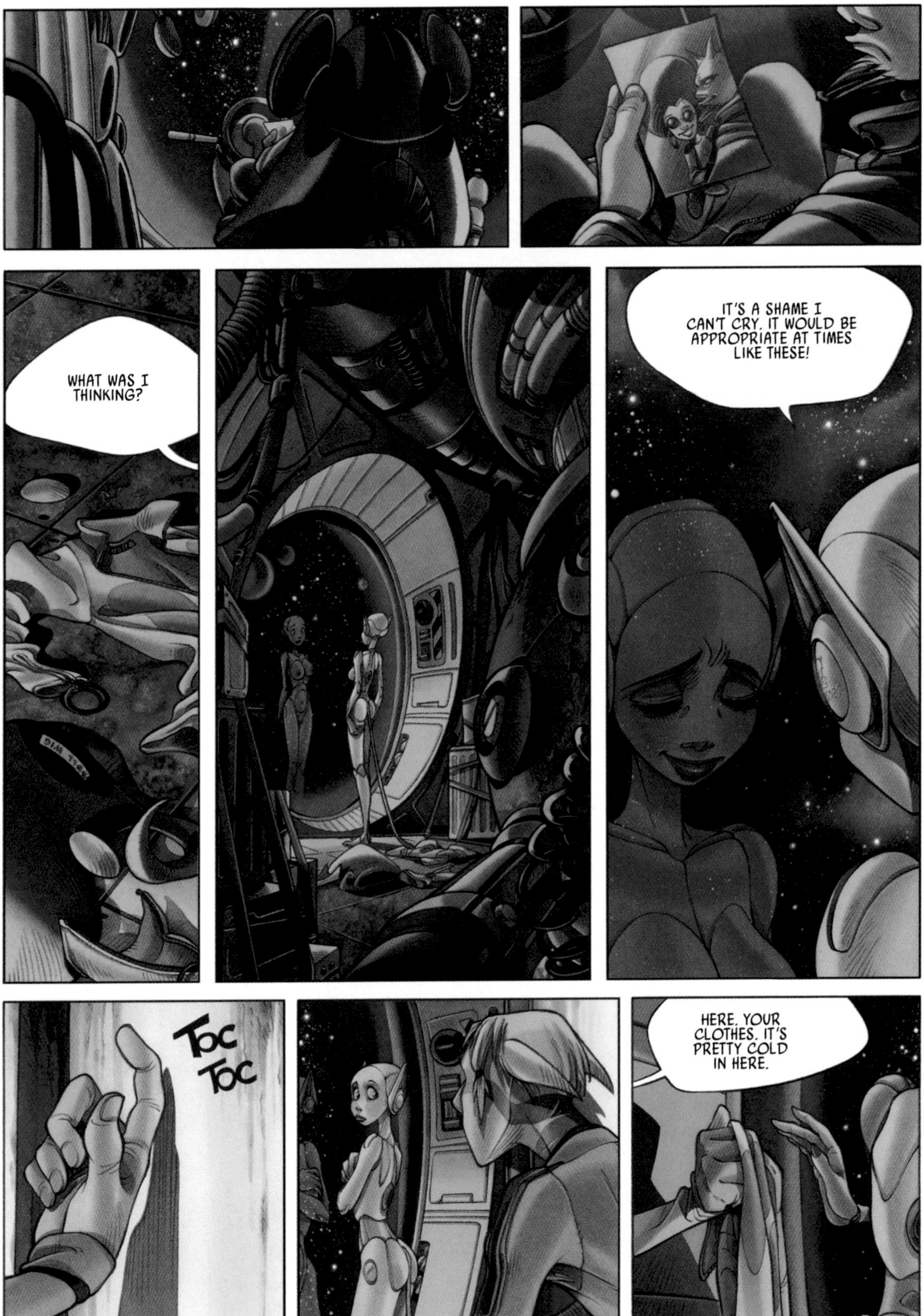
WHAT WAS I THINKING?
IT'S A SHAME I CAN'T CRY. IT WOULD BE APPROPRIATE AT TIMES LIKE THESE!
TOC TOC
HERE. YOUR CLOTHES. IT'S PRETTY COLD IN HERE.

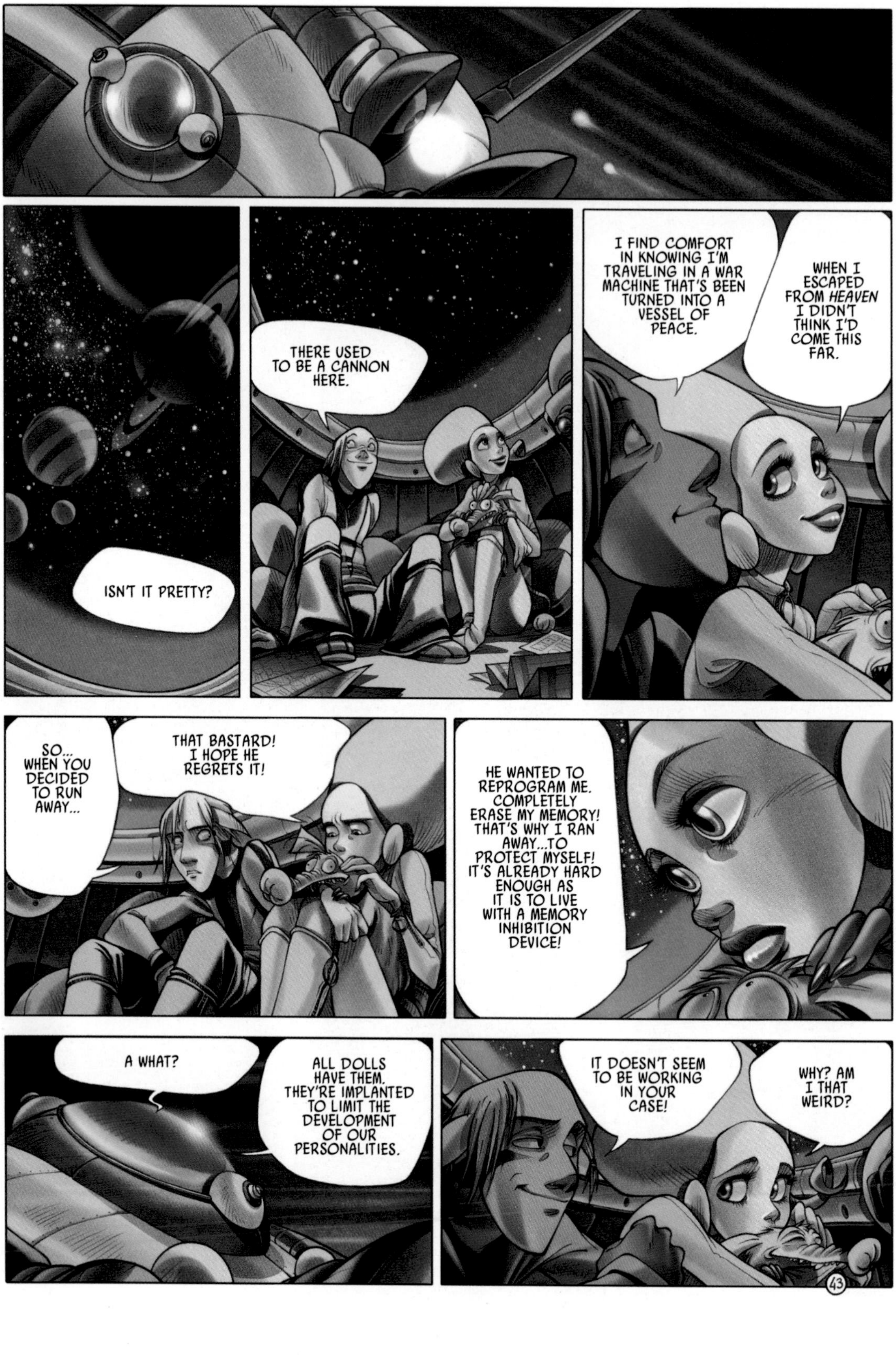
ISN'T IT PRETTY?
THERE USED TO BE A CANNON HERE.
I FIND COMFORT IN KNOWING I'M TRAVELING IN A WAR MACHINE THAT'S BEEN TURNED INTO A VESSEL OF PEACE.
WHEN I ESCAPED FROM *HEAVEN* I DIDN'T THINK I'D COME THIS FAR.
SO... WHEN YOU DECIDED TO RUN AWAY...
THAT BASTARD! I HOPE HE REGRETS IT!
HE WANTED TO REPROGRAM ME. COMPLETELY ERASE MY MEMORY! THAT'S WHY I RAN AWAY...TO PROTECT MYSELF! IT'S ALREADY HARD ENOUGH AS IT IS TO LIVE WITH A MEMORY INHIBITION DEVICE!
A WHAT?
ALL DOLLS HAVE THEM. THEY'RE IMPLANTED TO LIMIT THE DEVELOPMENT OF OUR PERSONALITIES.
IT DOESN'T SEEM TO BE WORKING IN YOUR CASE!
WHY? AM I THAT WEIRD?

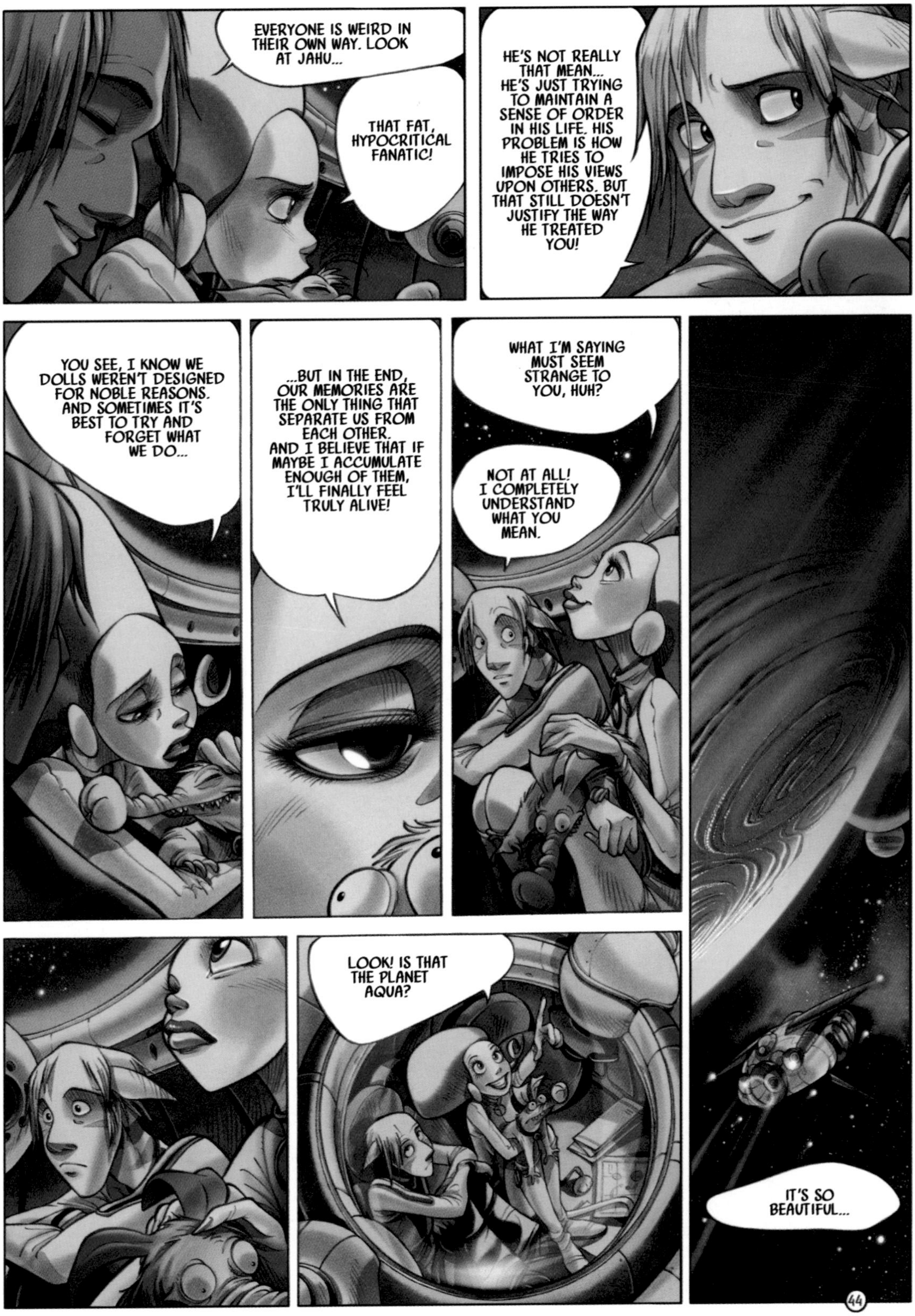
EVERYONE IS WEIRD IN THEIR OWN WAY. LOOK AT JAHU...
THAT FAT, HYPOCRITICAL FANATIC!
HE'S NOT REALLY THAT MEAN... HE'S JUST TRYING TO MAINTAIN A SENSE OF ORDER IN HIS LIFE. HIS PROBLEM IS HOW HE TRIES TO IMPOSE HIS VIEWS UPON OTHERS. BUT THAT STILL DOESN'T JUSTIFY THE WAY HE TREATED YOU!
YOU SEE, I KNOW WE DOLLS WEREN'T DESIGNED FOR NOBLE REASONS. AND SOMETIMES IT'S BEST TO TRY AND FORGET WHAT WE DO...
...BUT IN THE END, OUR MEMORIES ARE THE ONLY THING THAT SEPARATE US FROM EACH OTHER. AND I BELIEVE THAT IF MAYBE I ACCUMULATE ENOUGH OF THEM, I'LL FINALLY FEEL TRULY ALIVE!
WHAT I'M SAYING MUST SEEM STRANGE TO YOU, HUH?
NOT AT ALL! I COMPLETELY UNDERSTAND WHAT YOU MEAN.
LOOK! IS THAT THE PLANET AQUA?
IT'S SO BEAUTIFUL...

"...pure spirit is a pure lie..." - F. Nietzsche.

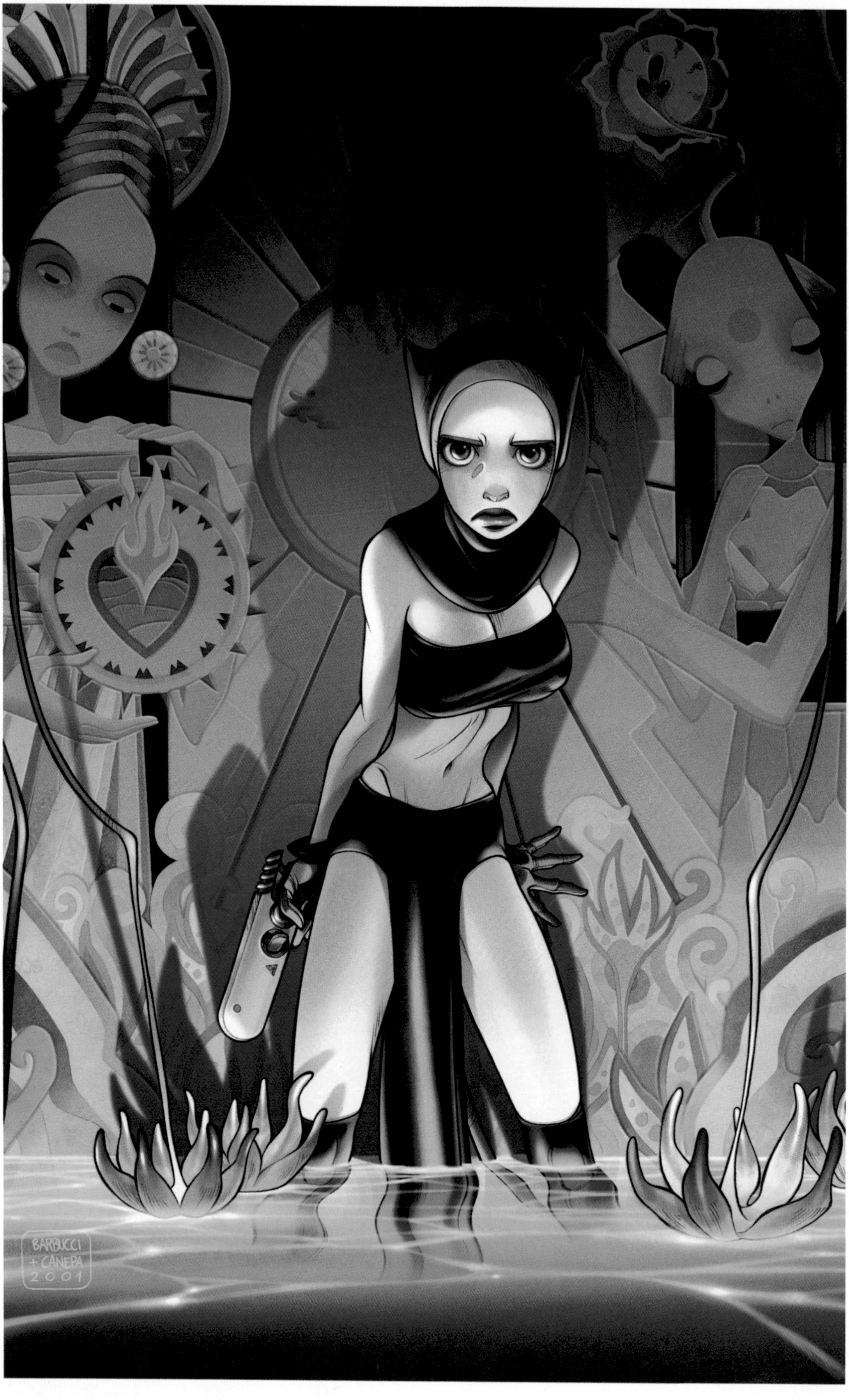
BARBUCCI
+ CANEPA
2001

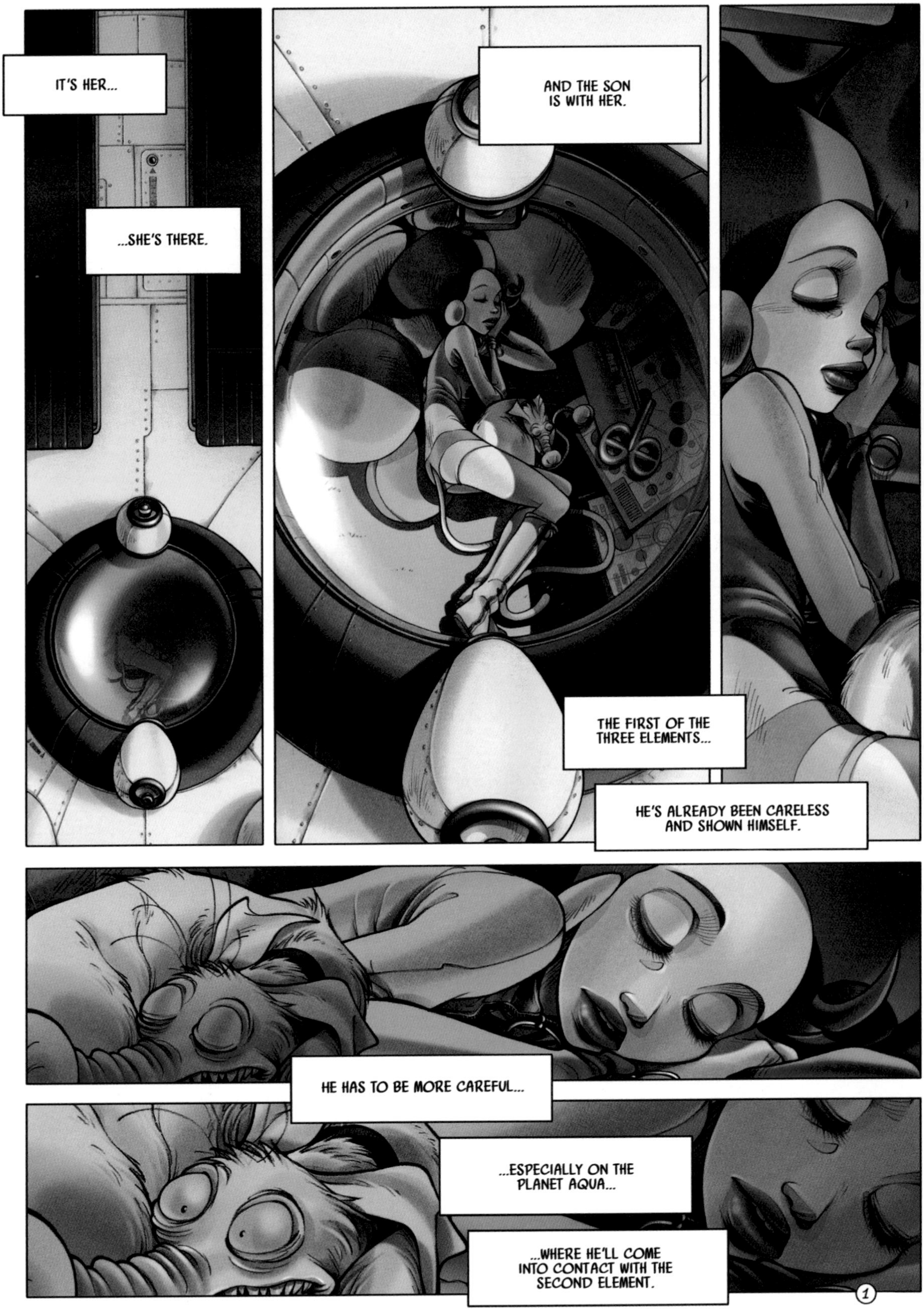
IT'S HER...
...SHE'S THERE.
AND THE SON IS WITH HER.
THE FIRST OF THE THREE ELEMENTS...
HE'S ALREADY BEEN CARELESS AND SHOWN HIMSELF.
HE HAS TO BE MORE CAREFUL...
...ESPECIALLY ON THE PLANET AQUA...
...WHERE HE'LL COME INTO CONTACT WITH THE SECOND ELEMENT.

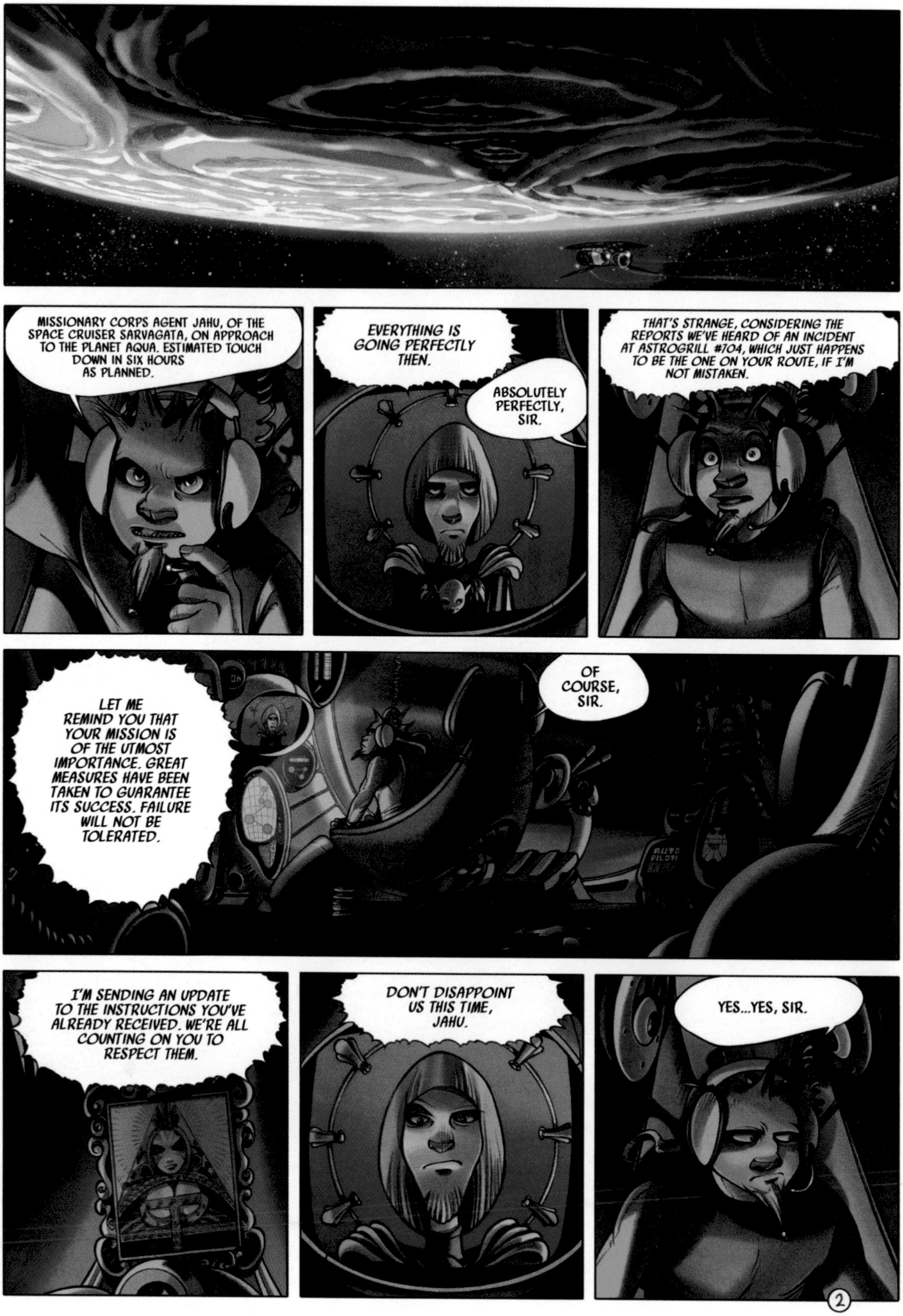
MISSIONARY CORPS AGENT JAHU, OF THE SPACE CRUISER SARVAGATA, ON APPROACH TO THE PLANET AQUA. ESTIMATED TOUCH DOWN IN SIX HOURS AS PLANNED.
EVERYTHING IS GOING PERFECTLY THEN.
ABSOLUTELY PERFECTLY, SIR.
THAT'S STRANGE, CONSIDERING THE REPORTS WE'VE HEARD OF AN INCIDENT AT ASTROGRILL #704, WHICH JUST HAPPENS TO BE THE ONE ON YOUR ROUTE, IF I'M NOT MISTAKEN.
LET ME REMIND YOU THAT YOUR MISSION IS OF THE UTMOST IMPORTANCE. GREAT MEASURES HAVE BEEN TAKEN TO GUARANTEE ITS SUCCESS. FAILURE WILL NOT BE TOLERATED.
OF COURSE, SIR.
I'M SENDING AN UPDATE TO THE INSTRUCTIONS YOU'VE ALREADY RECEIVED. WE'RE ALL COUNTING ON YOU TO RESPECT THEM.
DON'T DISAPPOINT US THIS TIME, JAHU.
YES...YES, SIR.

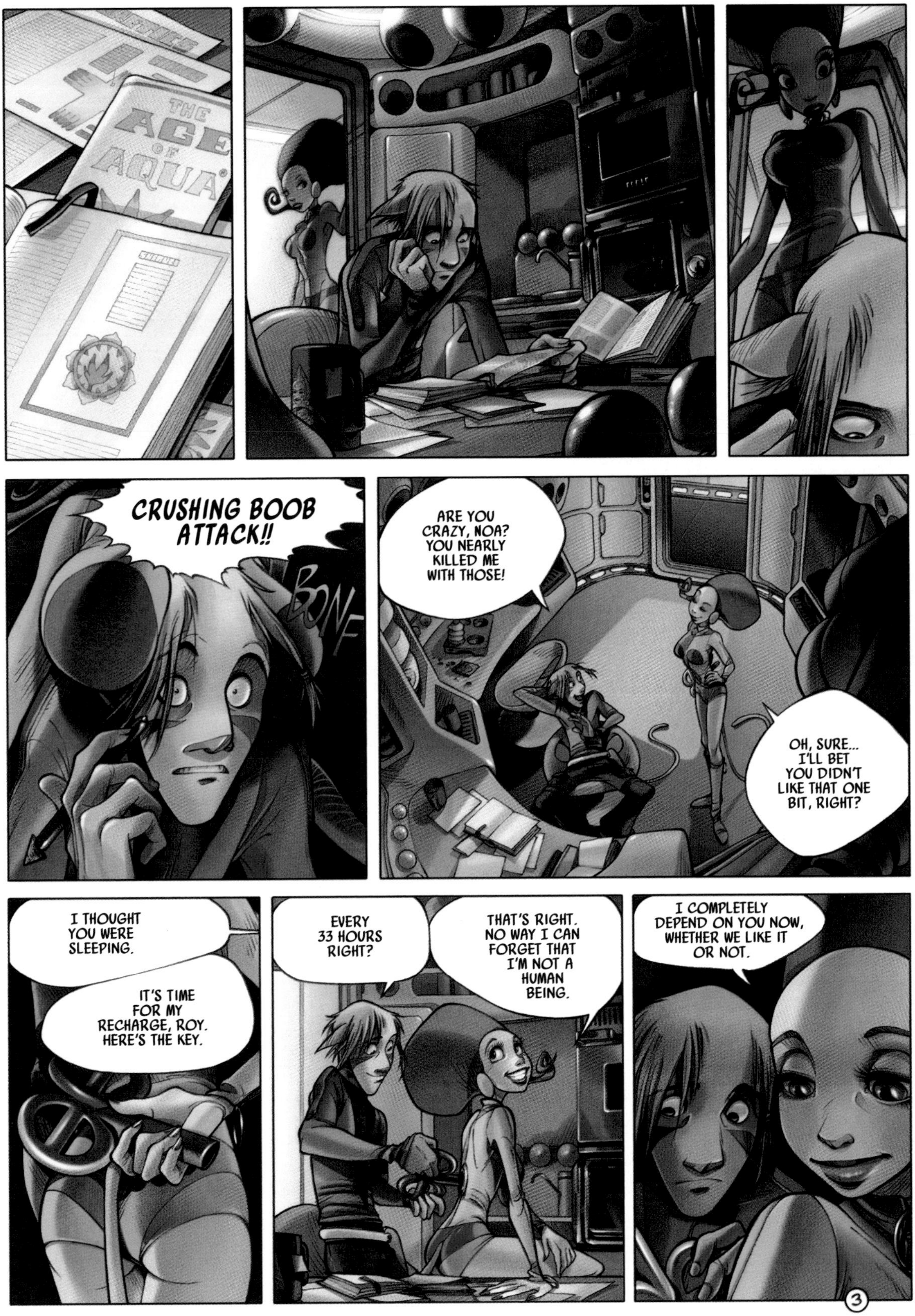
THE AGE OF AQUA
CRUSHING BOOB ATTACK!!
BONF
ARE YOU CRAZY, NOA? YOU NEARLY KILLED ME WITH THOSE!
OH, SURE... I'LL BET YOU DIDN'T LIKE THAT ONE BIT, RIGHT?
I THOUGHT YOU WERE SLEEPING.
IT'S TIME FOR MY RECHARGE, ROY. HERE'S THE KEY.
EVERY 33 HOURS RIGHT?
THAT'S RIGHT. NO WAY I CAN FORGET THAT I'M NOT A HUMAN BEING.
I COMPLETELY DEPEND ON YOU NOW, WHETHER WE LIKE IT OR NOT.

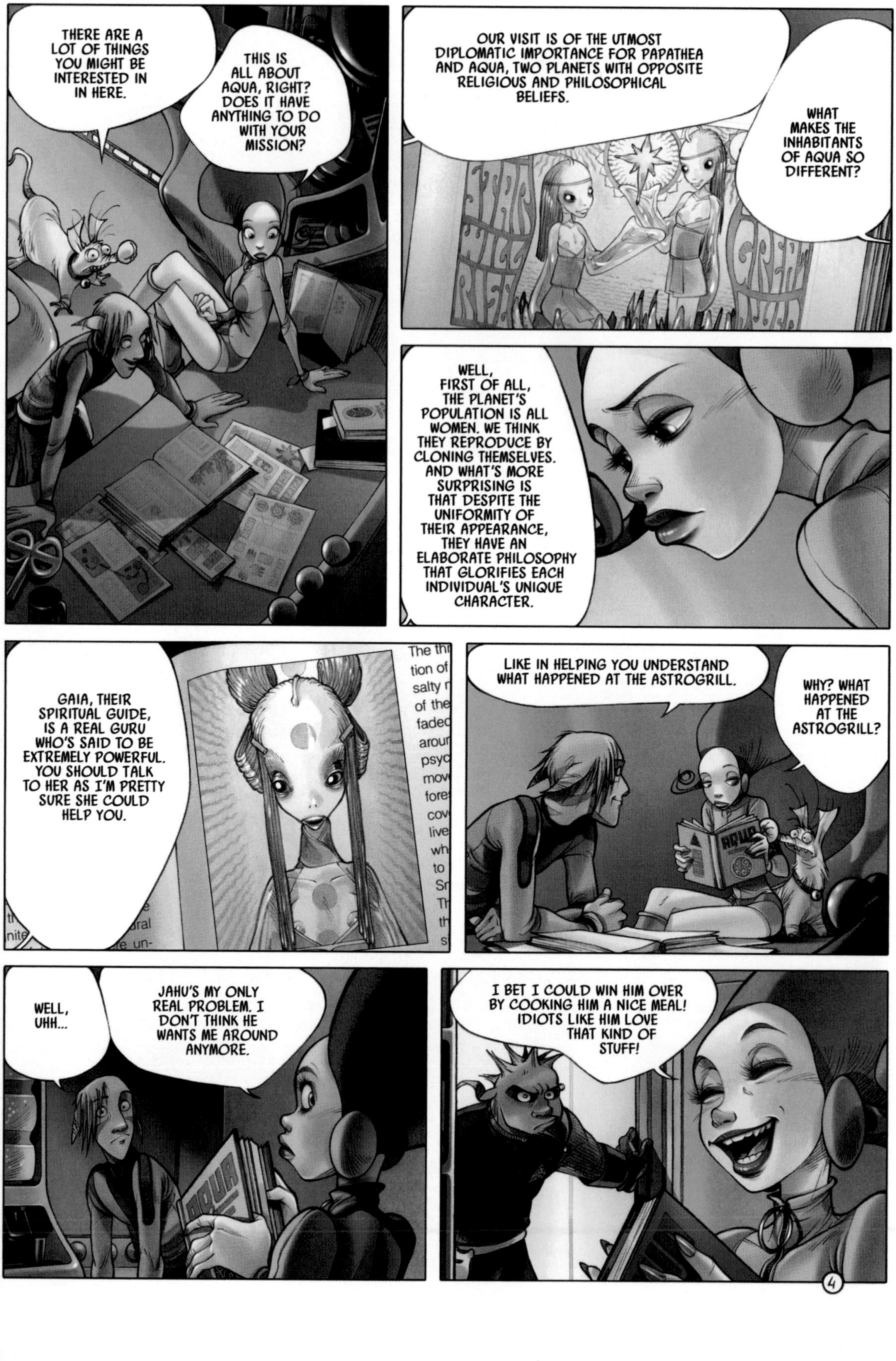
THERE ARE A LOT OF THINGS YOU MIGHT BE INTERESTED IN IN HERE.
THIS IS ALL ABOUT AQUA, RIGHT? DOES IT HAVE ANYTHING TO DO WITH YOUR MISSION?
OUR VISIT IS OF THE UTMOST DIPLOMATIC IMPORTANCE FOR PAPATHEA AND AQUA, TWO PLANETS WITH OPPOSITE RELIGIOUS AND PHILOSOPHICAL BELIEFS.
WHAT MAKES THE INHABITANTS OF AQUA SO DIFFERENT?
WELL, FIRST OF ALL, THE PLANET'S POPULATION IS ALL WOMEN. WE THINK THEY REPRODUCE BY CLONING THEMSELVES. AND WHAT'S MORE SURPRISING IS THAT DESPITE THE UNIFORMITY OF THEIR APPEARANCE, THEY HAVE AN ELABORATE PHILOSOPHY THAT GLORIFIES EACH INDIVIDUAL'S UNIQUE CHARACTER.
GAIA, THEIR SPIRITUAL GUIDE, IS A REAL GURU WHO'S SAID TO BE EXTREMELY POWERFUL. YOU SHOULD TALK TO HER AS I'M PRETTY SURE SHE COULD HELP YOU.
LIKE IN HELPING YOU UNDERSTAND WHAT HAPPENED AT THE ASTROGRILL.
WHY? WHAT HAPPENED AT THE ASTROGRILL?
WELL, UHH...
JAHU'S MY ONLY REAL PROBLEM. I DON'T THINK HE WANTS ME AROUND ANYMORE.
I BET I COULD WIN HIM OVER BY COOKING HIM A NICE MEAL! IDIOTS LIKE HIM LOVE THAT KIND OF STUFF!

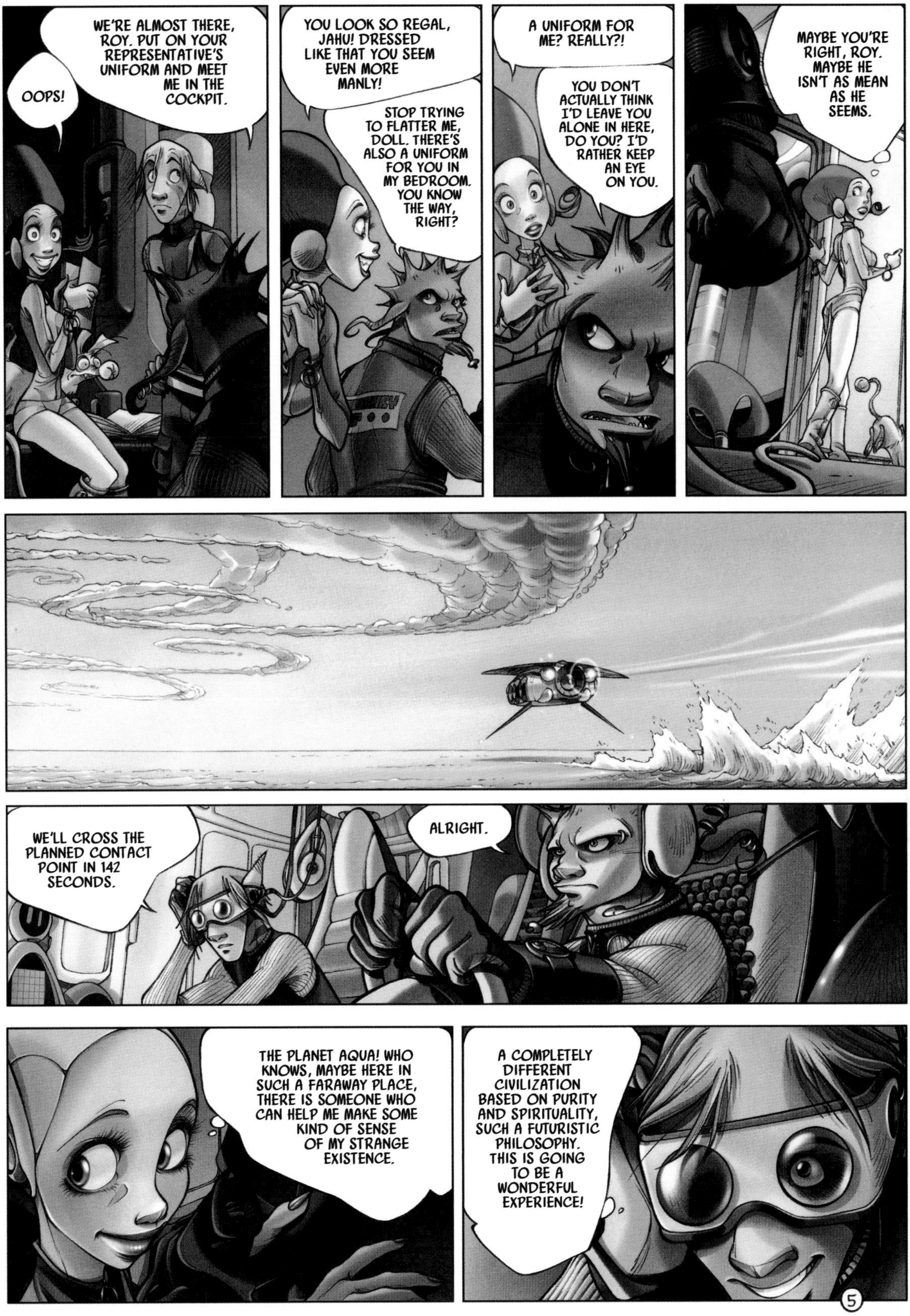
WE'RE ALMOST THERE, ROY. PUT ON YOUR REPRESENTATIVE'S UNIFORM AND MEET ME IN THE COCKPIT.
OOPS!
YOU LOOK SO REGAL, JAHU! DRESSED LIKE THAT YOU SEEM EVEN MORE MANLY!
STOP TRYING TO FLATTER ME, DOLL. THERE'S ALSO A UNIFORM FOR YOU IN MY BEDROOM. YOU KNOW THE WAY, RIGHT?
A UNIFORM FOR ME? REALLY?!
YOU DON'T ACTUALLY THINK I'D LEAVE YOU ALONE IN HERE, DO YOU? I'D RATHER KEEP AN EYE ON YOU.
MAYBE YOU'RE RIGHT, ROY. MAYBE HE ISN'T AS MEAN AS HE SEEMS.
WE'LL CROSS THE PLANNED CONTACT POINT IN 142 SECONDS.
ALRIGHT.
THE PLANET AQUA! WHO KNOWS, MAYBE HERE IN SUCH A FARAWAY PLACE, THERE IS SOMEONE WHO CAN HELP ME MAKE SOME KIND OF SENSE OF MY STRANGE EXISTENCE.
A COMPLETELY DIFFERENT CIVILIZATION BASED ON PURITY AND SPIRITUALITY, SUCH A FUTURISTIC PHILOSOPHY. THIS IS GOING TO BE A WONDERFUL EXPERIENCE!

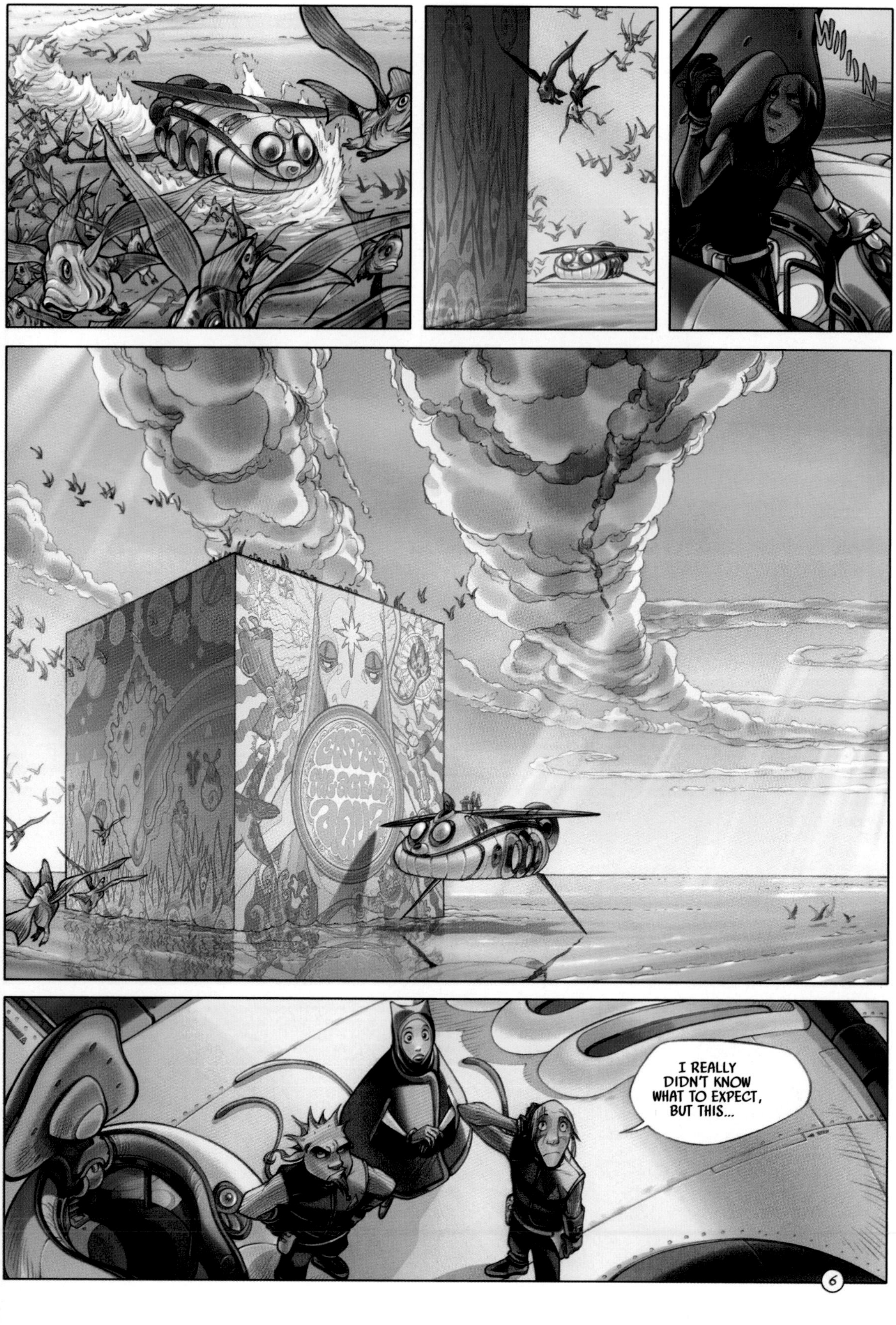
WIIIIIN
I REALLY DIDN'T KNOW WHAT TO EXPECT, BUT THIS...

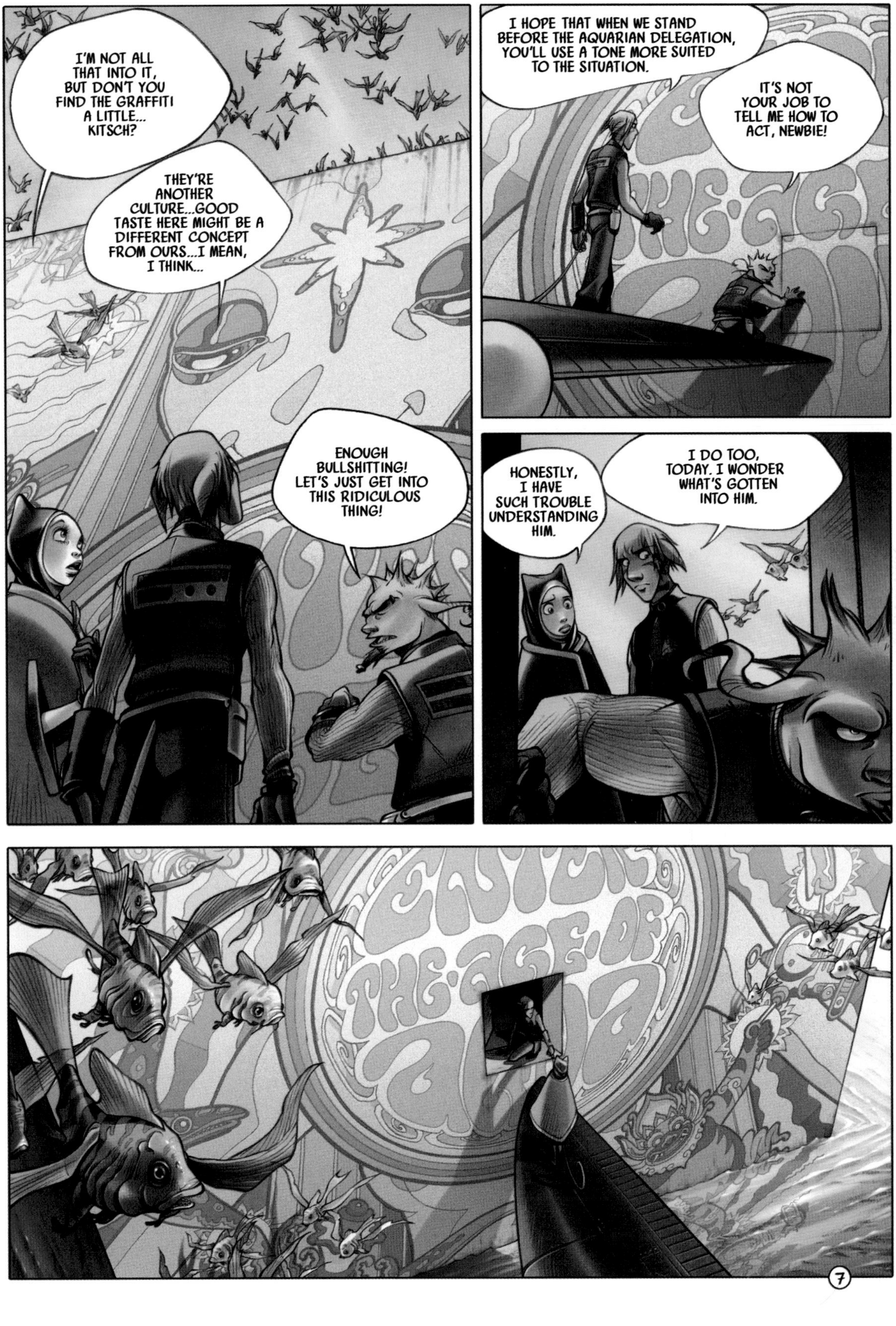
I'M NOT ALL THAT INTO IT, BUT DON'T YOU FIND THE GRAFFITI A LITTLE... KITSCH?
THEY'RE ANOTHER CULTURE...GOOD TASTE HERE MIGHT BE A DIFFERENT CONCEPT FROM OURS...I MEAN, I THINK...
ENOUGH BULLSHITTING! LET'S JUST GET INTO THIS RIDICULOUS THING!
I HOPE THAT WHEN WE STAND BEFORE THE AQUARIAN DELEGATION, YOU'LL USE A TONE MORE SUITED TO THE SITUATION.
IT'S NOT YOUR JOB TO TELL ME HOW TO ACT, NEWBIE!
HONESTLY, I HAVE SUCH TROUBLE UNDERSTANDING HIM.
I DO TOO, TODAY. I WONDER WHAT'S GOTTEN INTO HIM.
ENTER THE AGE OF AQUA

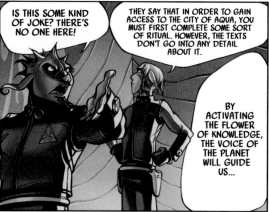

IS THIS SOME KIND OF JOKE? THERE'S NO ONE HERE!

THEY SAY THAT IN ORDER TO GAIN ACCESS TO THE CITY OF AQUA, YOU MUST FIRST COMPLETE SOME SORT OF RITUAL. HOWEVER, THE TEXTS DON'T GO INTO ANY DETAIL ABOUT IT.

BY ACTIVATING THE FLOWER OF KNOWLEDGE, THE VOICE OF THE PLANET WILL GUIDE US...

...AND ONCE WE'RE IN HARMONY WITH THE CYCLE OF THE UNIVERSE, THE DOORS OF AQUA WILL OPEN AND WELCOME US INTO ITS HEART OF PERFECTION.

HOW DO YOU KNOW ALL THAT?

EVERYTHING WAS WRITTEN IN THE BROCHURES AT THE ENTRANCE. DIDN'T YOU SEE THEM?

PERFECT! THE STUPID DOLL SEEMS RIGHT AT HOME.

"THE FLOWER OF KNOWLEDGE"? HMPH!

CLK

ZZZZ

ZZ

YOU BETTER LET ME DO THE TALKING HERE. I DON'T KNOW WHAT'S UP WITH YOU TODAY, BUT YOU'RE DEFINITELY NOT IN THE RIGHT STATE OF MIND FOR THIS MISSION.

DON'T WORRY, I'VE NEVER FAILED A MISSION.

WELCOME TO AQUA, DISCORDANT CREATURES. PLEASE TAKE A SEAT ON THE MEDITATION CUBES.

8

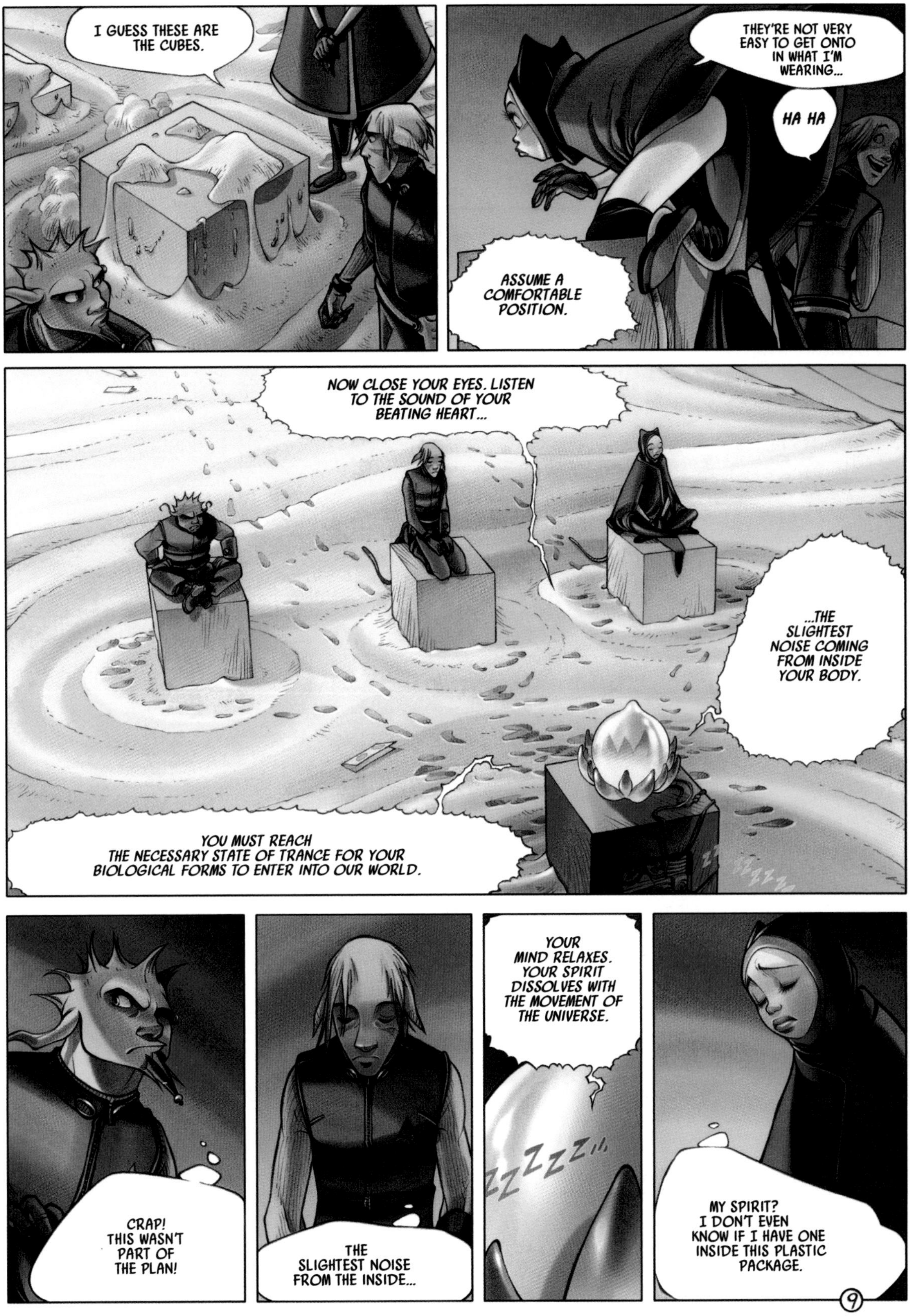

I GUESS THESE ARE THE CUBES.
THEY'RE NOT VERY EASY TO GET ONTO IN WHAT I'M WEARING...
HA HA
ASSUME A COMFORTABLE POSITION.
NOW CLOSE YOUR EYES. LISTEN TO THE SOUND OF YOUR BEATING HEART...
...THE SLIGHTEST NOISE COMING FROM INSIDE YOUR BODY.
YOU MUST REACH THE NECESSARY STATE OF TRANCE FOR YOUR BIOLOGICAL FORMS TO ENTER INTO OUR WORLD.
ZZZZZ
CRAP! THIS WASN'T PART OF THE PLAN!
THE SLIGHTEST NOISE FROM THE INSIDE...
YOUR MIND RELAXES. YOUR SPIRIT DISSOLVES WITH THE MOVEMENT OF THE UNIVERSE.
ZZZZZ
MY SPIRIT? I DON'T EVEN KNOW IF I HAVE ONE INSIDE THIS PLASTIC PACKAGE.

THIS IS THE FIRST TIME I'VE EVER BEEN ASKED TO UNDERGO ANY KIND OF MENTAL AND SPIRITUAL EXERCISE. IT'LL NEVER WORK!

OPEN THE SECRET DOOR THAT LEADS TO INTERNAL PEACE.

MAYBE I COULD TRY...BY SEARCHING INSIDE MYSELF.

OKAY! I'M GOING TO PRETEND I BELIEVE IN THIS NONSENSE. I JUST HAVE TO KEEP MY EYES CLOSED AND LOOK LIKE I'M AT PEACE.

HEY! WHERE DID THEY GO?!

I HEAR... THE SOUNDS OF MY BIOMECHANICAL INNARDS. THE CIRCULATION OF VITAL LIQUIDS...

...AND SOMETHING ELSE AS WELL...

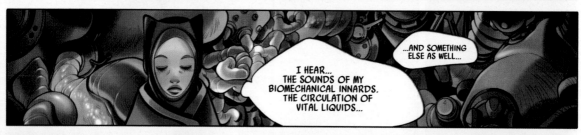

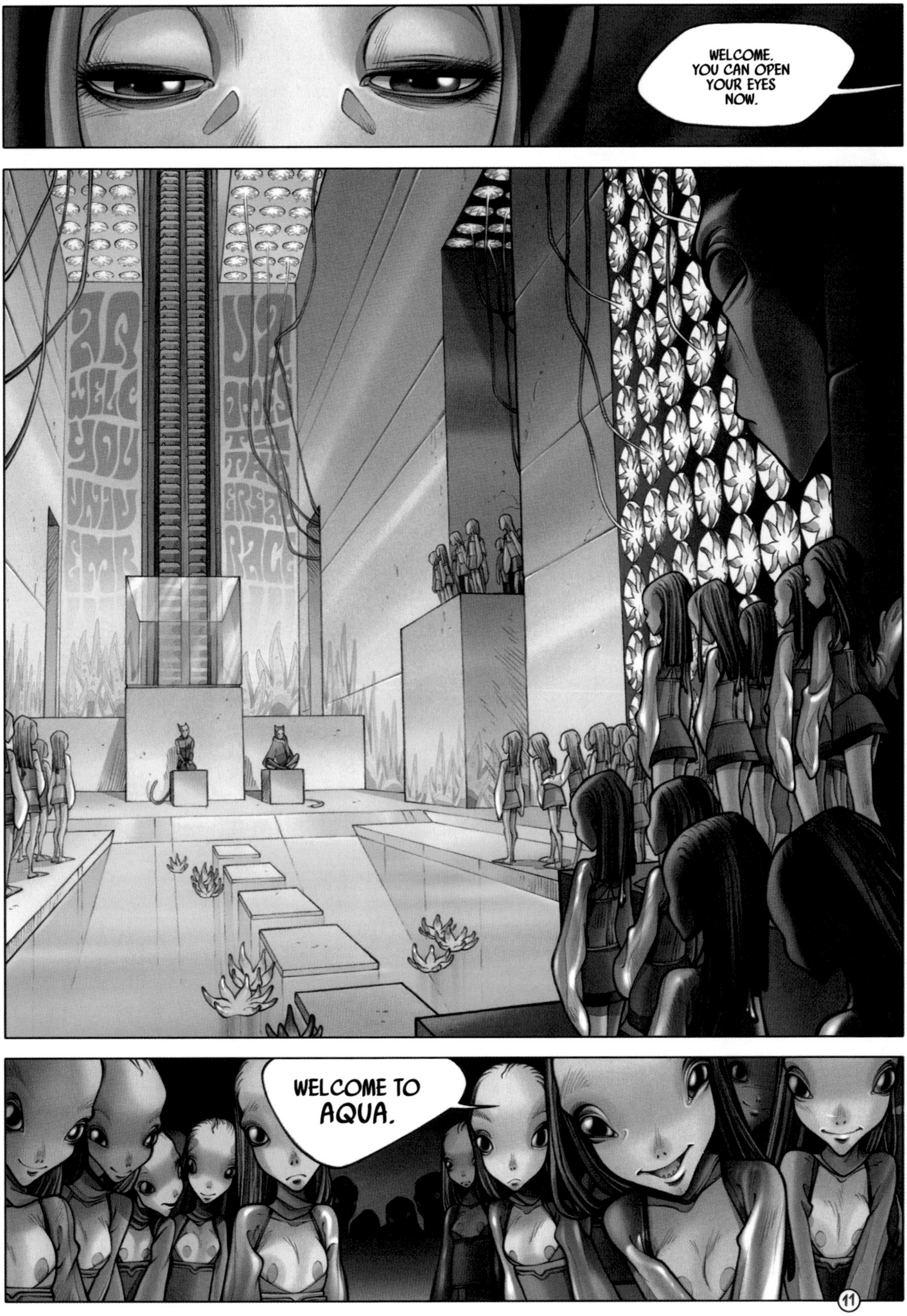
WELCOME. YOU CAN OPEN YOUR EYES NOW.
WELCOME TO AQUA.

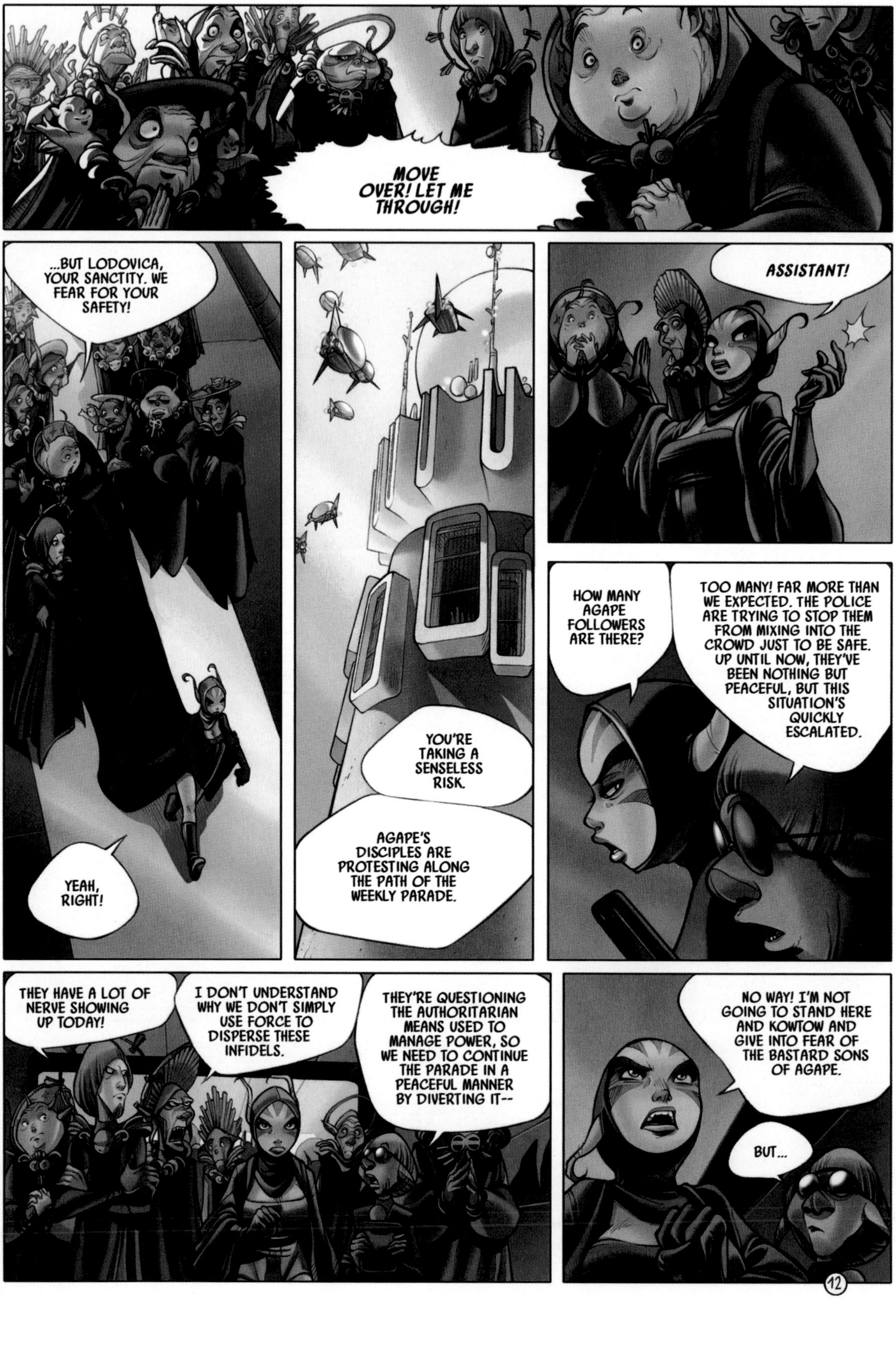
MOVE OVER! LET ME THROUGH!
...BUT LODOVICA, YOUR SANCTITY. WE FEAR FOR YOUR SAFETY!
YEAH, RIGHT!
YOU'RE TAKING A SENSELESS RISK.
AGAPE'S DISCIPLES ARE PROTESTING ALONG THE PATH OF THE WEEKLY PARADE.
ASSISTANT!
HOW MANY AGAPE FOLLOWERS ARE THERE?
TOO MANY! FAR MORE THAN WE EXPECTED. THE POLICE ARE TRYING TO STOP THEM FROM MIXING INTO THE CROWD JUST TO BE SAFE. UP UNTIL NOW, THEY'VE BEEN NOTHING BUT PEACEFUL, BUT THIS SITUATION'S QUICKLY ESCALATED.
THEY HAVE A LOT OF NERVE SHOWING UP TODAY!
I DON'T UNDERSTAND WHY WE DON'T SIMPLY USE FORCE TO DISPERSE THESE INFIDELS.
THEY'RE QUESTIONING THE AUTHORITARIAN MEANS USED TO MANAGE POWER, SO WE NEED TO CONTINUE THE PARADE IN A PEACEFUL MANNER BY DIVERTING IT--
NO WAY! I'M NOT GOING TO STAND HERE AND KOWTOW AND GIVE INTO FEAR OF THE BASTARD SONS OF AGAPE.
BUT...

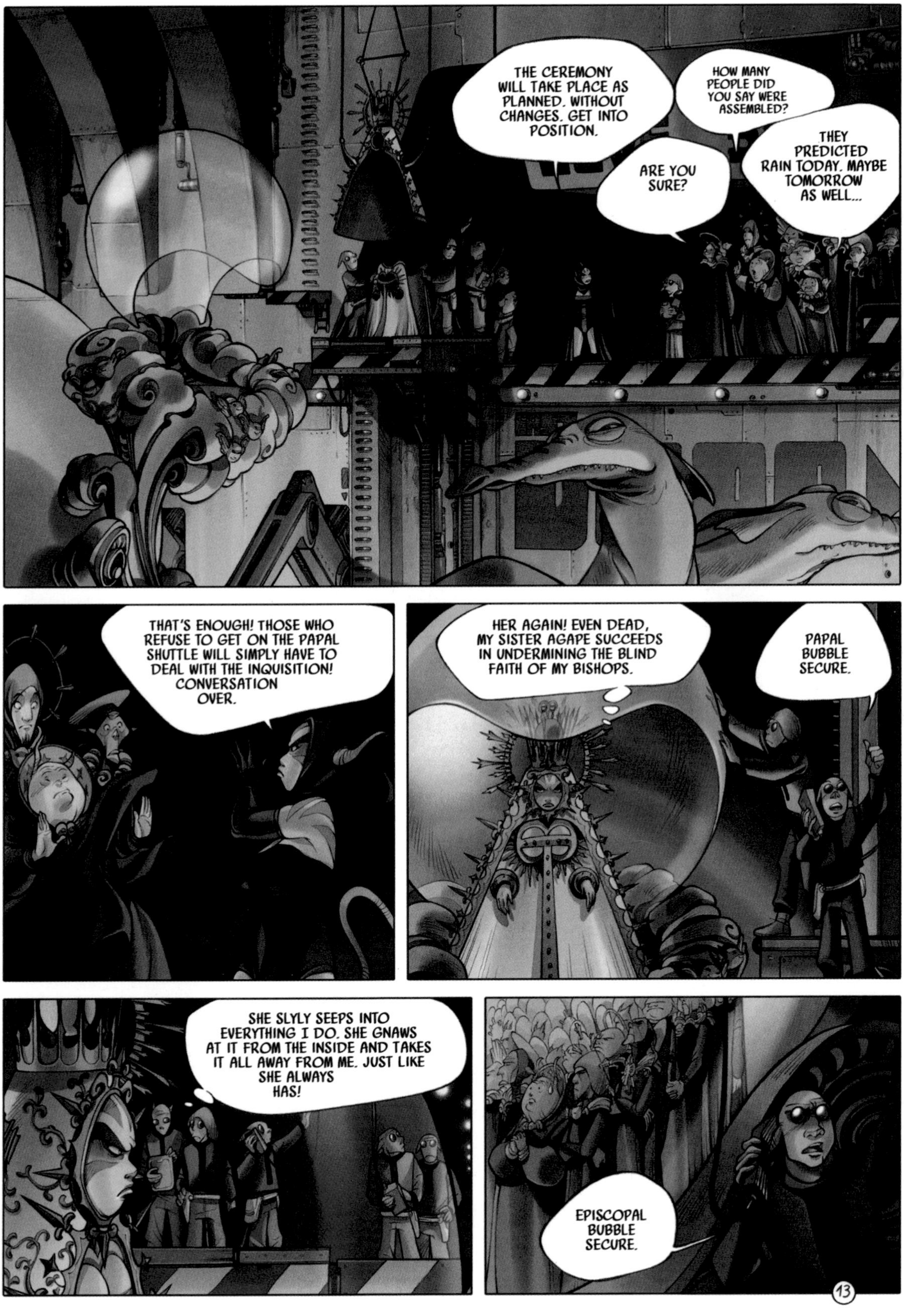
THE CEREMONY WILL TAKE PLACE AS PLANNED. WITHOUT CHANGES. GET INTO POSITION.
HOW MANY PEOPLE DID YOU SAY WERE ASSEMBLED?
ARE YOU SURE?
THEY PREDICTED RAIN TODAY. MAYBE TOMORROW AS WELL...
THAT'S ENOUGH! THOSE WHO REFUSE TO GET ON THE PAPAL SHUTTLE WILL SIMPLY HAVE TO DEAL WITH THE INQUISITION! CONVERSATION OVER.
HER AGAIN! EVEN DEAD, MY SISTER AGAPE SUCCEEDS IN UNDERMINING THE BLIND FAITH OF MY BISHOPS.
PAPAL BUBBLE SECURE.
SHE SLYLY SEEPS INTO EVERYTHING I DO. SHE GNAWS AT IT FROM THE INSIDE AND TAKES IT ALL AWAY FROM ME. JUST LIKE SHE ALWAYS HAS!
EPISCOPAL BUBBLE SECURE.

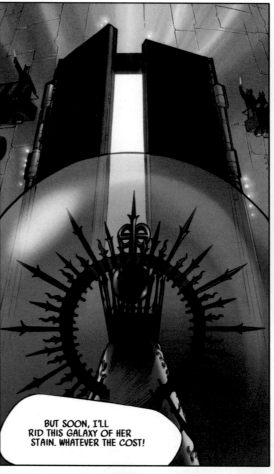

BUT SOON, I'LL RID THIS GALAXY OF HER STAIN. WHATEVER THE COST!

WISH ME LUCK, MIRACLE GENIE!

HERE WE ARE, MY BROTHERS. THE SACRED DOOR IS OPENING, AND IN A FEW SECONDS, THE PAPESS LODOVICA HERSELF WILL APPEAR BEFORE THE JOYOUS CROWDS.

THERE SHE IS! HALLELUJAH! HALLELUJAH!

APPROACH WITHOUT FEAR, MY LITTLE BITCH...

I'M WAITING FOR YOU AS WELL. WITH A NICE SURPRISE!

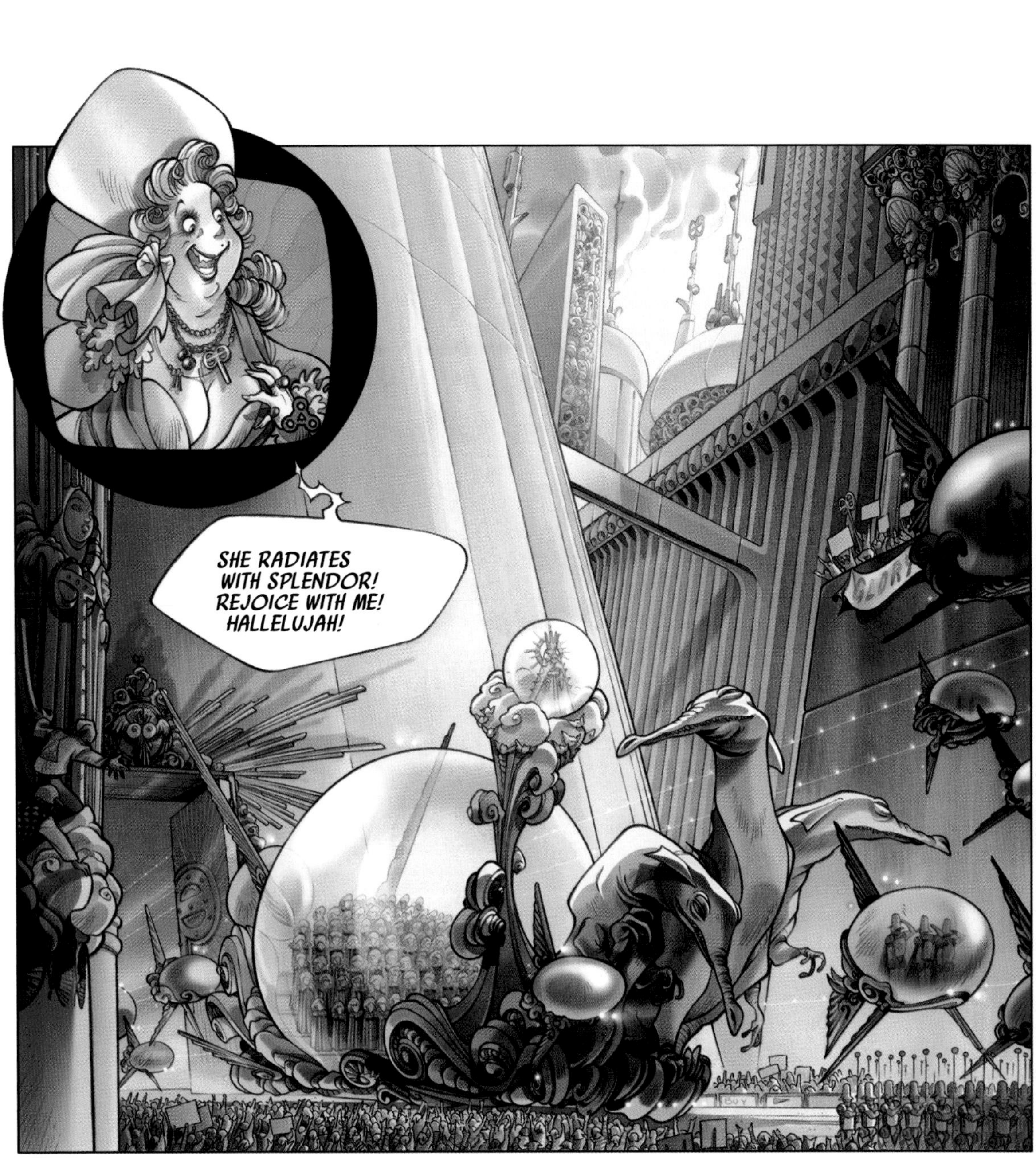
SHE RADIATES WITH SPLENDOR! REJOICE WITH ME! HALLELUJAH!

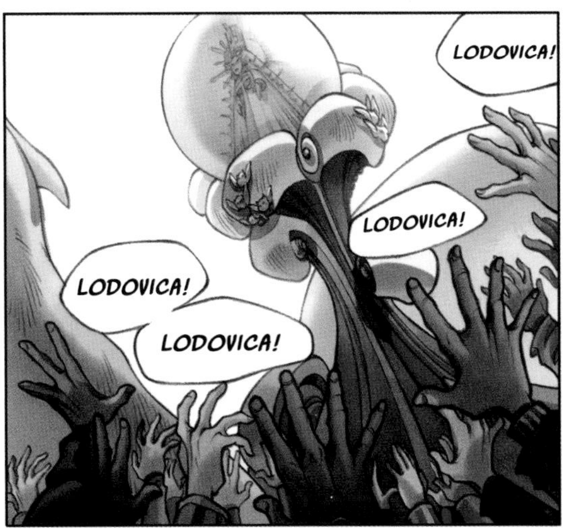
LODOVICA!
LODOVICA!
LODOVICA!
LODOVICA!

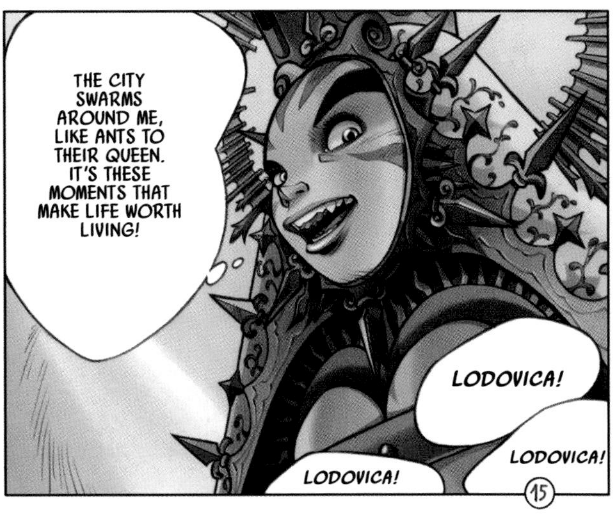
THE CITY SWARMS AROUND ME, LIKE ANTS TO THEIR QUEEN. IT'S THESE MOMENTS THAT MAKE LIFE WORTH LIVING!
LODOVICA!
LODOVICA!
LODOVICA!

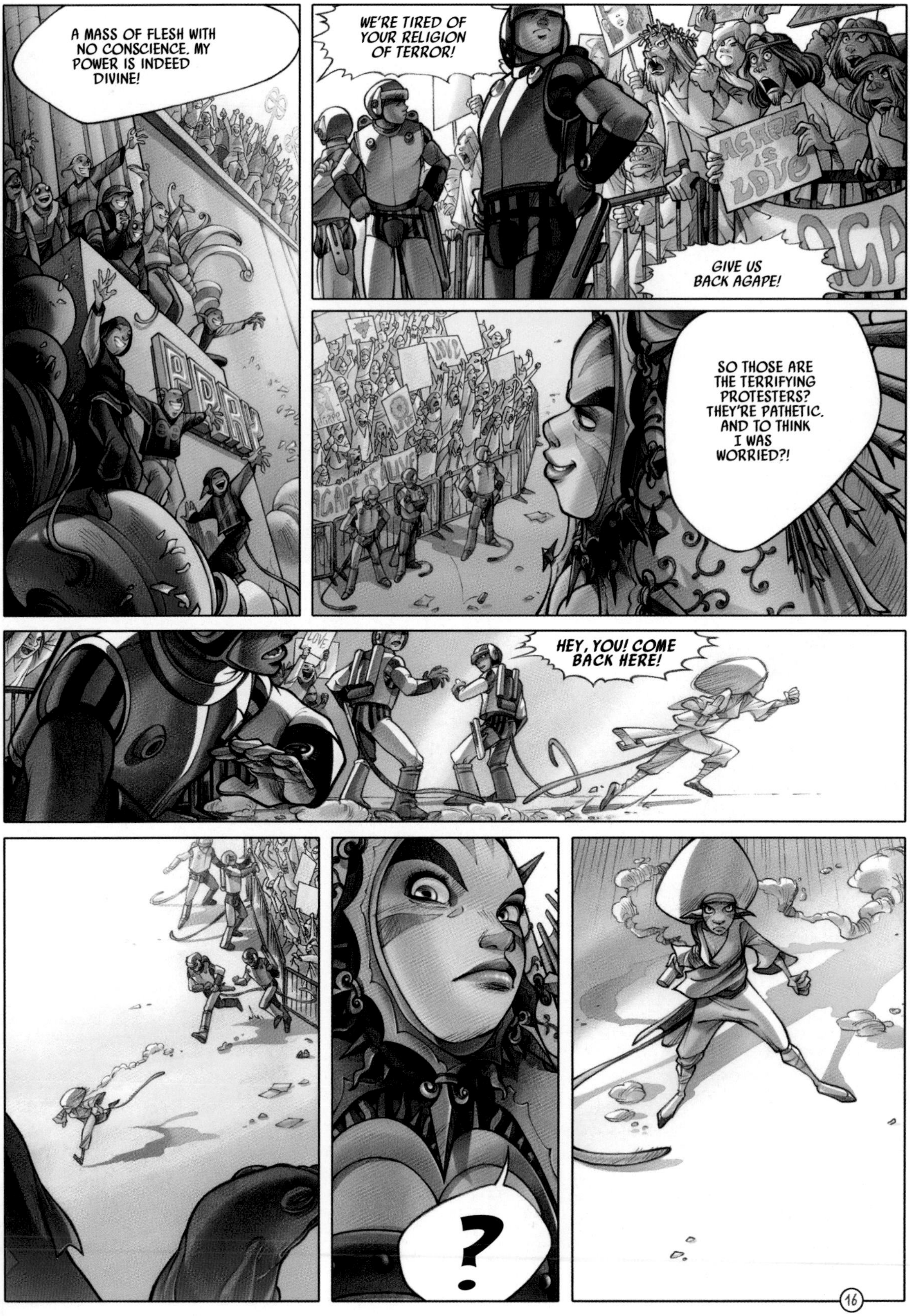
A MASS OF FLESH WITH NO CONSCIENCE. MY POWER IS INDEED DIVINE!
WE'RE TIRED OF YOUR RELIGION OF TERROR!
AGAPE IS LOVE
GIVE US BACK AGAPE!
SO THOSE ARE THE TERRIFYING PROTESTERS? THEY'RE PATHETIC. AND TO THINK I WAS WORRIED?!
HEY, YOU! COME BACK HERE!
?

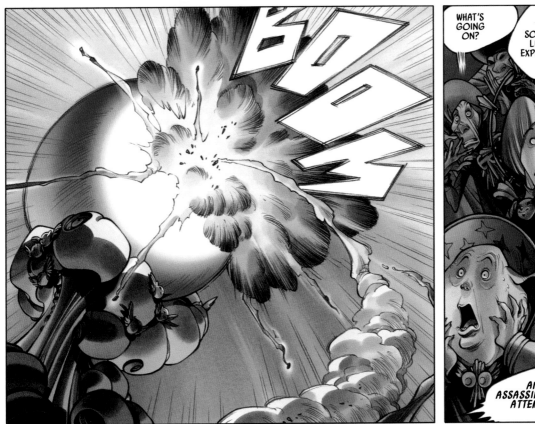

BOOM

WHAT'S GOING ON?

THAT SOUNDED LIKE AN EXPLOSION.

AN ASSASSINATION ATTEMPT!!

17

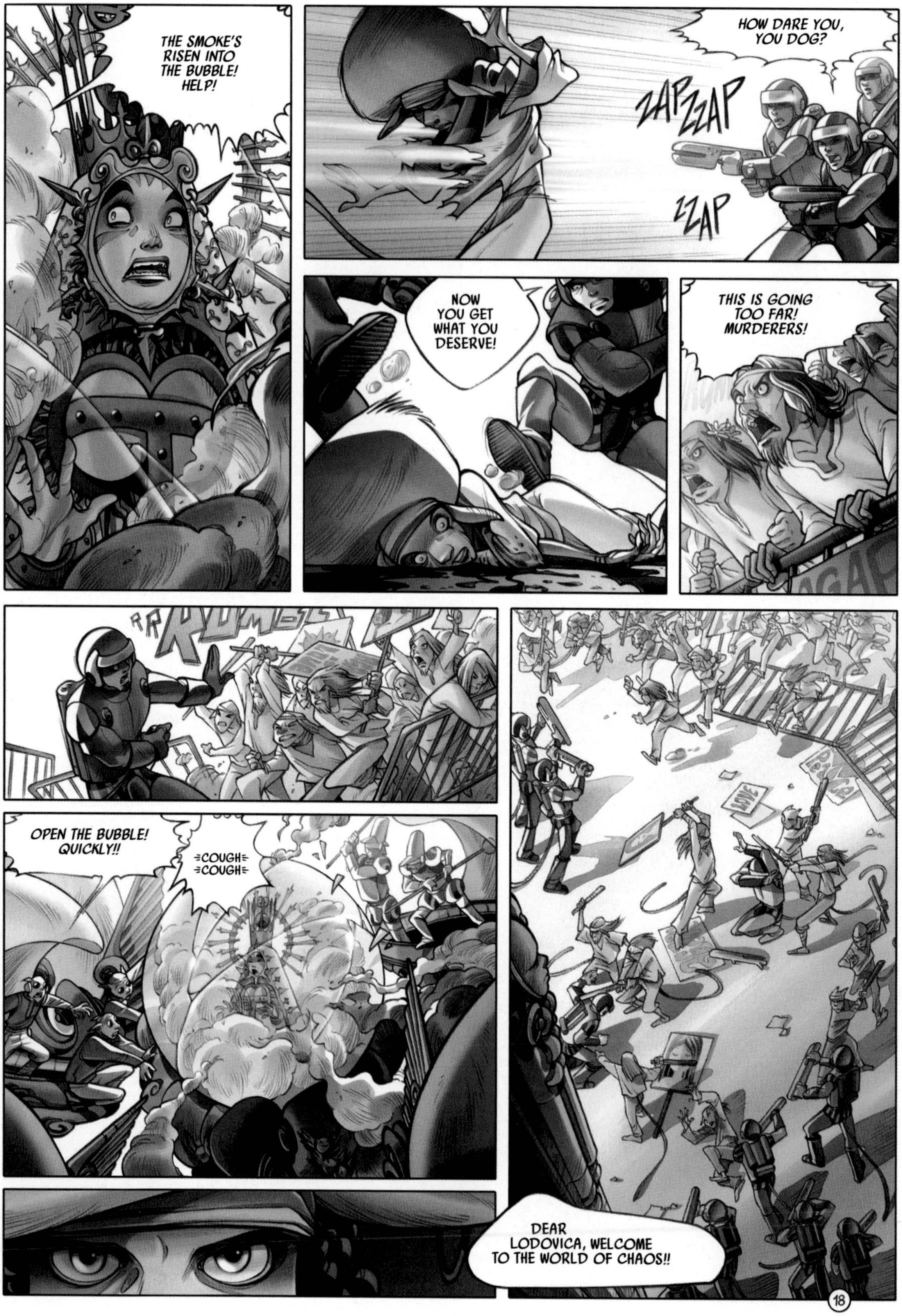
THE SMOKE'S RISEN INTO THE BUBBLE! HELP!
HOW DARE YOU, YOU DOG?
ZAP ZZAP
ZZAP
NOW YOU GET WHAT YOU DESERVE!
THIS IS GOING TOO FAR! MURDERERS!
LOVE
OPEN THE BUBBLE! QUICKLY!!
COUGH COUGH
DEAR LODOVICA, WELCOME TO THE WORLD OF CHAOS!!

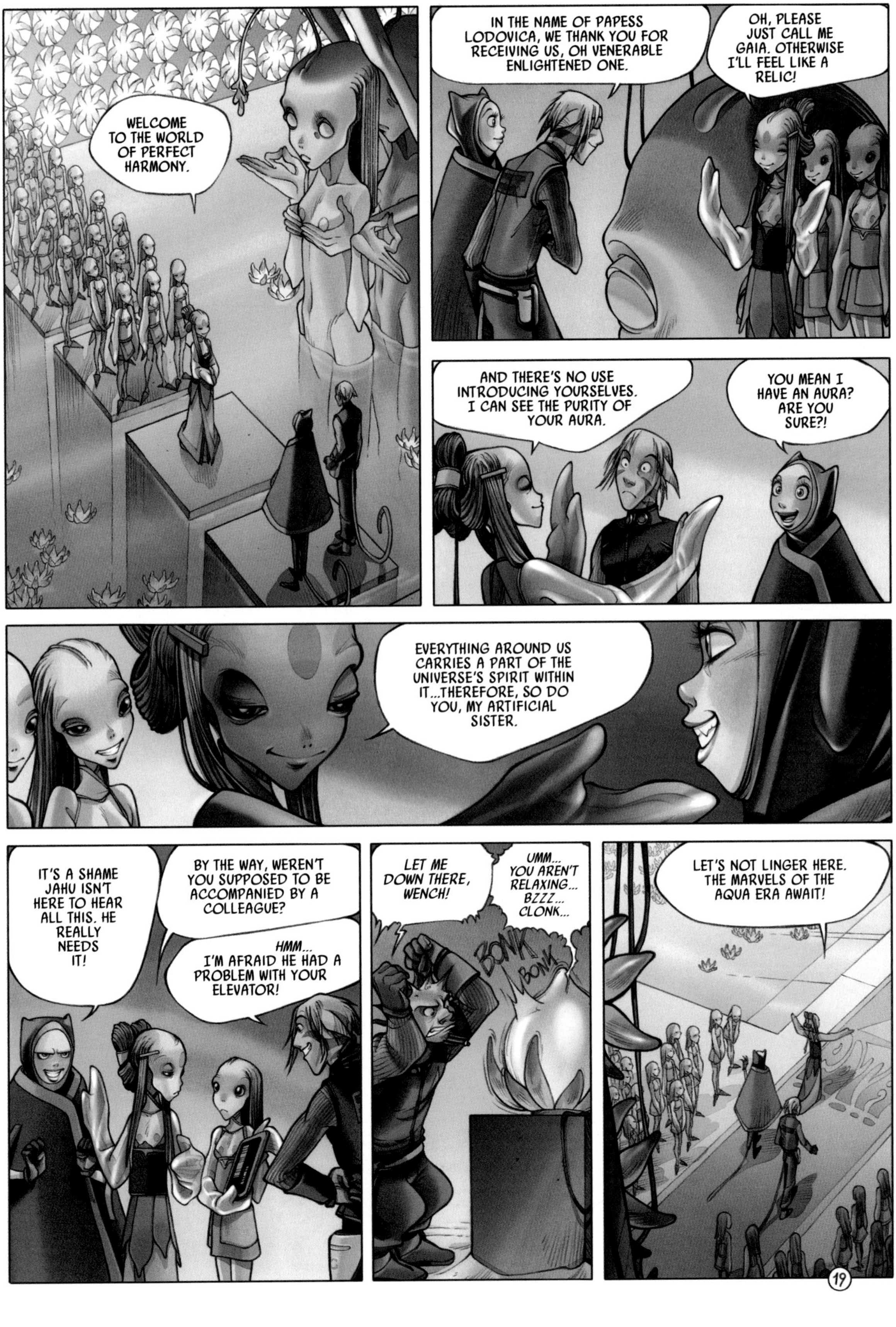
WELCOME TO THE WORLD OF PERFECT HARMONY.
IN THE NAME OF PAPESS LODOVICA, WE THANK YOU FOR RECEIVING US, OH VENERABLE ENLIGHTENED ONE.
OH, PLEASE JUST CALL ME GAIA. OTHERWISE I'LL FEEL LIKE A RELIC!
AND THERE'S NO USE INTRODUCING YOURSELVES. I CAN SEE THE PURITY OF YOUR AURA.
YOU MEAN I HAVE AN AURA? ARE YOU SURE?!
EVERYTHING AROUND US CARRIES A PART OF THE UNIVERSE'S SPIRIT WITHIN IT...THEREFORE, SO DO YOU, MY ARTIFICIAL SISTER.
IT'S A SHAME JAHU ISN'T HERE TO HEAR ALL THIS. HE REALLY NEEDS IT!
BY THE WAY, WEREN'T YOU SUPPOSED TO BE ACCOMPANIED BY A COLLEAGUE?
HMM... I'M AFRAID HE HAD A PROBLEM WITH YOUR ELEVATOR!
LET ME DOWN THERE, WENCH!
UMM... YOU AREN'T RELAXING... BZZZ... CLONK...
BONK
BONK
LET'S NOT LINGER HERE. THE MARVELS OF THE AQUA ERA AWAIT!

TO YOUR LEFT, YOU'LL SEE A TRAINING CLASS FOCUSING ON *"THE VISION OF LIFE."*

THERE, THE STUDENTS DELVE FURTHER INTO THE WRITINGS OF GAIA THE ILLUMINATED, WHICH IS THE ONLY WAY TO ACHIEVE FULL COMPREHENSION OF OUR EXISTENCE.

THE WRITINGS ARE COMPRISED OF MORE THAN 40 TEXTS, ALL AVAILABLE IN FIFTEEN LANGUAGES ON EASY-TO-UNDERSTAND CASSETTES.

AND HERE, PERSONAL *"HEARINGS"* HELP FOLLOWERS LEAVE BEHIND ANY REMAINING SPIRITUAL INABILITY.

THAT'S AMAZING! THEY'RE SO AHEAD OF THEIR TIME!

TO TELL THE TRUTH, I WAS EXPECTING SOMETHING RATHER DIFFERENT.

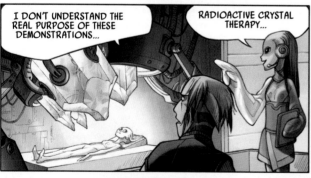

I DON'T UNDERSTAND THE REAL PURPOSE OF THESE DEMONSTRATIONS...

RADIOACTIVE CRYSTAL THERAPY...

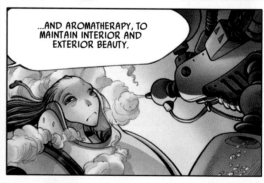

...AND AROMATHERAPY, TO MAINTAIN INTERIOR AND EXTERIOR BEAUTY.

OF COURSE, THE USE OF AQUARIAN PRODUCTS ARE ESSENTIAL FOR EACH AND EVERY ONE OF THESE TREATMENTS...

...FOR THE WELL-BEING OF THE BODY AND SOUL!

IT'S IMPOSSIBLE! I CAN'T DO IT!

THIS MEDITATION GARBAGE MIGHT RUIN EVERYTHING. I'M HERE TO ACT, DAMNIT!

I HAVE TO COME UP WITH SOMETHING QUICK. I'M RUNNING OUT OF TIME TO COMPLETE THE MISSION!

THIS MURAL REPRESENTS THE OVERALL DEVELOPMENT OF OUR FACILITIES IN QUADRANT 68 OVER THE PAST TEN YEARS.

SO THIS IS THE FAMOUS SO-CALLED "AQUA ERA"?

A CHAIN OF WELLNESS CENTERS SCATTERED ACROSS THE COSMOS?

OUR SPIRITUAL WAYS HELP TO BRING PEOPLE TOGETHER!

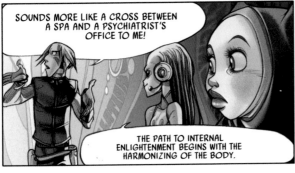

SOUNDS MORE LIKE A CROSS BETWEEN A SPA AND A PSYCHIATRIST'S OFFICE TO ME!

THE PATH TO INTERNAL ENLIGHTENMENT BEGINS WITH THE HARMONIZING OF THE BODY.

OUR AQUA CENTERS PROVIDE ALL THE NECESSARY MEANS TO ACHIEVE THIS--

TO ANYONE WITH ENOUGH MONEY TO SHELL OUT FOR IT, I'M SURE!

21

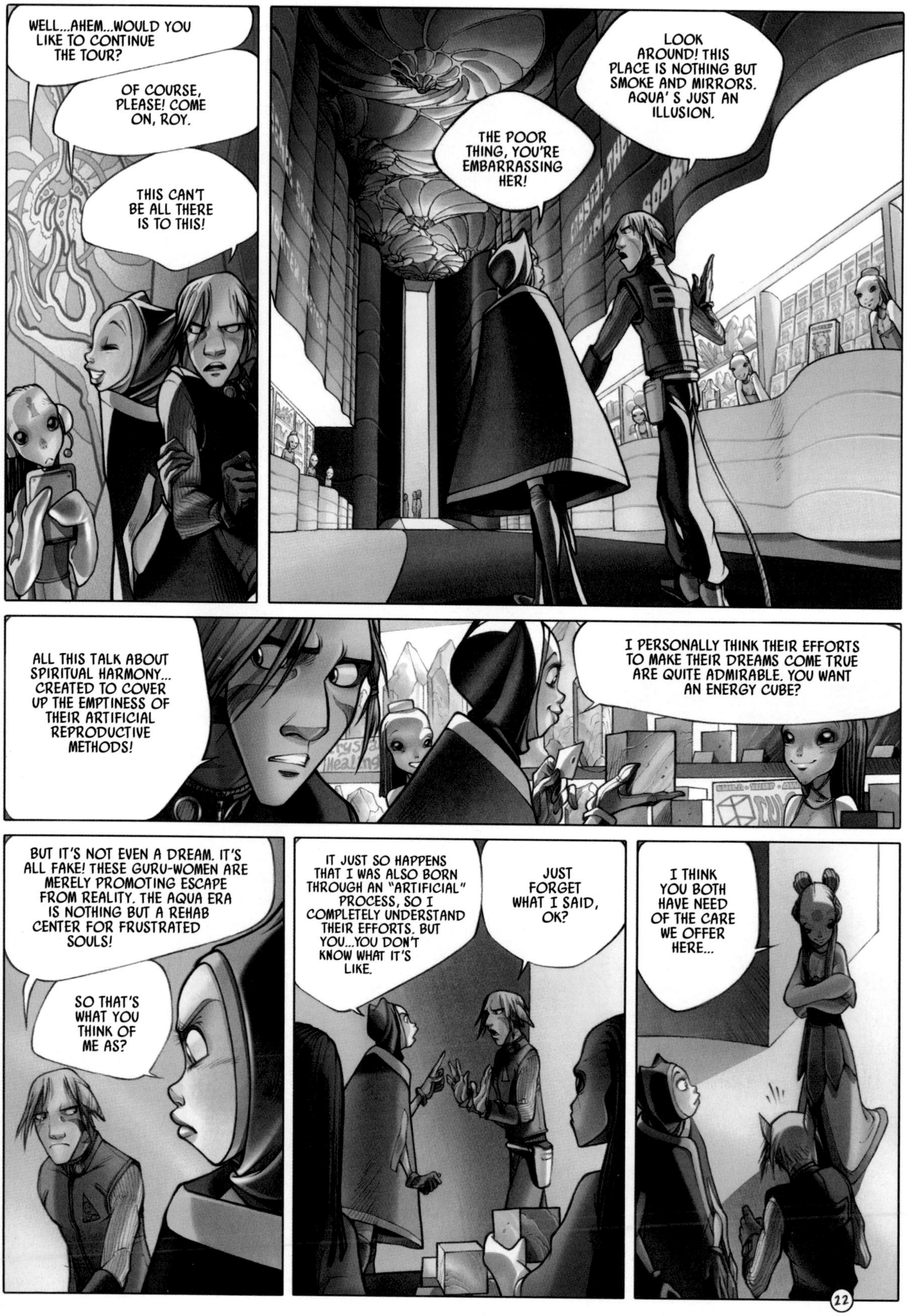
WELL...AHEM...WOULD YOU LIKE TO CONTINUE THE TOUR?
OF COURSE, PLEASE! COME ON, ROY.
THIS CAN'T BE ALL THERE IS TO THIS!
THE POOR THING, YOU'RE EMBARRASSING HER!
LOOK AROUND! THIS PLACE IS NOTHING BUT SMOKE AND MIRRORS. AQUA'S JUST AN ILLUSION.
ALL THIS TALK ABOUT SPIRITUAL HARMONY... CREATED TO COVER UP THE EMPTINESS OF THEIR ARTIFICIAL REPRODUCTIVE METHODS!
I PERSONALLY THINK THEIR EFFORTS TO MAKE THEIR DREAMS COME TRUE ARE QUITE ADMIRABLE. YOU WANT AN ENERGY CUBE?
BUT IT'S NOT EVEN A DREAM. IT'S ALL FAKE! THESE GURU-WOMEN ARE MERELY PROMOTING ESCAPE FROM REALITY. THE AQUA ERA IS NOTHING BUT A REHAB CENTER FOR FRUSTRATED SOULS!
SO THAT'S WHAT YOU THINK OF ME AS?
IT JUST SO HAPPENS THAT I WAS ALSO BORN THROUGH AN "ARTIFICIAL" PROCESS, SO I COMPLETELY UNDERSTAND THEIR EFFORTS. BUT YOU...YOU DON'T KNOW WHAT IT'S LIKE.
JUST FORGET WHAT I SAID, OK?
I THINK YOU BOTH HAVE NEED OF THE CARE WE OFFER HERE...

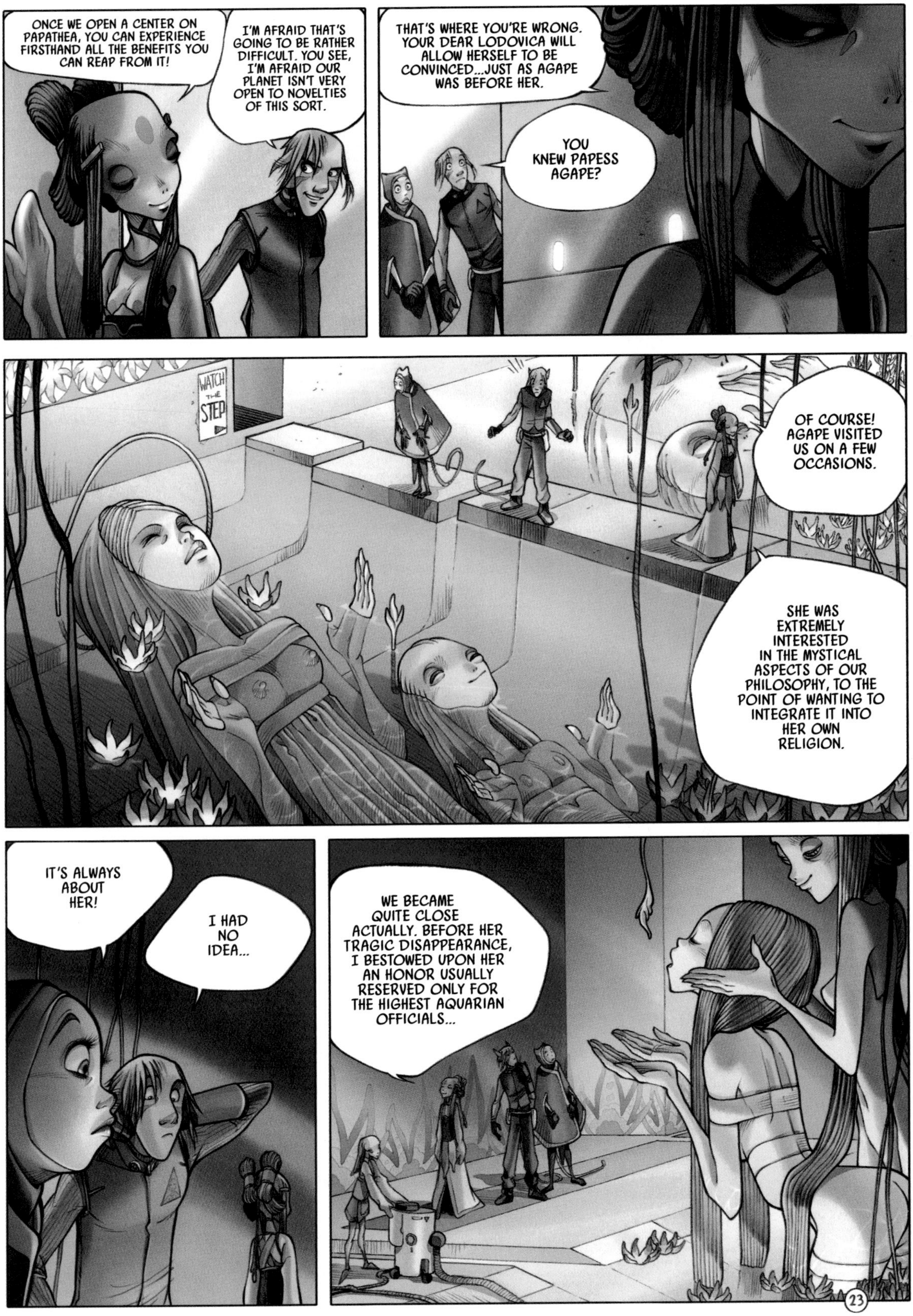
ONCE WE OPEN A CENTER ON PAPATHEA, YOU CAN EXPERIENCE FIRSTHAND ALL THE BENEFITS YOU CAN REAP FROM IT!
I'M AFRAID THAT'S GOING TO BE RATHER DIFFICULT. YOU SEE, I'M AFRAID OUR PLANET ISN'T VERY OPEN TO NOVELTIES OF THIS SORT.
THAT'S WHERE YOU'RE WRONG. YOUR DEAR LODOVICA WILL ALLOW HERSELF TO BE CONVINCED...JUST AS AGAPE WAS BEFORE HER.
YOU KNEW PAPESS AGAPE?
WATCH THE STEP
OF COURSE! AGAPE VISITED US ON A FEW OCCASIONS.
SHE WAS EXTREMELY INTERESTED IN THE MYSTICAL ASPECTS OF OUR PHILOSOPHY, TO THE POINT OF WANTING TO INTEGRATE IT INTO HER OWN RELIGION.
IT'S ALWAYS ABOUT HER!
I HAD NO IDEA...
WE BECAME QUITE CLOSE ACTUALLY. BEFORE HER TRAGIC DISAPPEARANCE, I BESTOWED UPON HER AN HONOR USUALLY RESERVED ONLY FOR THE HIGHEST AQUARIAN OFFICIALS...

I ALLOWED HER TO EXPERIENCE THE SPLENDOR OF THE SACRED FISH.

THE...THE SACRED FISH?

YOU SEE THIS IMAGE? THAT'S WHAT IT REPRESENTS, THE HEART OF ALL COSMIC ENERGY.

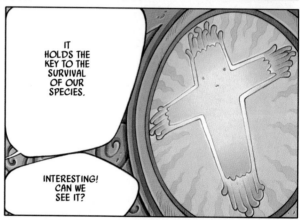

IT HOLDS THE KEY TO THE SURVIVAL OF OUR SPECIES.

INTERESTING! CAN WE SEE IT?

NO, THAT WOULD BE IMPOSSIBLE.

IT'S NOW TIME FOR OUR DAILY MEDITATION HOUR. ALL ACTIVITIES STOP.

FIGURES!

BIP!

YOU CAN PARTICIPATE IF YOU'D LIKE.

I WOULD LOVE TO!

NO, THANKS! I'VE HAD ENOUGH EMOTION FOR ONE DAY.

IN THAT CASE, ROY, YOU'LL NEED TO STAY WITH THE TUTOR DROIDS.

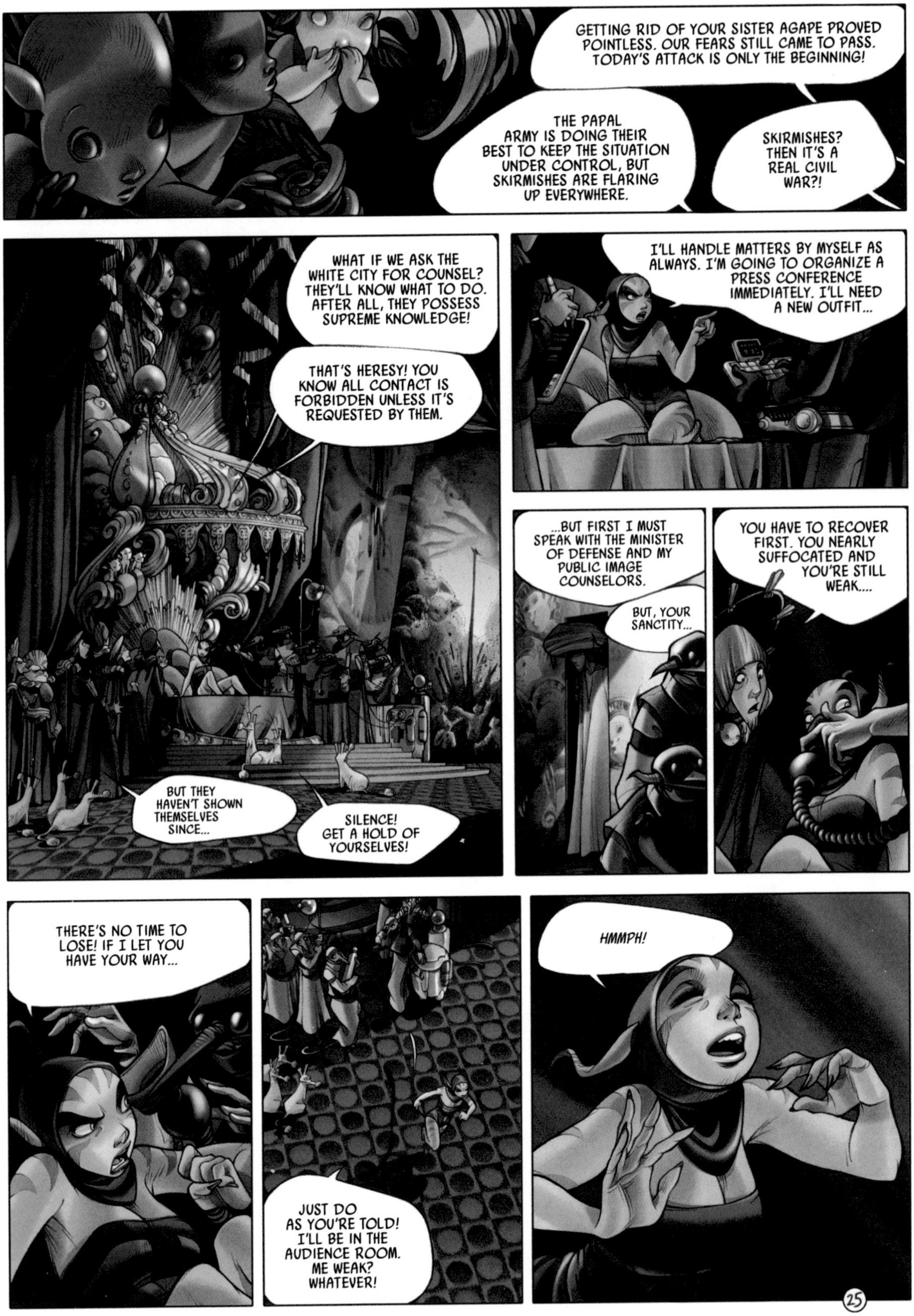

GETTING RID OF YOUR SISTER AGAPE PROVED POINTLESS. OUR FEARS STILL CAME TO PASS. TODAY'S ATTACK IS ONLY THE BEGINNING!
THE PAPAL ARMY IS DOING THEIR BEST TO KEEP THE SITUATION UNDER CONTROL, BUT SKIRMISHES ARE FLARING UP EVERYWHERE.
SKIRMISHES? THEN IT'S A REAL CIVIL WAR?!
WHAT IF WE ASK THE WHITE CITY FOR COUNSEL? THEY'LL KNOW WHAT TO DO. AFTER ALL, THEY POSSESS SUPREME KNOWLEDGE!
THAT'S HERESY! YOU KNOW ALL CONTACT IS FORBIDDEN UNLESS IT'S REQUESTED BY THEM.
BUT THEY HAVEN'T SHOWN THEMSELVES SINCE...
SILENCE! GET A HOLD OF YOURSELVES!
I'LL HANDLE MATTERS BY MYSELF AS ALWAYS. I'M GOING TO ORGANIZE A PRESS CONFERENCE IMMEDIATELY. I'LL NEED A NEW OUTFIT...
...BUT FIRST I MUST SPEAK WITH THE MINISTER OF DEFENSE AND MY PUBLIC IMAGE COUNSELORS.
BUT, YOUR SANCTITY...
YOU HAVE TO RECOVER FIRST. YOU NEARLY SUFFOCATED AND YOU'RE STILL WEAK....
THERE'S NO TIME TO LOSE! IF I LET YOU HAVE YOUR WAY...
JUST DO AS YOU'RE TOLD! I'LL BE IN THE AUDIENCE ROOM. ME WEAK? WHATEVER!
HMMPH!

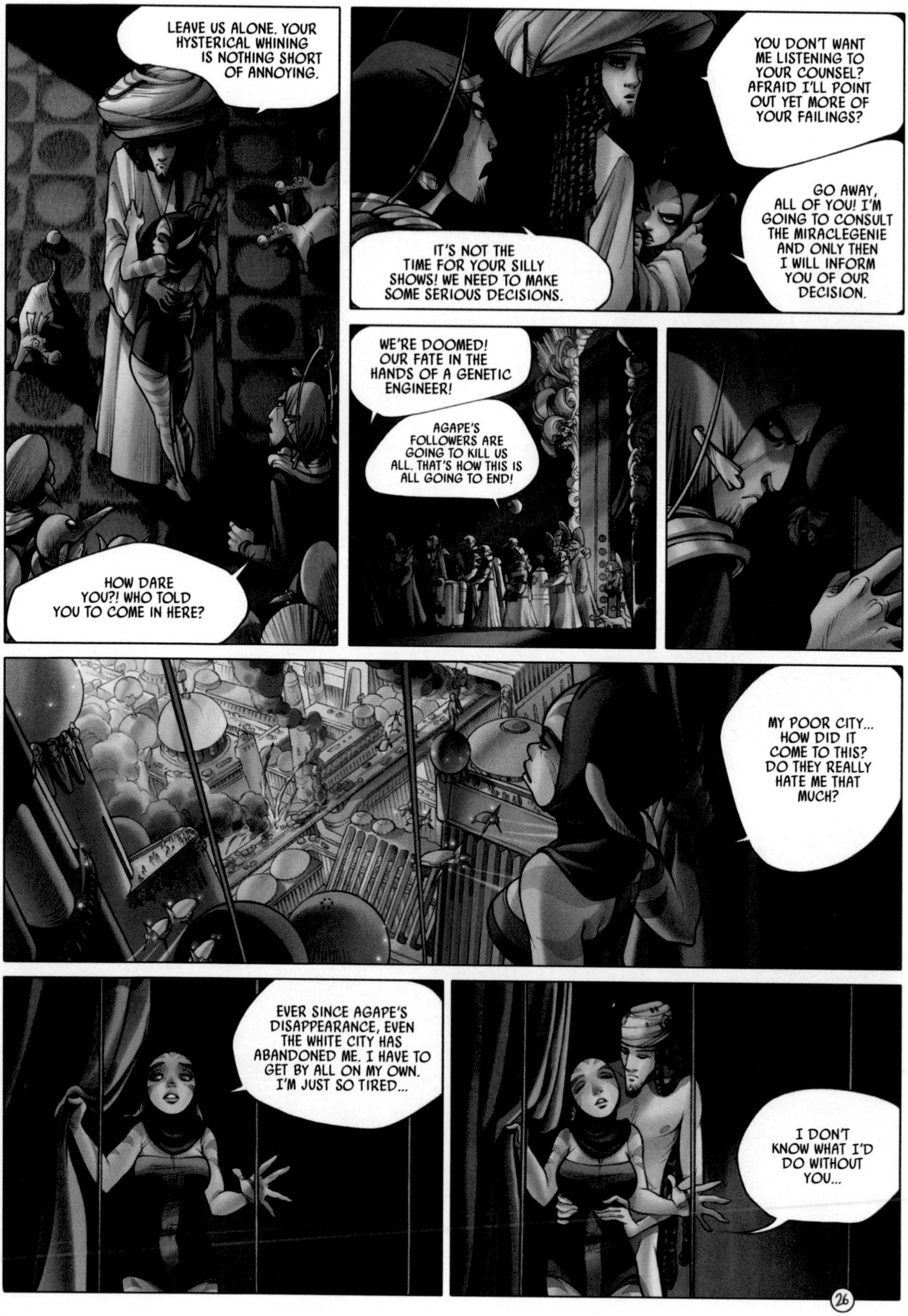
LEAVE US ALONE. YOUR HYSTERICAL WHINING IS NOTHING SHORT OF ANNOYING.
HOW DARE YOU?! WHO TOLD YOU TO COME IN HERE?
YOU DON'T WANT ME LISTENING TO YOUR COUNSEL? AFRAID I'LL POINT OUT YET MORE OF YOUR FAILINGS?
IT'S NOT THE TIME FOR YOUR SILLY SHOWS! WE NEED TO MAKE SOME SERIOUS DECISIONS.
GO AWAY, ALL OF YOU! I'M GOING TO CONSULT THE MIRACLEGENIE AND ONLY THEN I WILL INFORM YOU OF OUR DECISION.
WE'RE DOOMED! OUR FATE IN THE HANDS OF A GENETIC ENGINEER!
AGAPE'S FOLLOWERS ARE GOING TO KILL US ALL. THAT'S HOW THIS IS ALL GOING TO END!
MY POOR CITY... HOW DID IT COME TO THIS? DO THEY REALLY HATE ME THAT MUCH?
EVER SINCE AGAPE'S DISAPPEARANCE, EVEN THE WHITE CITY HAS ABANDONED ME. I HAVE TO GET BY ALL ON MY OWN. I'M JUST SO TIRED...
I DON'T KNOW WHAT I'D DO WITHOUT YOU...

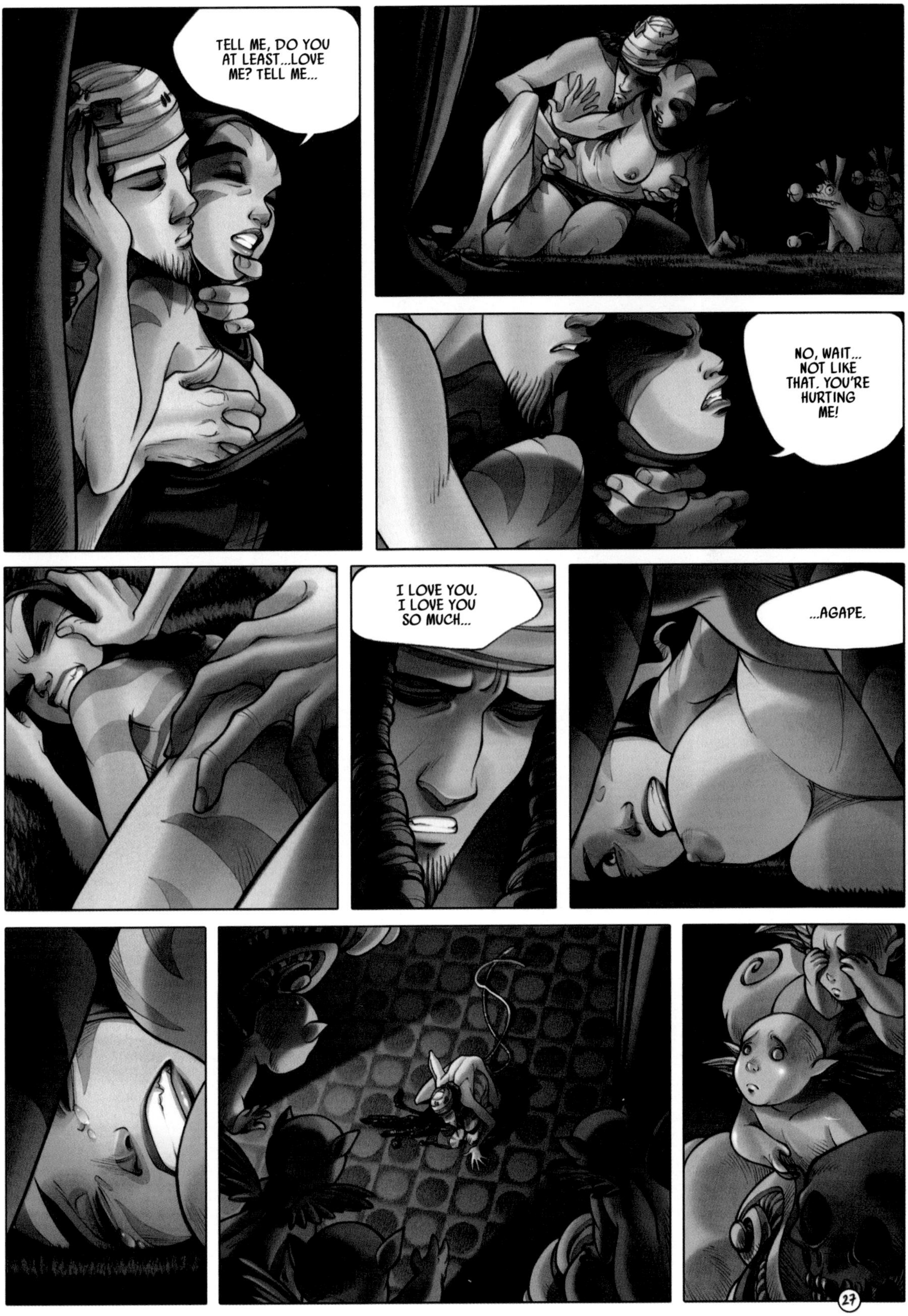
TELL ME, DO YOU AT LEAST...LOVE ME? TELL ME...
NO, WAIT... NOT LIKE THAT. YOU'RE HURTING ME!
I LOVE YOU. I LOVE YOU SO MUCH...
...AGAPE.

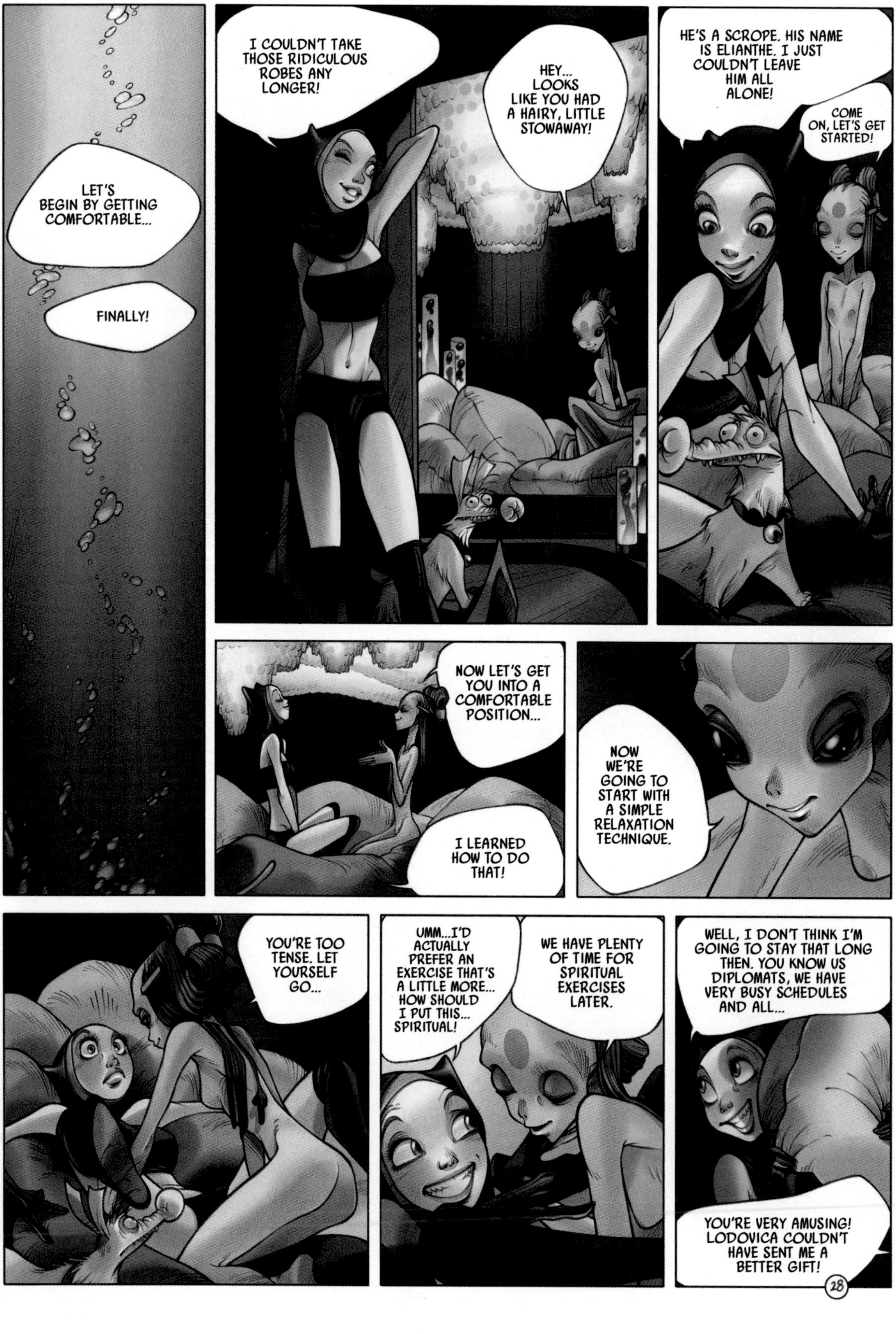
LET'S BEGIN BY GETTING COMFORTABLE...
FINALLY!
I COULDN'T TAKE THOSE RIDICULOUS ROBES ANY LONGER!
HEY... LOOKS LIKE YOU HAD A HAIRY, LITTLE STOWAWAY!
HE'S A SCROPE. HIS NAME IS ELIANTHE. I JUST COULDN'T LEAVE HIM ALL ALONE!
COME ON, LET'S GET STARTED!
NOW LET'S GET YOU INTO A COMFORTABLE POSITION...
I LEARNED HOW TO DO THAT!
NOW WE'RE GOING TO START WITH A SIMPLE RELAXATION TECHNIQUE.
YOU'RE TOO TENSE. LET YOURSELF GO...
UMM...I'D ACTUALLY PREFER AN EXERCISE THAT'S A LITTLE MORE... HOW SHOULD I PUT THIS... SPIRITUAL!
WE HAVE PLENTY OF TIME FOR SPIRITUAL EXERCISES LATER.
WELL, I DON'T THINK I'M GOING TO STAY THAT LONG THEN. YOU KNOW US DIPLOMATS, WE HAVE VERY BUSY SCHEDULES AND ALL...
YOU'RE VERY AMUSING! LODOVICA COULDN'T HAVE SENT ME A BETTER GIFT!

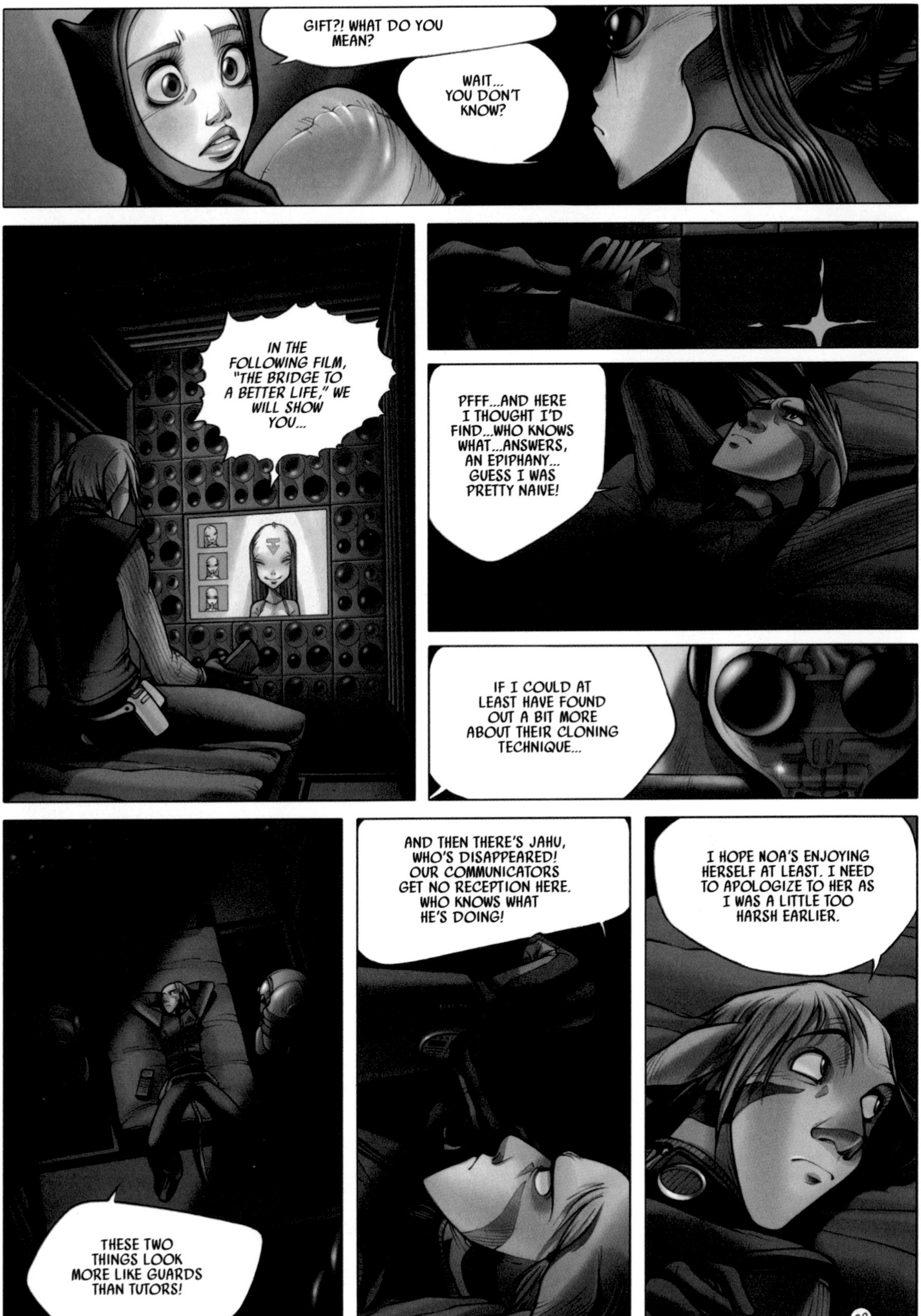
GIFT?! WHAT DO YOU MEAN?
WAIT... YOU DON'T KNOW?
IN THE FOLLOWING FILM, "THE BRIDGE TO A BETTER LIFE," WE WILL SHOW YOU...
CLIK
PFFF...AND HERE I THOUGHT I'D FIND...WHO KNOWS WHAT...ANSWERS, AN EPIPHANY... GUESS I WAS PRETTY NAIVE!
IF I COULD AT LEAST HAVE FOUND OUT A BIT MORE ABOUT THEIR CLONING TECHNIQUE...
THESE TWO THINGS LOOK MORE LIKE GUARDS THAN TUTORS!
AND THEN THERE'S JAHU, WHO'S DISAPPEARED! OUR COMMUNICATORS GET NO RECEPTION HERE. WHO KNOWS WHAT HE'S DOING!
I HOPE NOA'S ENJOYING HERSELF AT LEAST. I NEED TO APOLOGIZE TO HER AS I WAS A LITTLE TOO HARSH EARLIER.

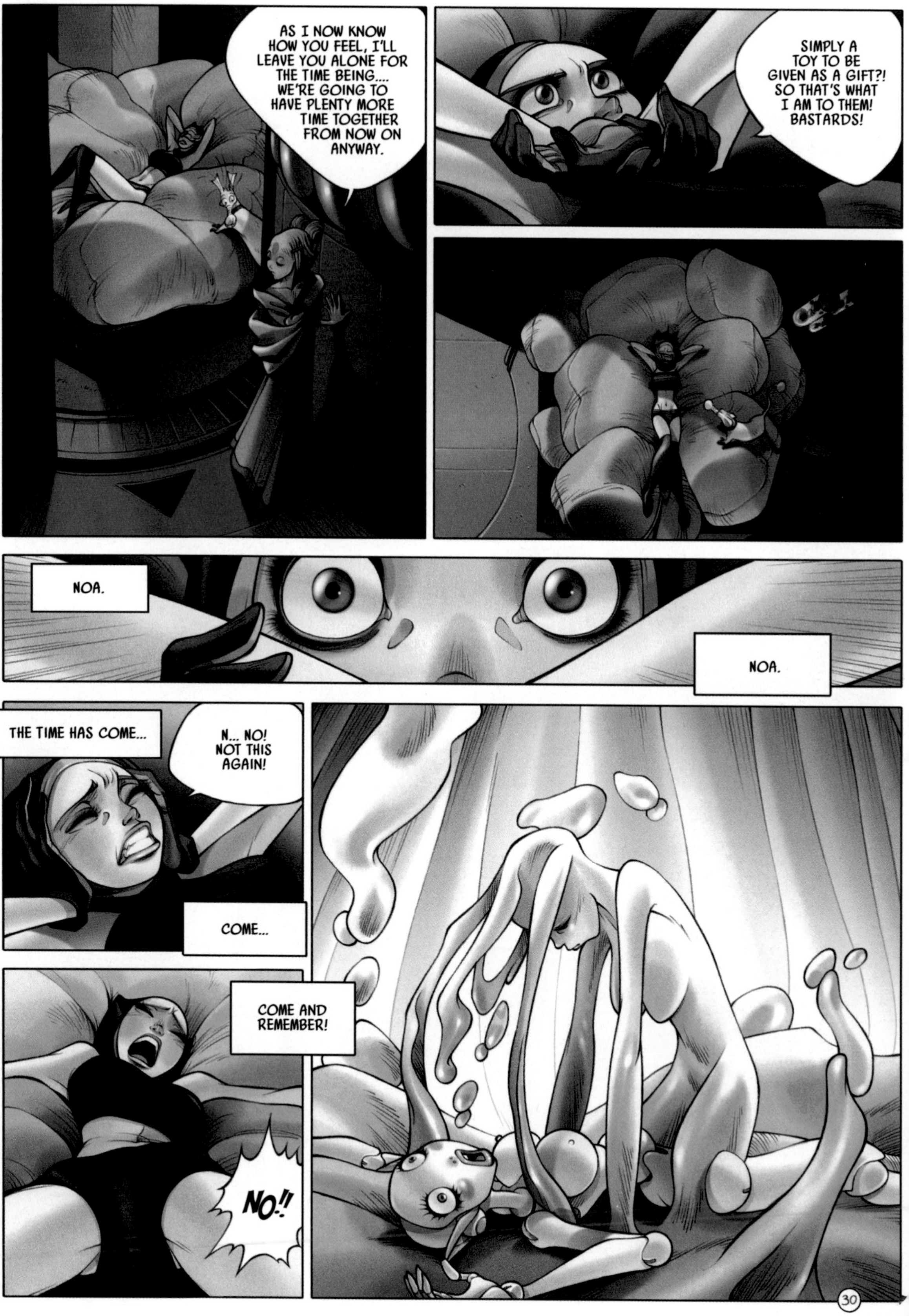
AS I NOW KNOW HOW YOU FEEL, I'LL LEAVE YOU ALONE FOR THE TIME BEING.... WE'RE GOING TO HAVE PLENTY MORE TIME TOGETHER FROM NOW ON ANYWAY.
SIMPLY A TOY TO BE GIVEN AS A GIFT?! SO THAT'S WHAT I AM TO THEM! BASTARDS!
NOA.
NOA.
THE TIME HAS COME...
N... NO! NOT THIS AGAIN!
COME...
COME AND REMEMBER!
NO!!

I CAN'T AFFORD TO WASTE ANY MORE TIME! I NEED TO ACT NOW!

IF IT TAKES AN ALTERED STATE OF MIND TO GET ONTO THIS DAMN PLANET, I GUESS I'LL JUST HAVE TO GET THERE ANOTHER WAY.

IT TOOK ME THREE YEARS TO GET CLEAN...BUT I KEPT THIS PILL ON ME SO I'D NEVER FORGET...

BY TAKING IT I RISK GOING BACK TO HELL...BUT THIS MISSION'S SUCCESS DEPENDS ON ME. I CAN'T FAIL!

FOR HER SANCTITY LODOVICA... COME WHAT MAY!

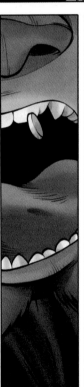

TRANCE LEVEL ACHIEVED. WELCOME TO AQUA.

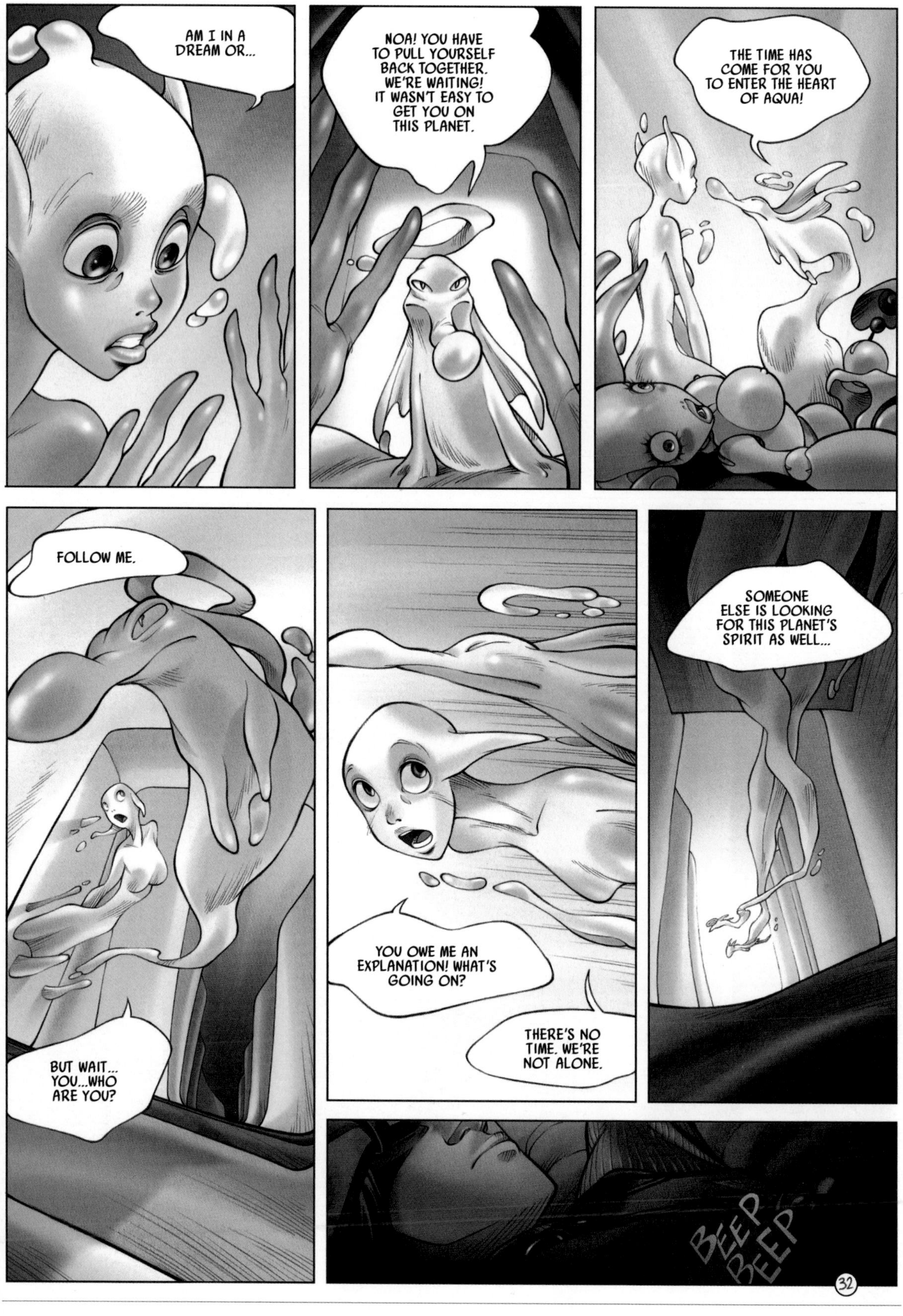
AM I IN A DREAM OR...
NOA! YOU HAVE TO PULL YOURSELF BACK TOGETHER. WE'RE WAITING! IT WASN'T EASY TO GET YOU ON THIS PLANET.
THE TIME HAS COME FOR YOU TO ENTER THE HEART OF AQUA!
FOLLOW ME.
BUT WAIT... YOU...WHO ARE YOU?
YOU OWE ME AN EXPLANATION! WHAT'S GOING ON?
THERE'S NO TIME. WE'RE NOT ALONE.
SOMEONE ELSE IS LOOKING FOR THIS PLANET'S SPIRIT AS WELL...
BEEP BEEP

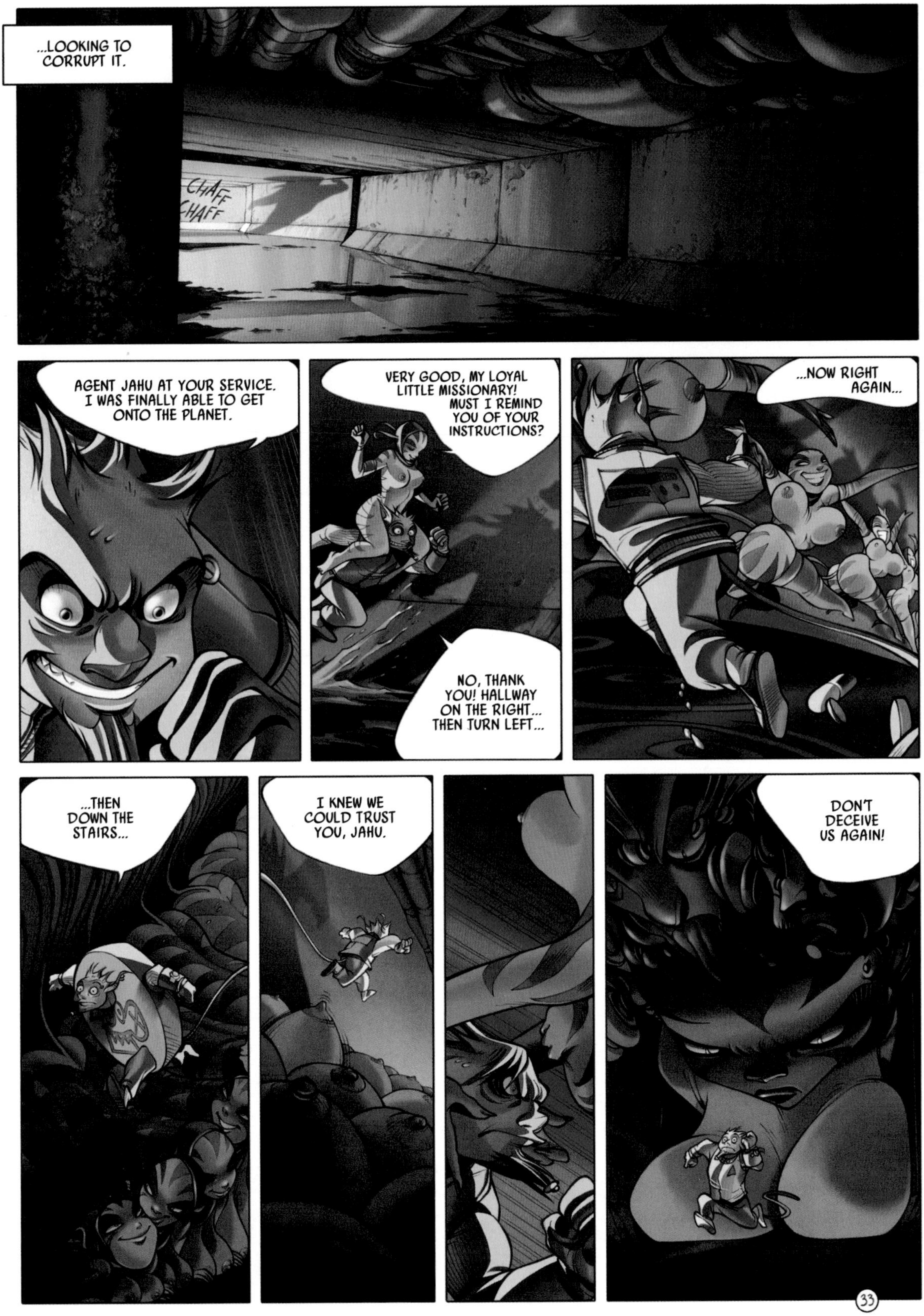
...LOOKING TO CORRUPT IT.
CHAFF CHAFF
AGENT JAHU AT YOUR SERVICE. I WAS FINALLY ABLE TO GET ONTO THE PLANET.
VERY GOOD, MY LOYAL LITTLE MISSIONARY! MUST I REMIND YOU OF YOUR INSTRUCTIONS?
NO, THANK YOU! HALLWAY ON THE RIGHT... THEN TURN LEFT...
...NOW RIGHT AGAIN...
...THEN DOWN THE STAIRS...
I KNEW WE COULD TRUST YOU, JAHU.
DON'T DECEIVE US AGAIN!

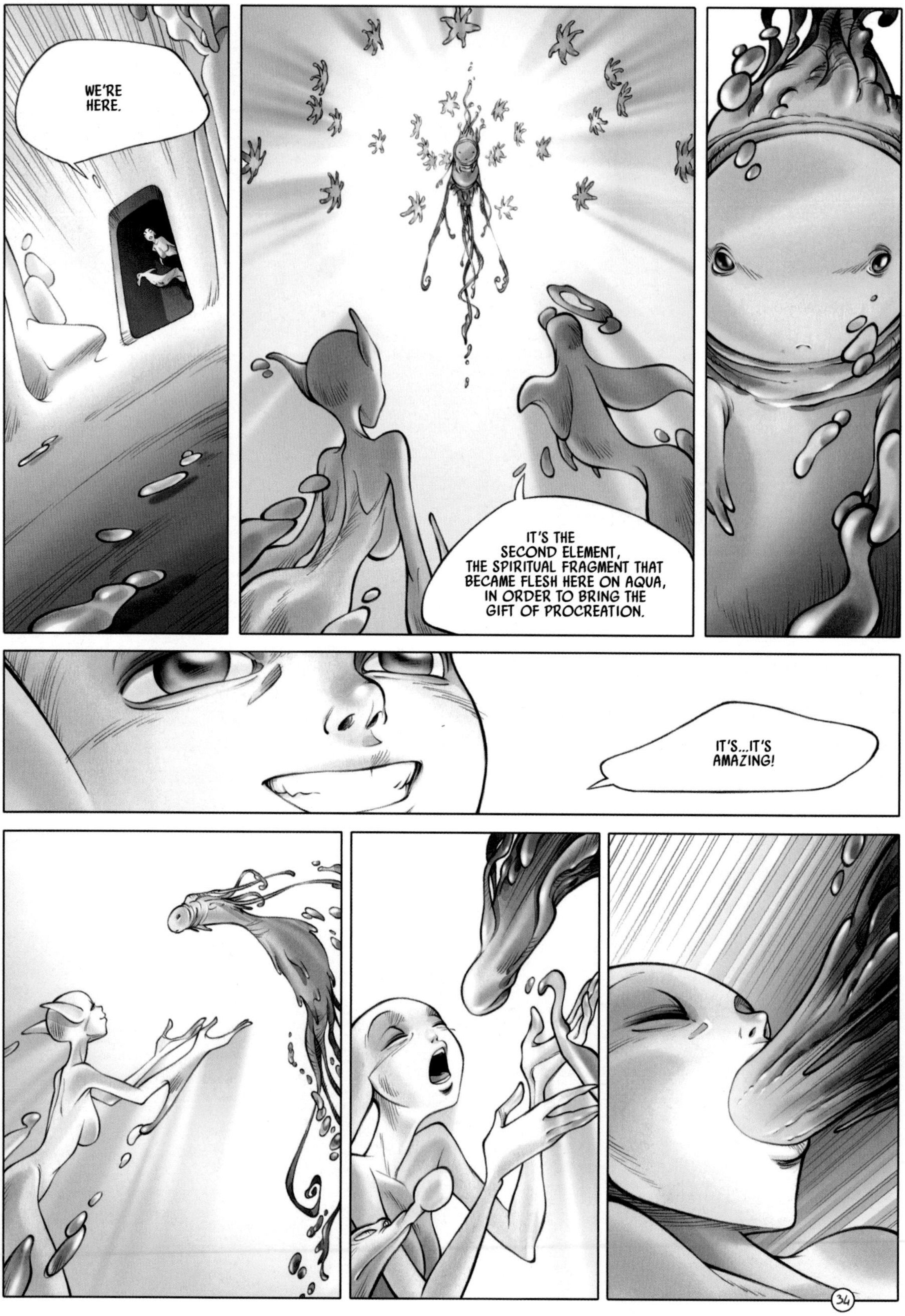
WE'RE HERE.
IT'S THE SECOND ELEMENT, THE SPIRITUAL FRAGMENT THAT BECAME FLESH HERE ON AQUA, IN ORDER TO BRING THE GIFT OF PROCREATION.
IT'S...IT'S AMAZING!

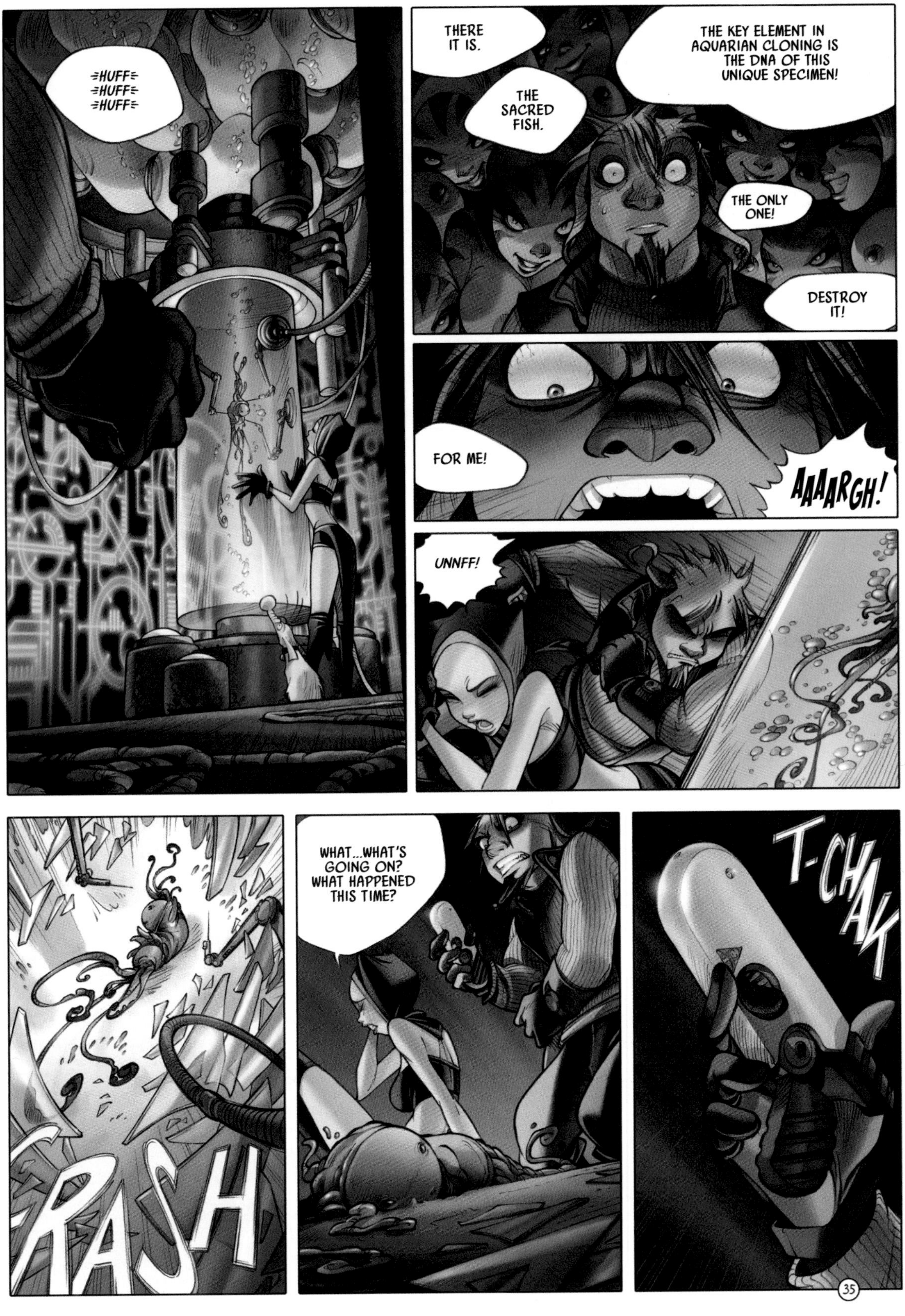

≠HUFF≠
≠HUFF≠
≠HUFF≠
THERE IT IS.
THE SACRED FISH.
THE KEY ELEMENT IN AQUARIAN CLONING IS THE DNA OF THIS UNIQUE SPECIMEN!
THE ONLY ONE!
DESTROY IT!
FOR ME!
AAAARGH!
UNNFF!
CRASH
WHAT...WHAT'S GOING ON? WHAT HAPPENED THIS TIME?
T-CHAK

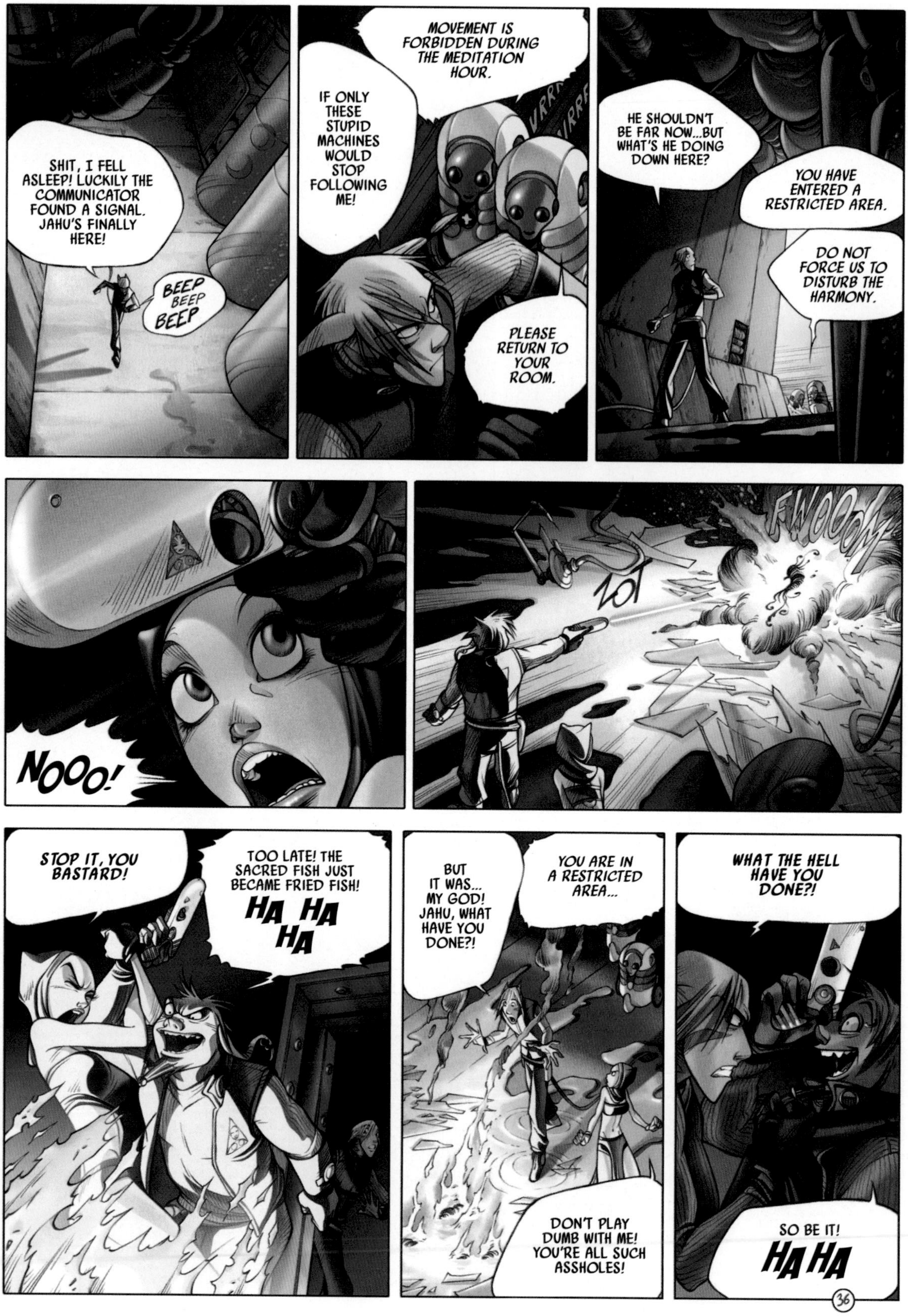
SHIT, I FELL ASLEEP! LUCKILY THE COMMUNICATOR FOUND A SIGNAL. JAHU'S FINALLY HERE!
BEEP BEEP BEEP
MOVEMENT IS FORBIDDEN DURING THE MEDITATION HOUR.
IF ONLY THESE STUPID MACHINES WOULD STOP FOLLOWING ME!
PLEASE RETURN TO YOUR ROOM.
HE SHOULDN'T BE FAR NOW...BUT WHAT'S HE DOING DOWN HERE?
YOU HAVE ENTERED A RESTRICTED AREA.
DO NOT FORCE US TO DISTURB THE HARMONY.
NOOO!
ZOT
FWOOOM
STOP IT, YOU BASTARD!
TOO LATE! THE SACRED FISH JUST BECAME FRIED FISH!
HA HA HA
BUT IT WAS... MY GOD! JAHU, WHAT HAVE YOU DONE?!
YOU ARE IN A RESTRICTED AREA...
DON'T PLAY DUMB WITH ME! YOU'RE ALL SUCH ASSHOLES!
WHAT THE HELL HAVE YOU DONE?!
SO BE IT!
HA HA

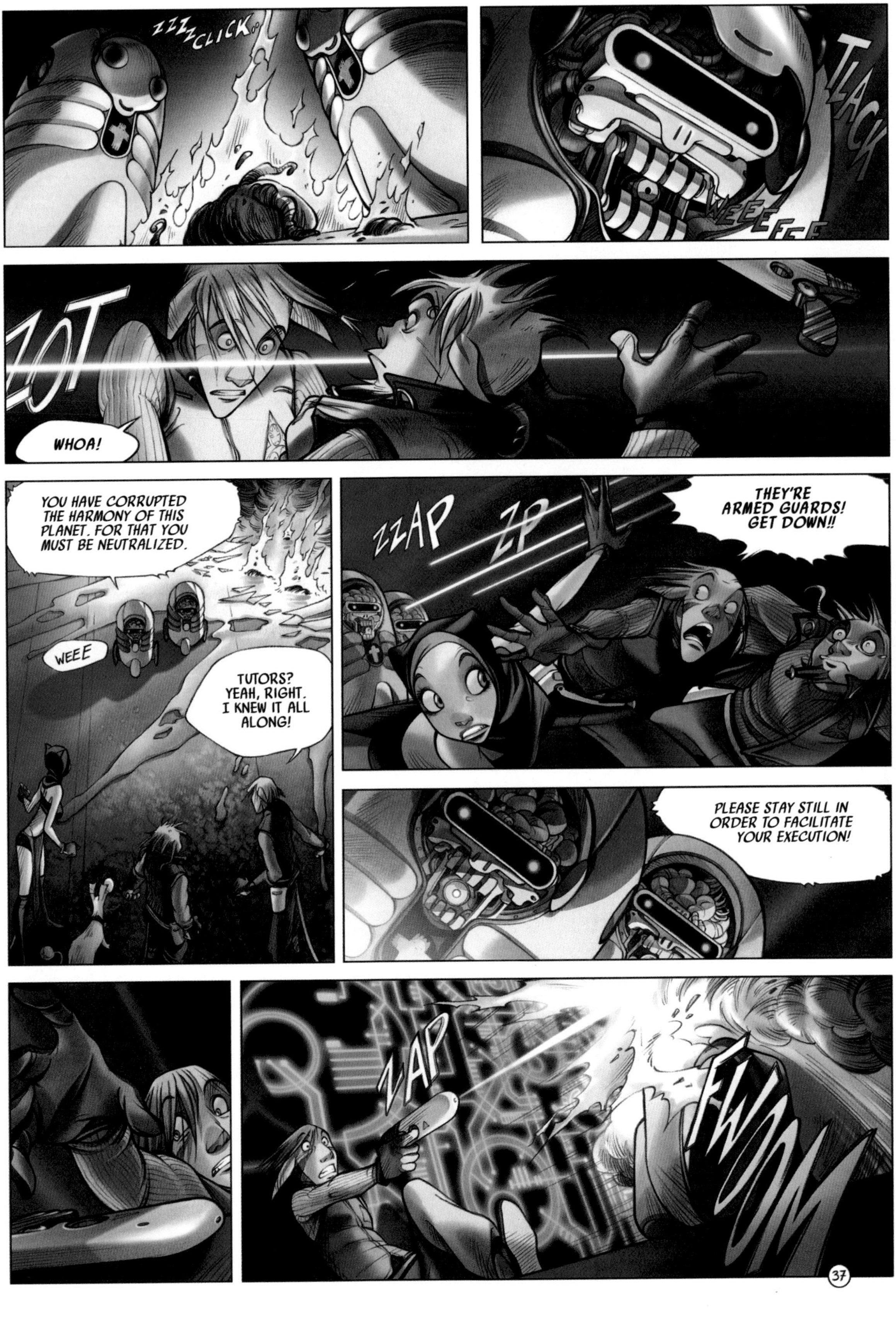
ZZZZCLICK
TLACK
WEEEEEE
ZOT
WHOA!
YOU HAVE CORRUPTED THE HARMONY OF THIS PLANET. FOR THAT YOU MUST BE NEUTRALIZED.
WEEE
TUTORS? YEAH, RIGHT. I KNEW IT ALL ALONG!
ZZAP
ZP
THEY'RE ARMED GUARDS! GET DOWN!!
PLEASE STAY STILL IN ORDER TO FACILITATE YOUR EXECUTION!
ZAP
FWOOM

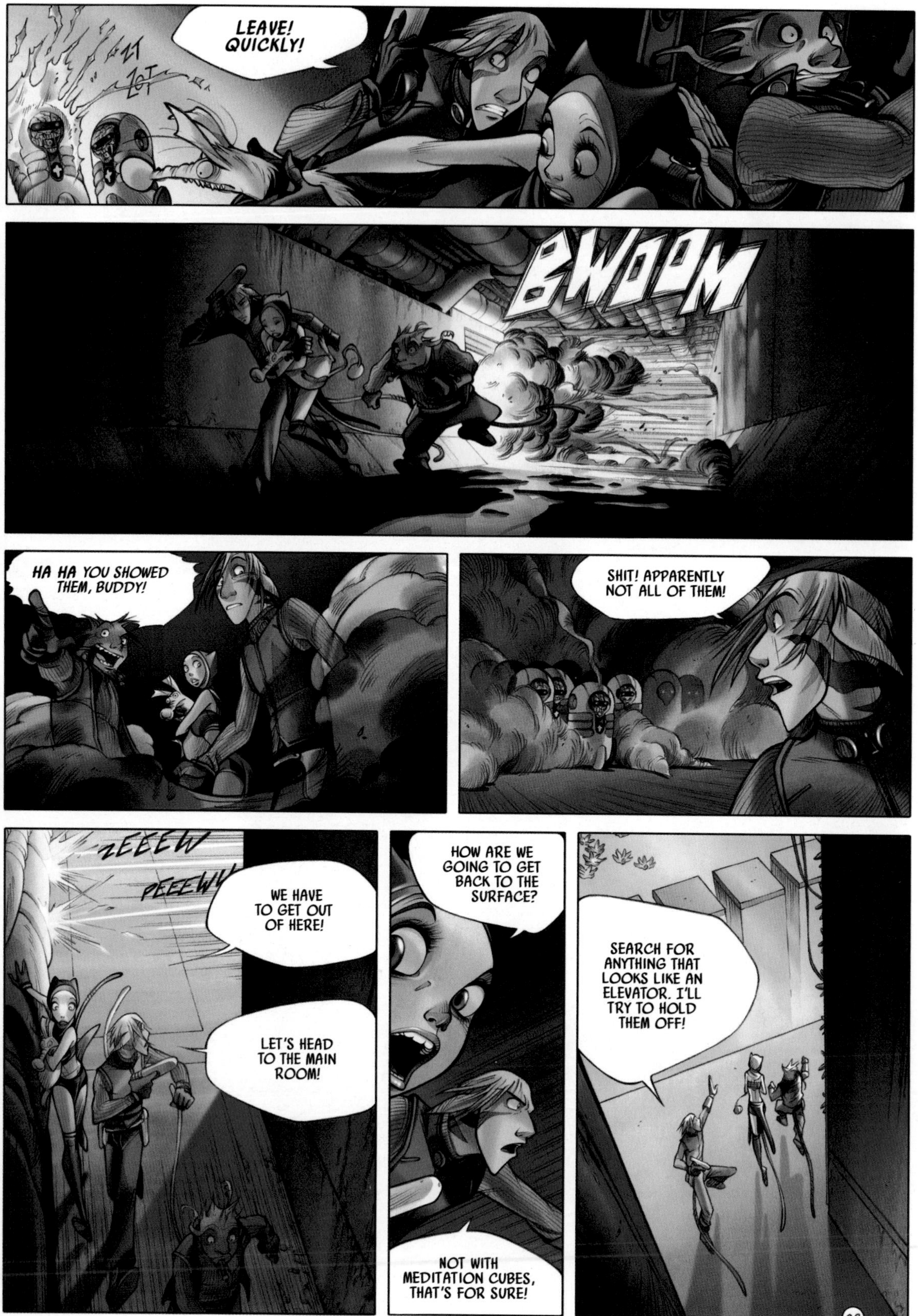

ZT
ZOT
LEAVE! QUICKLY!
BWOOM
HA HA YOU SHOWED THEM, BUDDY!
SHIT! APPARENTLY NOT ALL OF THEM!
ZEEEW
PEEEWU
WE HAVE TO GET OUT OF HERE!
LET'S HEAD TO THE MAIN ROOM!
HOW ARE WE GOING TO GET BACK TO THE SURFACE?
NOT WITH MEDITATION CUBES, THAT'S FOR SURE!
SEARCH FOR ANYTHING THAT LOOKS LIKE AN ELEVATOR. I'LL TRY TO HOLD THEM OFF!

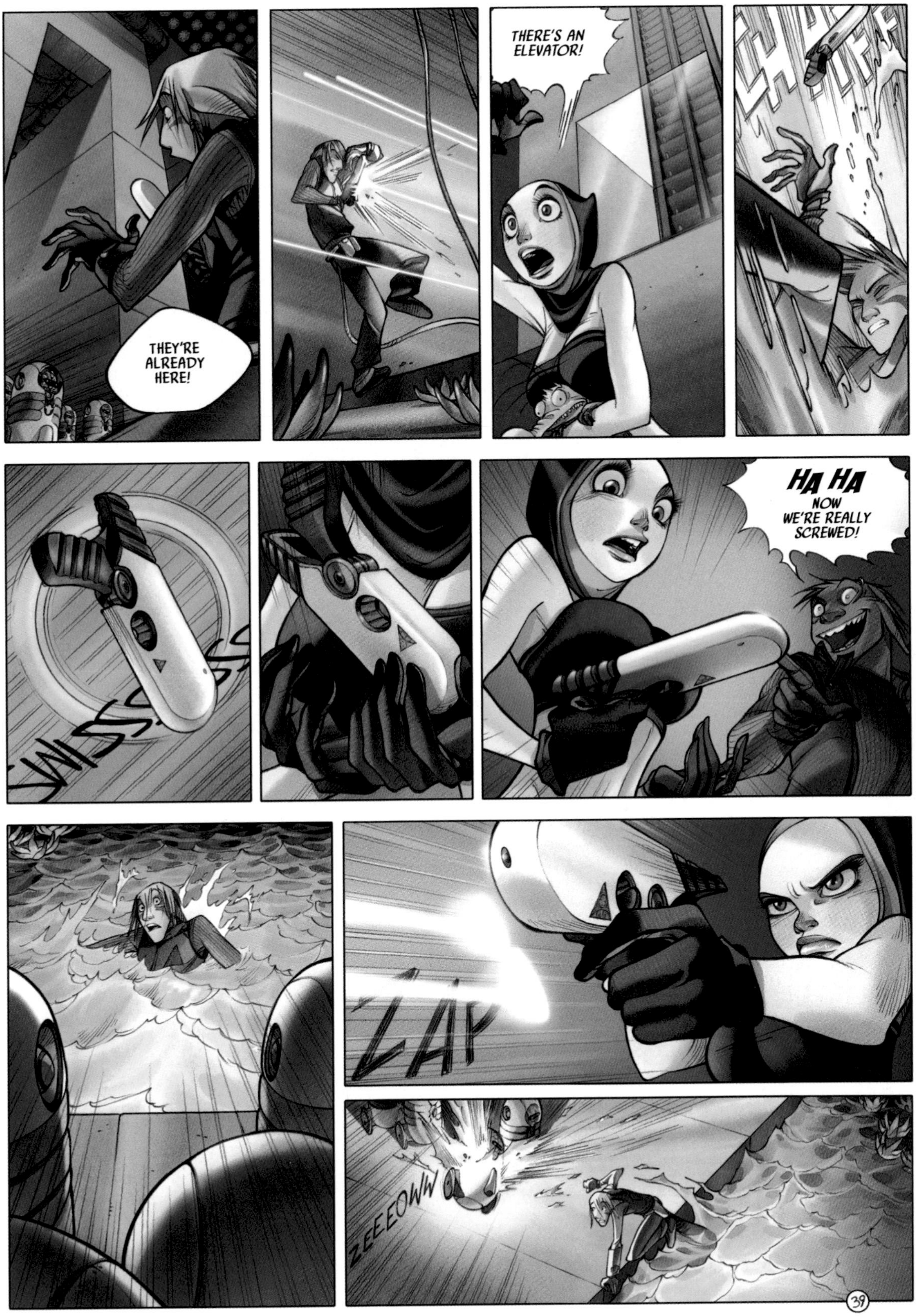
THEY'RE ALREADY HERE!
THERE'S AN ELEVATOR!
HA HA NOW WE'RE REALLY SCREWED!
ZEEEOWW

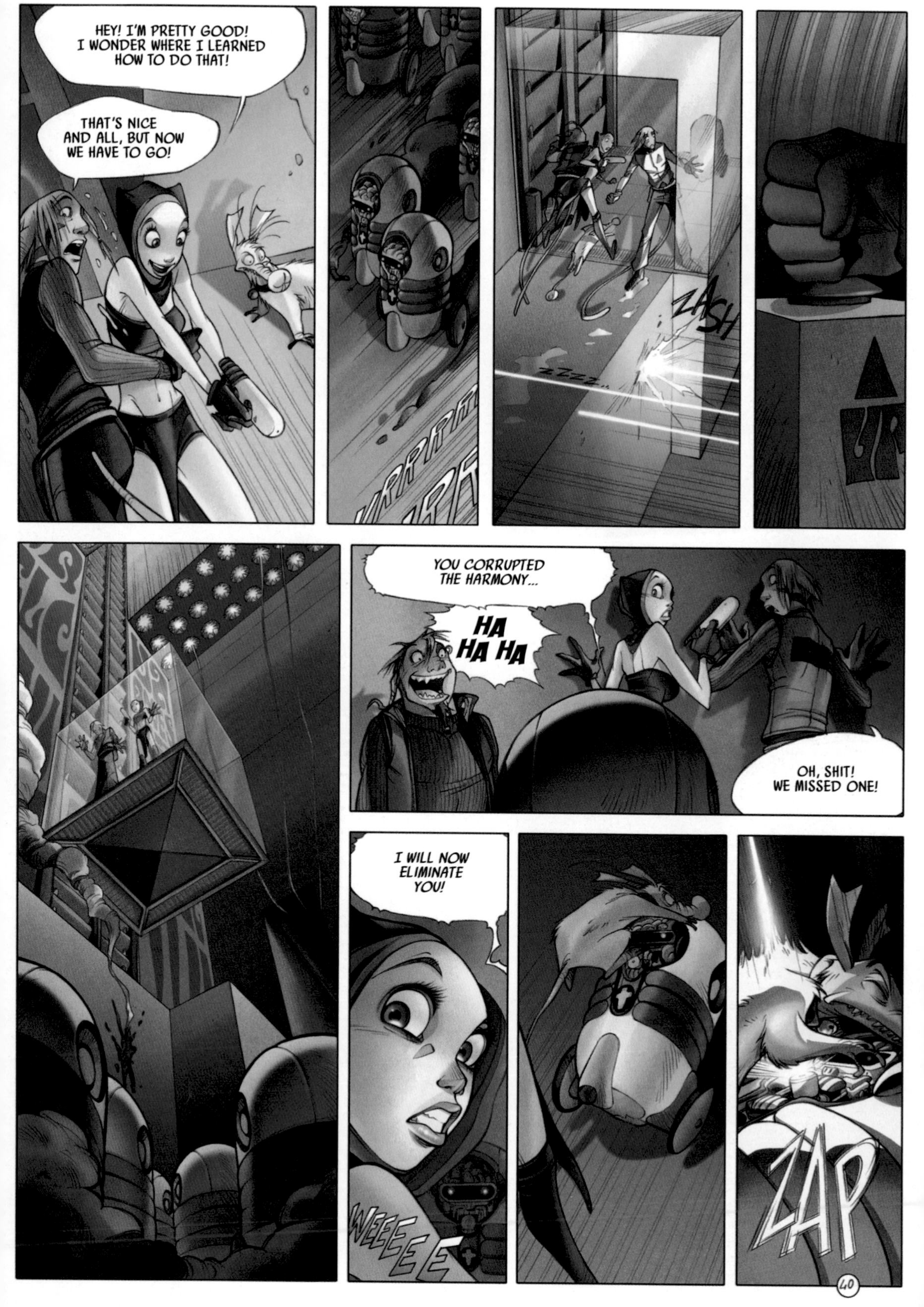
HEY! I'M PRETTY GOOD! I WONDER WHERE I LEARNED HOW TO DO THAT!
THAT'S NICE AND ALL, BUT NOW WE HAVE TO GO!
URRRRRR URRR
ZASH
ZZZZZ...
YOU CORRUPTED THE HARMONY...
HA HA HA
OH, SHIT! WE MISSED ONE!
I WILL NOW ELIMINATE YOU!
WEEEEE
ZAP

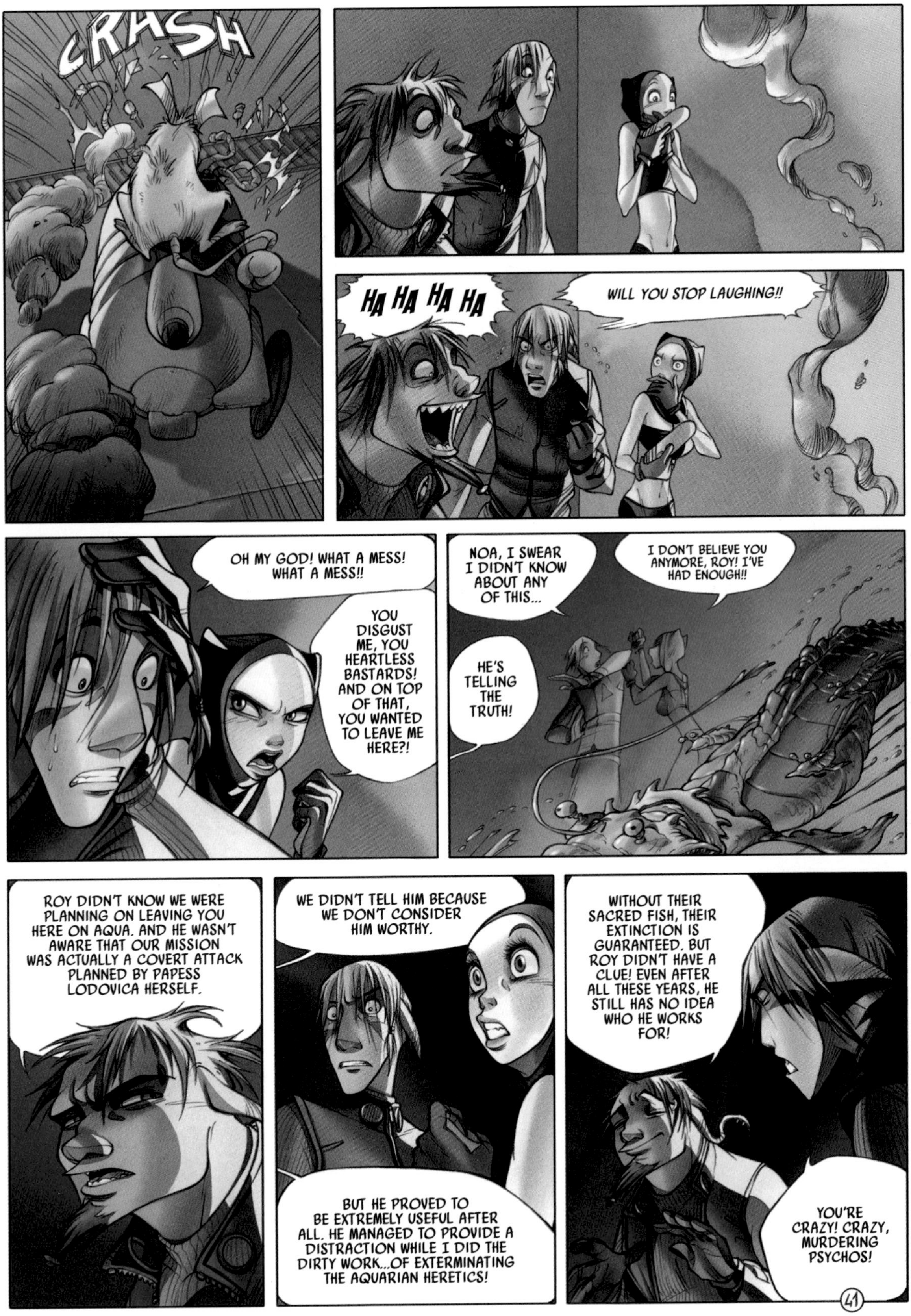
CRASH
HA HA HA HA
WILL YOU STOP LAUGHING!!
OH MY GOD! WHAT A MESS! WHAT A MESS!!
YOU DISGUST ME, YOU HEARTLESS BASTARDS! AND ON TOP OF THAT, YOU WANTED TO LEAVE ME HERE?!
NOA, I SWEAR I DIDN'T KNOW ABOUT ANY OF THIS...
I DON'T BELIEVE YOU ANYMORE, ROY! I'VE HAD ENOUGH!!
HE'S TELLING THE TRUTH!
ROY DIDN'T KNOW WE WERE PLANNING ON LEAVING YOU HERE ON AQUA, AND HE WASN'T AWARE THAT OUR MISSION WAS ACTUALLY A COVERT ATTACK PLANNED BY PAPESS LODOVICA HERSELF.
WE DIDN'T TELL HIM BECAUSE WE DON'T CONSIDER HIM WORTHY.
BUT HE PROVED TO BE EXTREMELY USEFUL AFTER ALL. HE MANAGED TO PROVIDE A DISTRACTION WHILE I DID THE DIRTY WORK...OF EXTERMINATING THE AQUARIAN HERETICS!
WITHOUT THEIR SACRED FISH, THEIR EXTINCTION IS GUARANTEED. BUT ROY DIDN'T HAVE A CLUE! EVEN AFTER ALL THESE YEARS, HE STILL HAS NO IDEA WHO HE WORKS FOR!
YOU'RE CRAZY! CRAZY, MURDERING PSYCHOS!

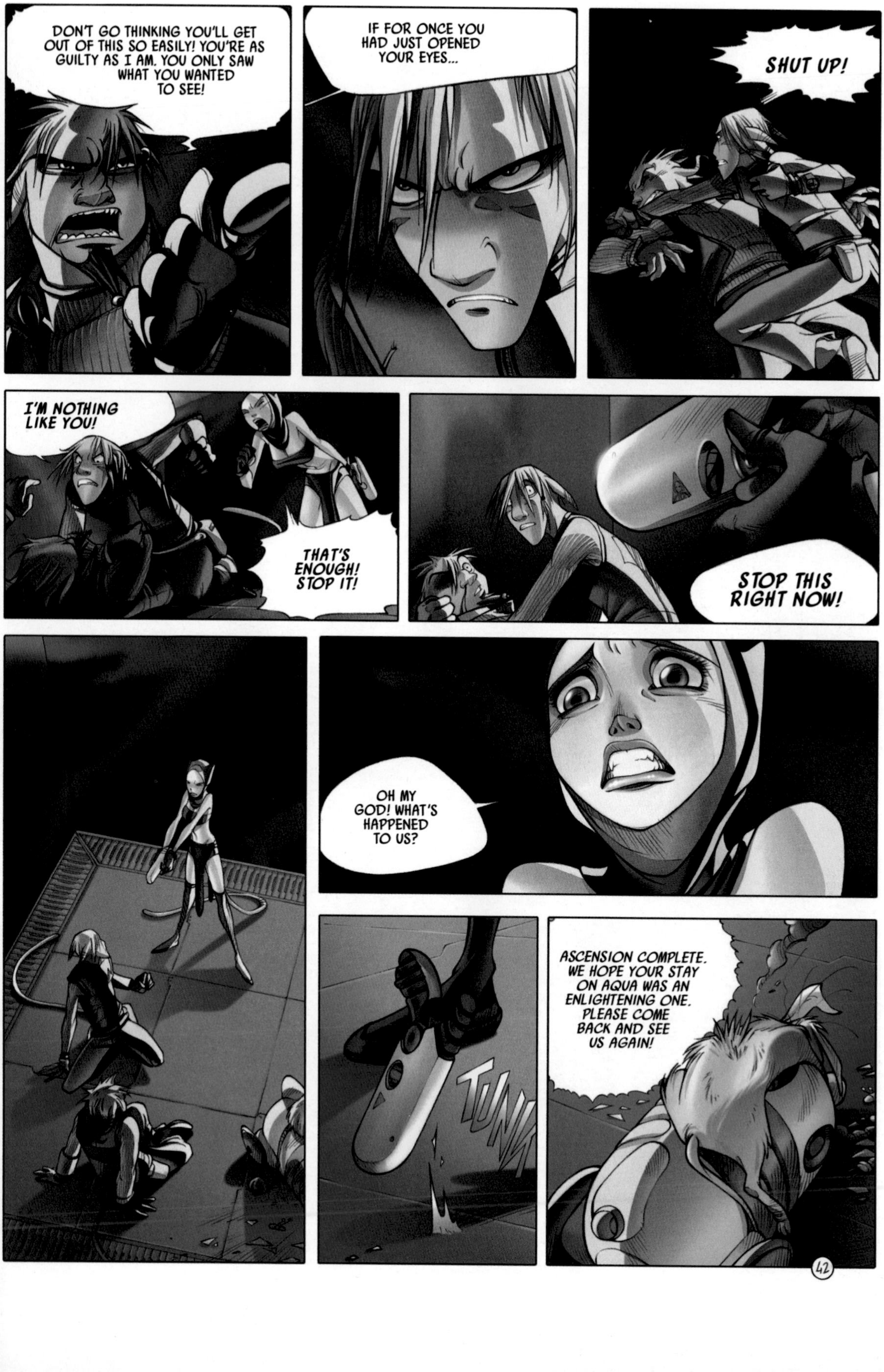
DON'T GO THINKING YOU'LL GET OUT OF THIS SO EASILY! YOU'RE AS GUILTY AS I AM. YOU ONLY SAW WHAT YOU WANTED TO SEE!
IF FOR ONCE YOU HAD JUST OPENED YOUR EYES...
SHUT UP!
I'M NOTHING LIKE YOU!
THAT'S ENOUGH! STOP IT!
STOP THIS RIGHT NOW!
OH MY GOD! WHAT'S HAPPENED TO US?
TUNK
ASCENSION COMPLETE. WE HOPE YOUR STAY ON AQUA WAS AN ENLIGHTENING ONE. PLEASE COME BACK AND SEE US AGAIN!

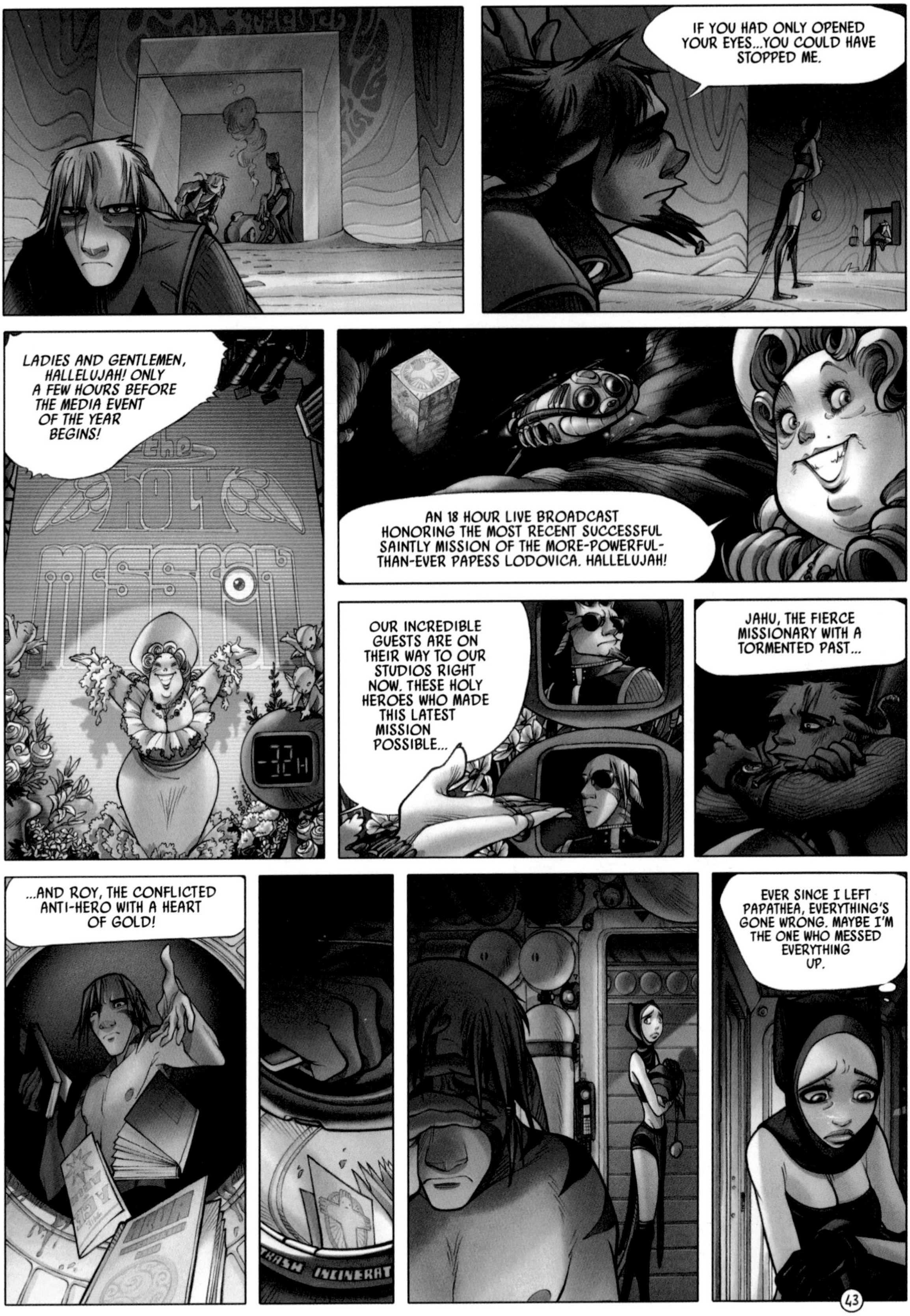
IF YOU HAD ONLY OPENED YOUR EYES...YOU COULD HAVE STOPPED ME.
LADIES AND GENTLEMEN, HALLELUJAH! ONLY A FEW HOURS BEFORE THE MEDIA EVENT OF THE YEAR BEGINS!
AN 18 HOUR LIVE BROADCAST HONORING THE MOST RECENT SUCCESSFUL SAINTLY MISSION OF THE MORE-POWERFUL-THAN-EVER PAPESS LODOVICA. HALLELUJAH!
OUR INCREDIBLE GUESTS ARE ON THEIR WAY TO OUR STUDIOS RIGHT NOW. THESE HOLY HEROES WHO MADE THIS LATEST MISSION POSSIBLE...
JAHU, THE FIERCE MISSIONARY WITH A TORMENTED PAST...
...AND ROY, THE CONFLICTED ANTI-HERO WITH A HEART OF GOLD!
TRASH INCINERAT
EVER SINCE I LEFT PAPATHEA, EVERYTHING'S GONE WRONG. MAYBE I'M THE ONE WHO MESSED EVERYTHING UP.

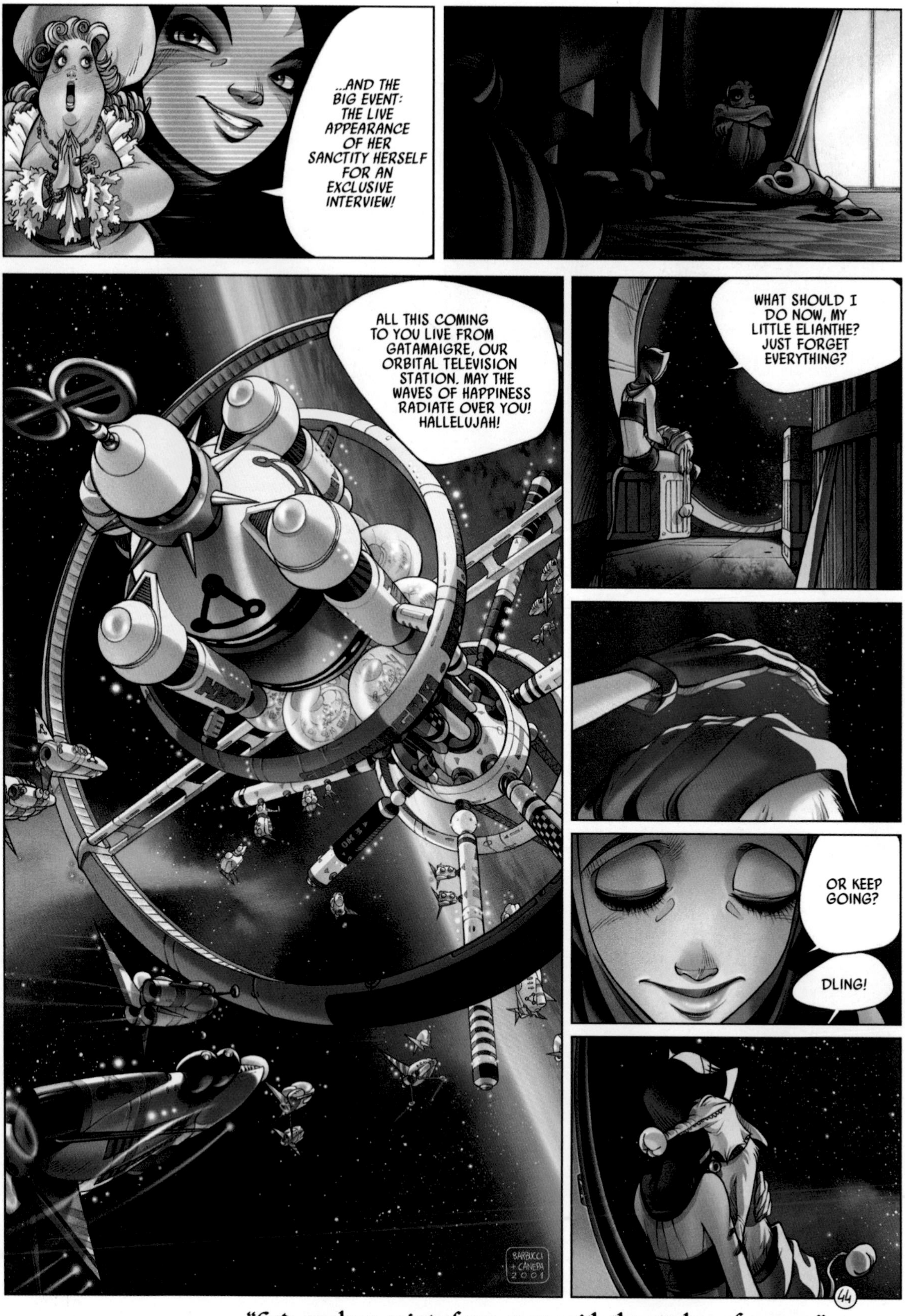
...AND THE BIG EVENT: THE LIVE APPEARANCE OF HER SANCTITY HERSELF FOR AN EXCLUSIVE INTERVIEW!
ALL THIS COMING TO YOU LIVE FROM GATAMAIGRE, OUR ORBITAL TELEVISION STATION. MAY THE WAVES OF HAPPINESS RADIATE OVER YOU! HALLELUJAH!
WHAT SHOULD I DO NOW, MY LITTLE ELIANTHE? JUST FORGET EVERYTHING?
OR KEEP GOING?
DLING!
BARBUCCI + CANEPA 2001
44

"God, make a saint of me, even with the strokes of a cane."
J. Escriva de Balaguer

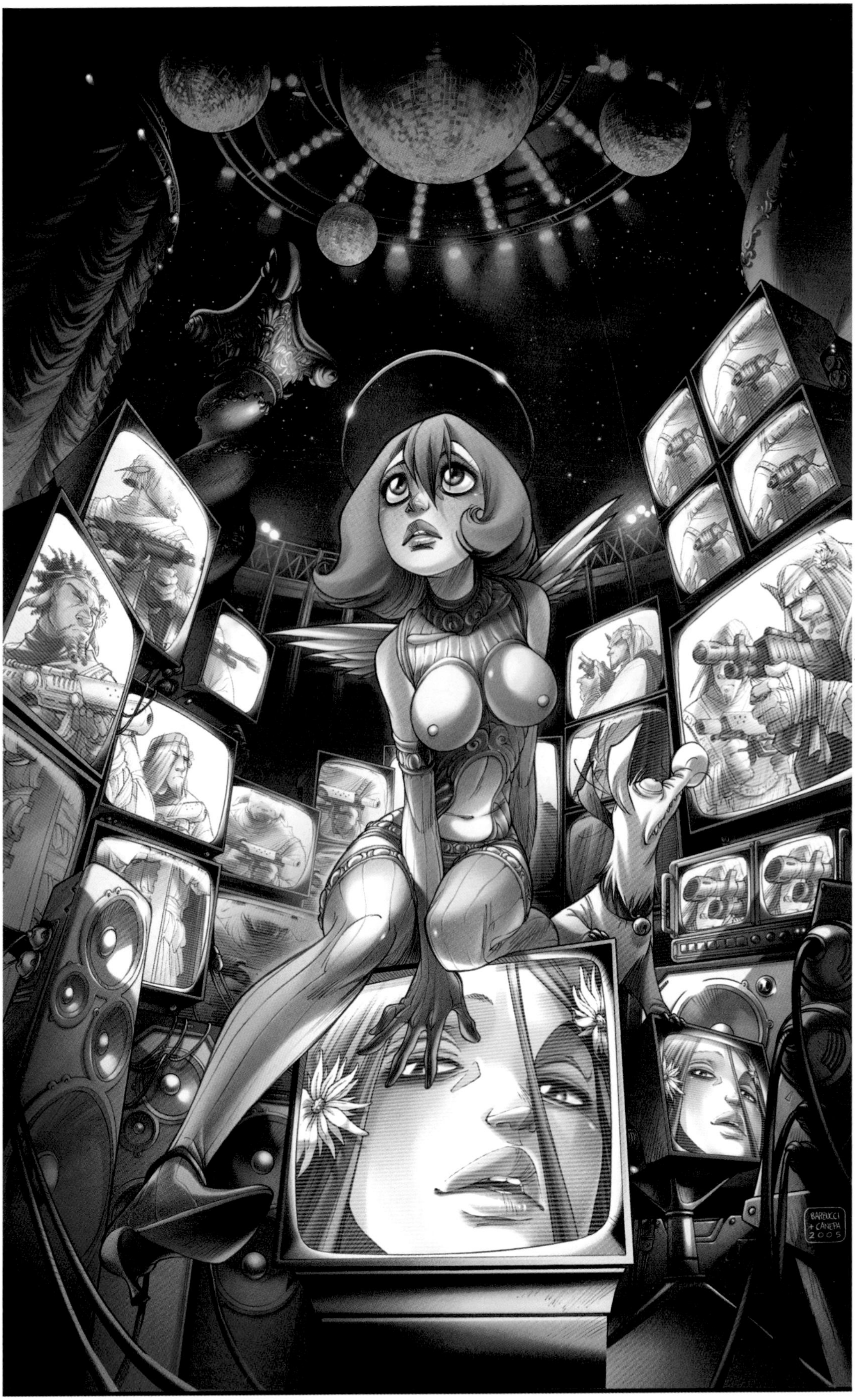
BARBUCCI
+ CANEPA
2005

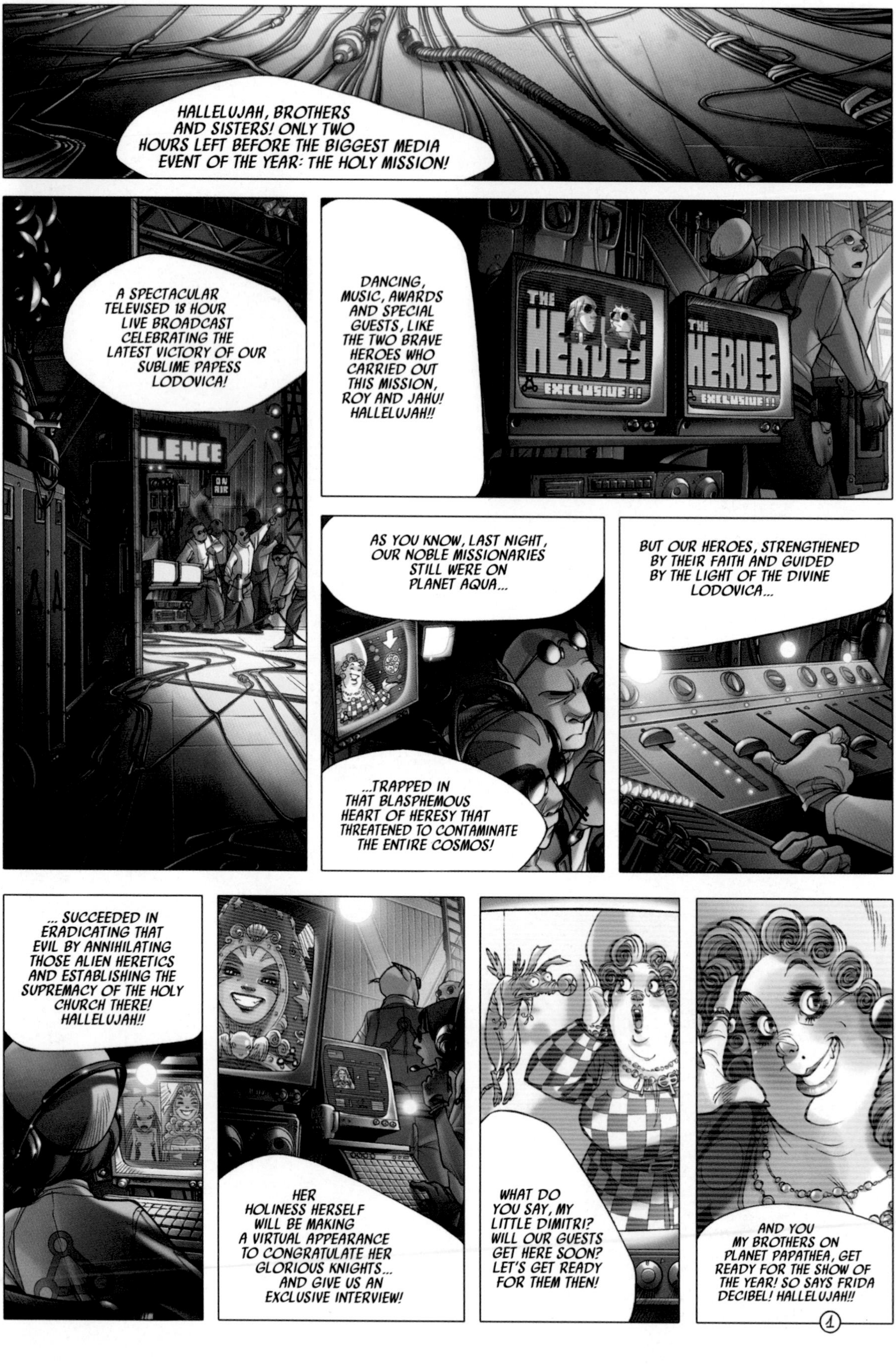
HALLELUJAH, BROTHERS AND SISTERS! ONLY TWO HOURS LEFT BEFORE THE BIGGEST MEDIA EVENT OF THE YEAR: THE HOLY MISSION!
A SPECTACULAR TELEVISED 18 HOUR LIVE BROADCAST CELEBRATING THE LATEST VICTORY OF OUR SUBLIME PAPESS LODOVICA!
ILENCE
ON AIR
DANCING, MUSIC, AWARDS AND SPECIAL GUESTS, LIKE THE TWO BRAVE HEROES WHO CARRIED OUT THIS MISSION, ROY AND JAHU! HALLELUJAH!!
THE HEROES EXCLUSIVE!!
THE HEROES EXCLUSIVE!!
AS YOU KNOW, LAST NIGHT, OUR NOBLE MISSIONARIES STILL WERE ON PLANET AQUA...
...TRAPPED IN THAT BLASPHEMOUS HEART OF HERESY THAT THREATENED TO CONTAMINATE THE ENTIRE COSMOS!
BUT OUR HEROES, STRENGTHENED BY THEIR FAITH AND GUIDED BY THE LIGHT OF THE DIVINE LODOVICA...
... SUCCEEDED IN ERADICATING THAT EVIL BY ANNIHILATING THOSE ALIEN HERETICS AND ESTABLISHING THE SUPREMACY OF THE HOLY CHURCH THERE! HALLELUJAH!!
HER HOLINESS HERSELF WILL BE MAKING A VIRTUAL APPEARANCE TO CONGRATULATE HER GLORIOUS KNIGHTS... AND GIVE US AN EXCLUSIVE INTERVIEW!
WHAT DO YOU SAY, MY LITTLE DIMITRI? WILL OUR GUESTS GET HERE SOON? LET'S GET READY FOR THEM THEN!
AND YOU MY BROTHERS ON PLANET PAPATHEA, GET READY FOR THE SHOW OF THE YEAR! SO SAYS FRIDA DECIBEL! HALLELUJAH!!

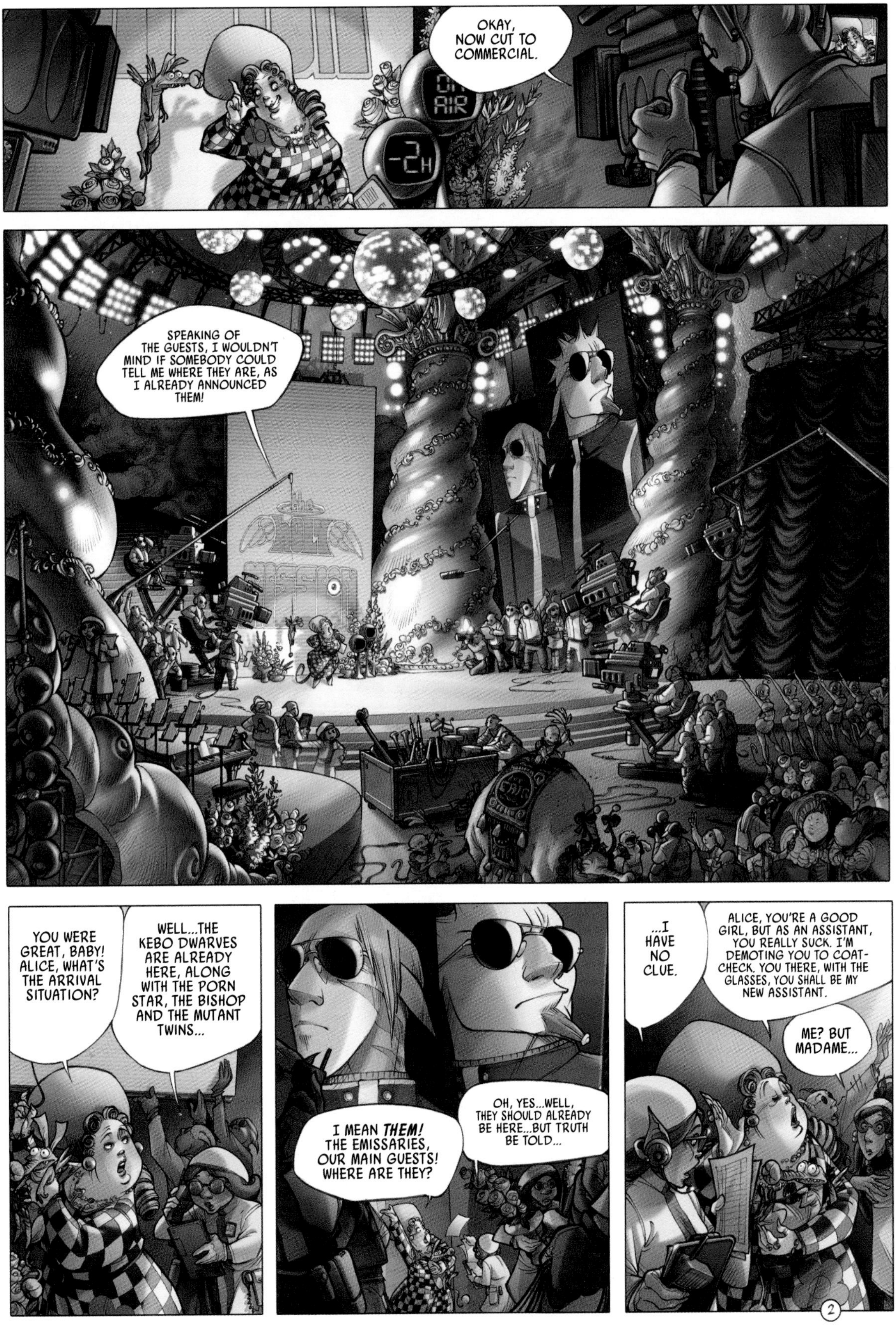
OKAY, NOW CUT TO COMMERCIAL.
ON AIR
-2H
SPEAKING OF THE GUESTS, I WOULDN'T MIND IF SOMEBODY COULD TELL ME WHERE THEY ARE, AS I ALREADY ANNOUNCED THEM!
YOU WERE GREAT, BABY! ALICE, WHAT'S THE ARRIVAL SITUATION?
WELL...THE KEBO DWARVES ARE ALREADY HERE, ALONG WITH THE PORN STAR, THE BISHOP AND THE MUTANT TWINS...
I MEAN *THEM!* THE EMISSARIES, OUR MAIN GUESTS! WHERE ARE THEY?
OH, YES...WELL, THEY SHOULD ALREADY BE HERE...BUT TRUTH BE TOLD...
...I HAVE NO CLUE.
ALICE, YOU'RE A GOOD GIRL, BUT AS AN ASSISTANT, YOU REALLY SUCK. I'M DEMOTING YOU TO COAT-CHECK. YOU THERE, WITH THE GLASSES, YOU SHALL BE MY NEW ASSISTANT.
ME? BUT MADAME...

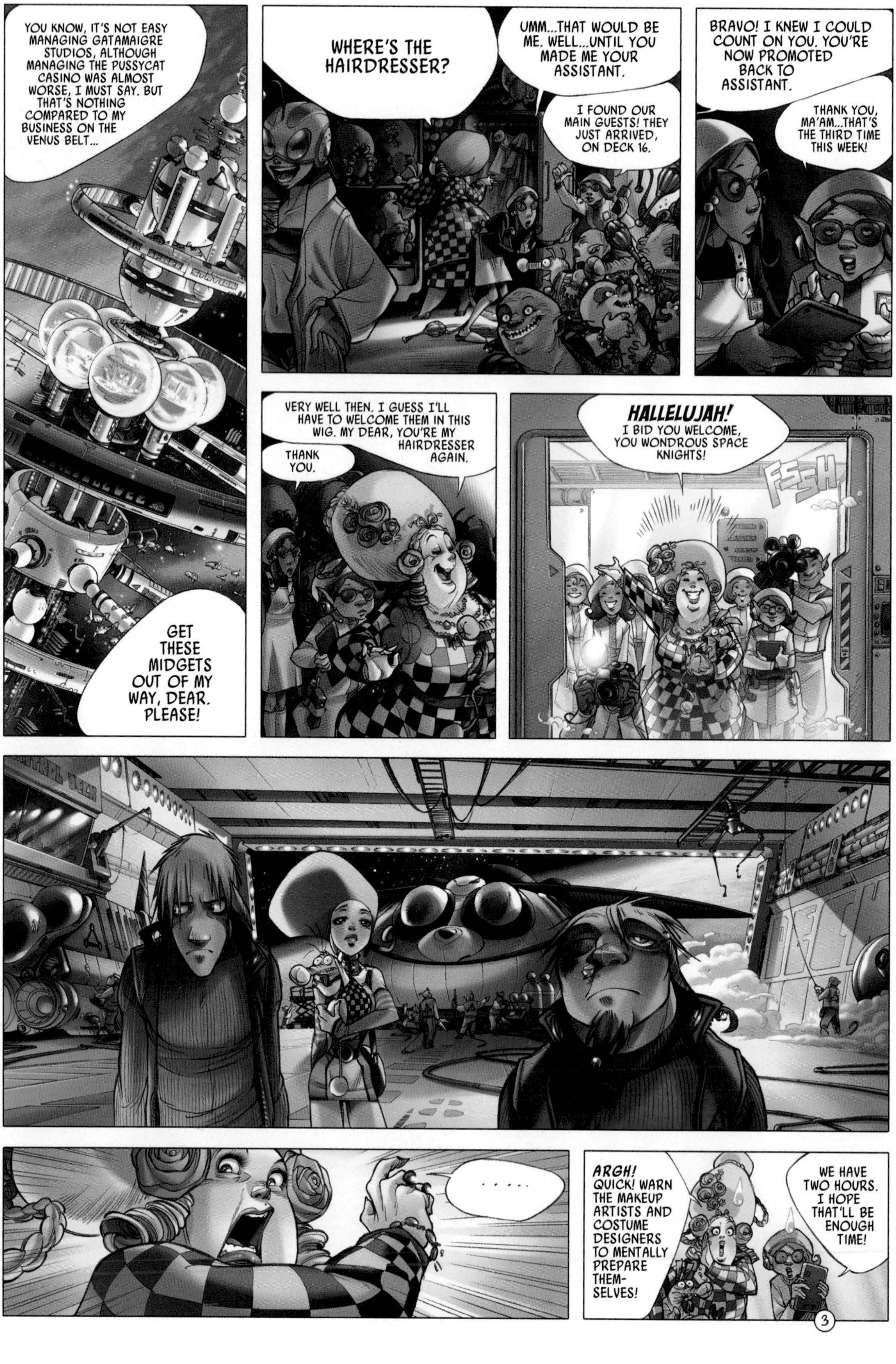
YOU KNOW, IT'S NOT EASY MANAGING GATAMAIGRE STUDIOS, ALTHOUGH MANAGING THE PUSSYCAT CASINO WAS ALMOST WORSE, I MUST SAY. BUT THAT'S NOTHING COMPARED TO MY BUSINESS ON THE VENUS BELT...
GET THESE MIDGETS OUT OF MY WAY, DEAR. PLEASE!
WHERE'S THE HAIRDRESSER?
UMM...THAT WOULD BE ME. WELL...UNTIL YOU MADE ME YOUR ASSISTANT.
I FOUND OUR MAIN GUESTS! THEY JUST ARRIVED, ON DECK 16.
BRAVO! I KNEW I COULD COUNT ON YOU. YOU'RE NOW PROMOTED BACK TO ASSISTANT.
THANK YOU, MA'AM...THAT'S THE THIRD TIME THIS WEEK!
VERY WELL THEN. I GUESS I'LL HAVE TO WELCOME THEM IN THIS WIG. MY DEAR, YOU'RE MY HAIRDRESSER AGAIN.
THANK YOU.
HALLELUJAH! I BID YOU WELCOME, YOU WONDROUS SPACE KNIGHTS!
FSSH
. . . . .
ARGH! QUICK! WARN THE MAKEUP ARTISTS AND COSTUME DESIGNERS TO MENTALLY PREPARE THEM-SELVES!
WE HAVE TWO HOURS. I HOPE THAT'LL BE ENOUGH TIME!

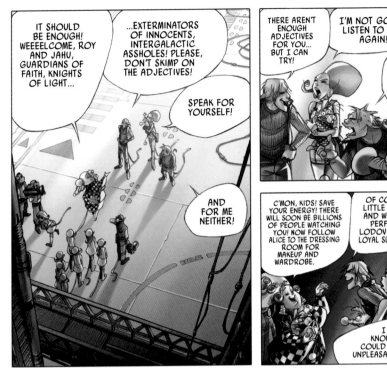

IT SHOULD BE ENOUGH! WEEEELCOME, ROY AND JAHU, GUARDIANS OF FAITH, KNIGHTS OF LIGHT...

...EXTERMINATORS OF INNOCENTS, INTERGALACTIC ASSHOLES! PLEASE, DON'T SKIMP ON THE ADJECTIVES!

SPEAK FOR YOURSELF!

AND FOR ME NEITHER!

THERE AREN'T ENOUGH ADJECTIVES FOR YOU... BUT I CAN TRY!

I'M NOT GONNA LISTEN TO THIS AGAIN!

YOU WANNA FIGHT AGAIN? SAY IT! JUST SAY IT!

HMMM...EMOTIONAL STRESS, BETRAYED AFFECTIONS... WELL, WELL, THIS IS ALL VERY INTERESTING!

C'MON, KIDS! SAVE YOUR ENERGY! THERE WILL SOON BE BILLIONS OF PEOPLE WATCHING YOU! NOW FOLLOW ALICE TO THE DRESSING ROOM FOR MAKEUP AND WARDROBE.

OF COURSE! A LITTLE MAKEUP AND WE'LL BE PERFECT! LODOVICA'S LOYAL SLUTS!

I DIDN'T KNOW YOU COULD BE SO UNPLEASANT, ROY!

IF YOU DON'T LIKE HANGING AROUND ME, THEN STOP TAGGING ALONG! AND TAKE THAT THING WITH YOU. HEY, WASN'T IT DEAD? HOW DID YOU...?

I HAVE POWERS YOU CAN'T EVEN IMAGINE! BUT APPARENTLY, YOU'RE NOT ALL THAT INTERESTED.

WHATEVER! GO TO HELL, ALL OF YOU!

HOW COULD I BE SO STUPID...?

IT HURTS ME TO SEE HIM LIKE THAT TOO. HE USED TO BE SO INNOCENT...NOW HE'S JUST AS CYNICAL AS EVERYONE ELSE. AND IT'S ALL MY FAULT.

I DESTROYED A PLANET...AS WELL AS MY FRIENDSHIP WITH ROY. NOW I JUST NEED TO GET THROUGH TONIGHT. I HOPE IT WAS ALL WORTH IT!

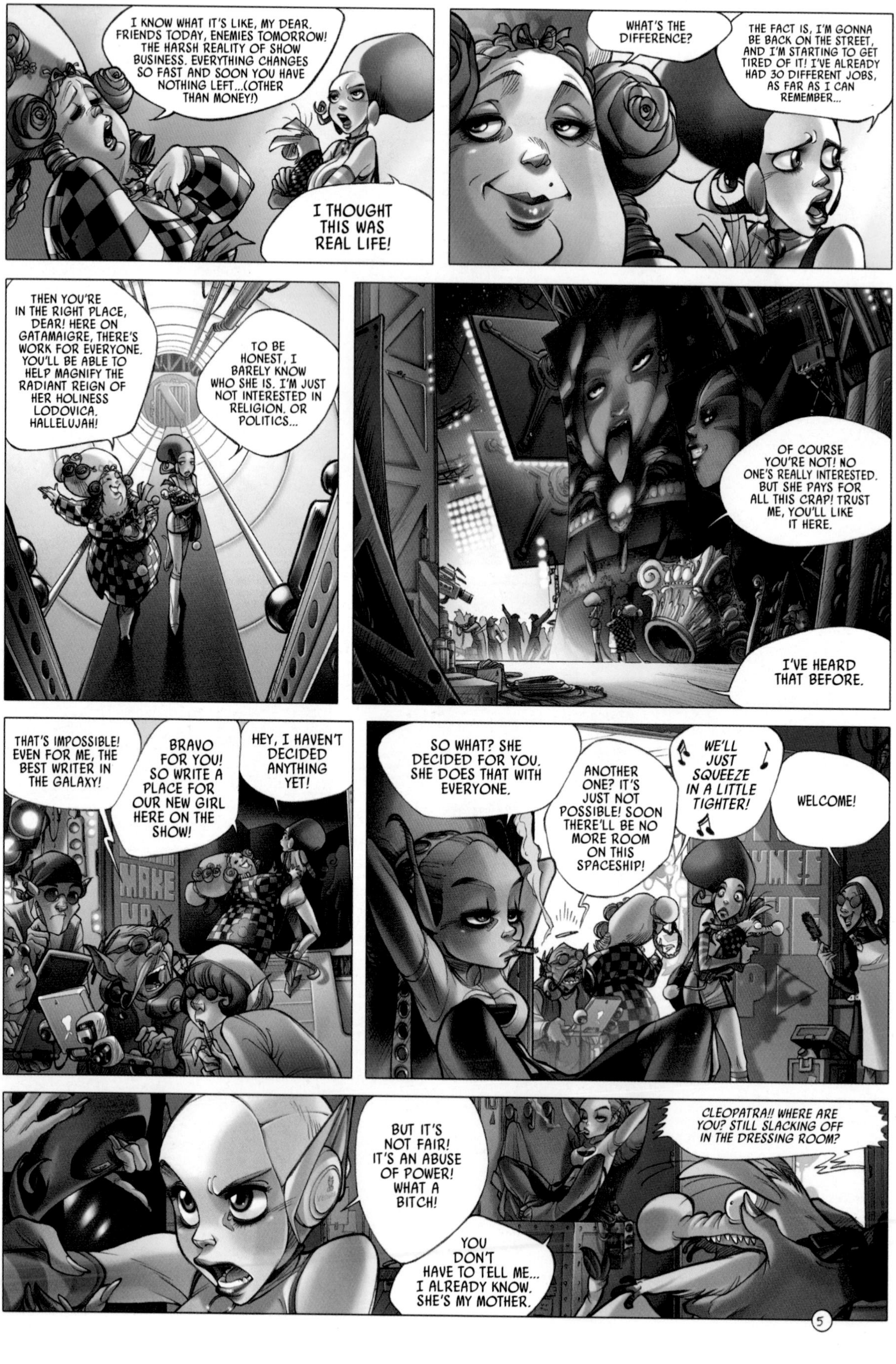
I KNOW WHAT IT'S LIKE, MY DEAR. FRIENDS TODAY, ENEMIES TOMORROW! THE HARSH REALITY OF SHOW BUSINESS. EVERYTHING CHANGES SO FAST AND SOON YOU HAVE NOTHING LEFT...(OTHER THAN MONEY!)
I THOUGHT THIS WAS REAL LIFE!
WHAT'S THE DIFFERENCE?
THE FACT IS, I'M GONNA BE BACK ON THE STREET, AND I'M STARTING TO GET TIRED OF IT! I'VE ALREADY HAD 30 DIFFERENT JOBS, AS FAR AS I CAN REMEMBER...
THEN YOU'RE IN THE RIGHT PLACE, DEAR! HERE ON GATAMAIGRE, THERE'S WORK FOR EVERYONE. YOU'LL BE ABLE TO HELP MAGNIFY THE RADIANT REIGN OF HER HOLINESS LODOVICA. HALLELUJAH!
TO BE HONEST, I BARELY KNOW WHO SHE IS. I'M JUST NOT INTERESTED IN RELIGION. OR POLITICS...
OF COURSE YOU'RE NOT! NO ONE'S REALLY INTERESTED. BUT SHE PAYS FOR ALL THIS CRAP! TRUST ME, YOU'LL LIKE IT HERE.
I'VE HEARD THAT BEFORE.
THAT'S IMPOSSIBLE! EVEN FOR ME, THE BEST WRITER IN THE GALAXY!
BRAVO FOR YOU! SO WRITE A PLACE FOR OUR NEW GIRL HERE ON THE SHOW!
HEY, I HAVEN'T DECIDED ANYTHING YET!
MAKE UP
SO WHAT? SHE DECIDED FOR YOU. SHE DOES THAT WITH EVERYONE.
ANOTHER ONE? IT'S JUST NOT POSSIBLE! SOON THERE'LL BE NO MORE ROOM ON THIS SPACESHIP!
WE'LL JUST SQUEEZE IN A LITTLE TIGHTER!
WELCOME!
BUT IT'S NOT FAIR! IT'S AN ABUSE OF POWER! WHAT A BITCH!
YOU DON'T HAVE TO TELL ME... I ALREADY KNOW. SHE'S MY MOTHER.
CLEOPATRA!! WHERE ARE YOU? STILL SLACKING OFF IN THE DRESSING ROOM?

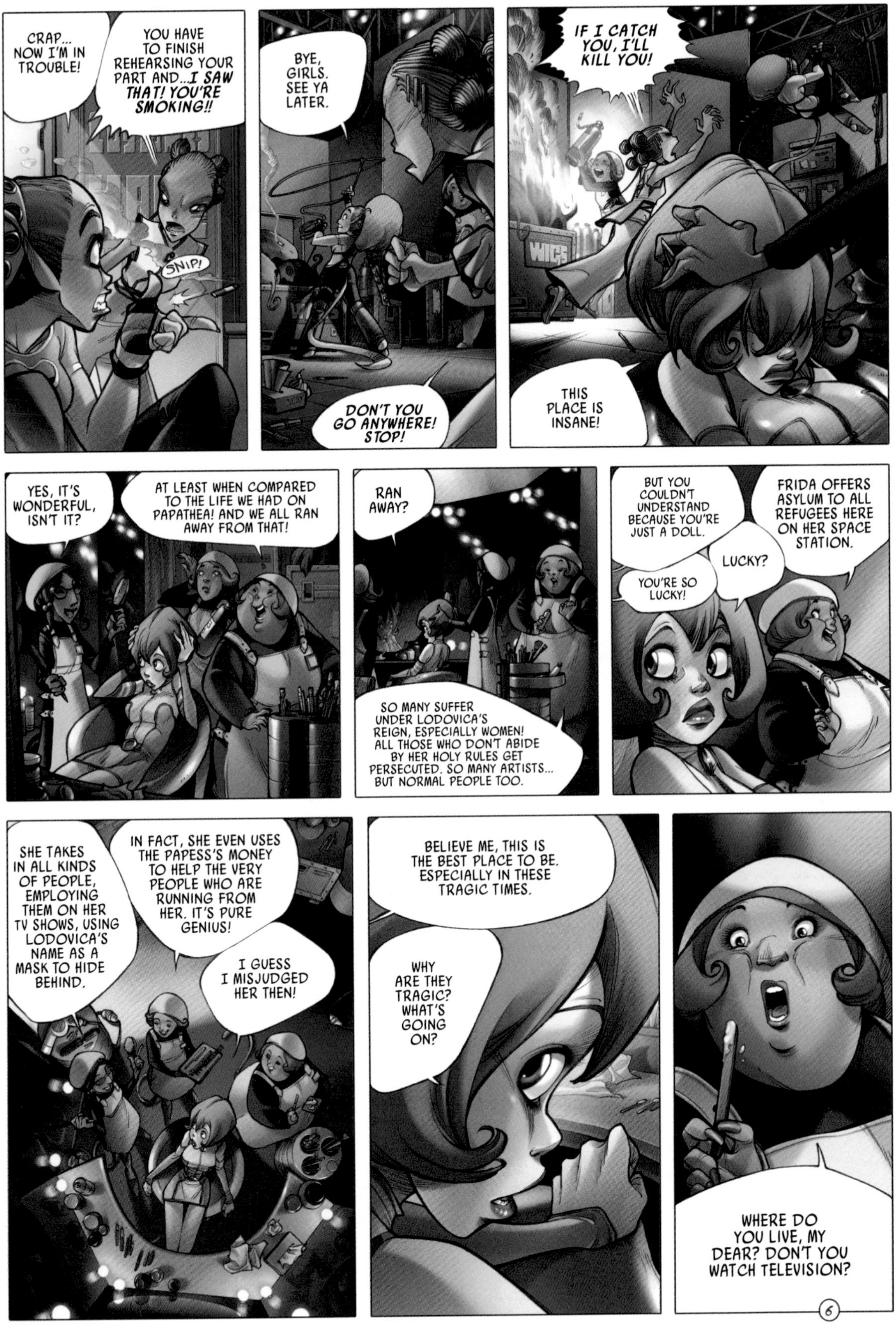

CRAP... NOW I'M IN TROUBLE!
YOU HAVE TO FINISH REHEARSING YOUR PART AND... I SAW THAT! YOU'RE SMOKING!!
SNIP!
BYE, GIRLS. SEE YA LATER.
DON'T YOU GO ANYWHERE! STOP!
IF I CATCH YOU, I'LL KILL YOU!
THIS PLACE IS INSANE!
YES, IT'S WONDERFUL, ISN'T IT?
AT LEAST WHEN COMPARED TO THE LIFE WE HAD ON PAPATHEA! AND WE ALL RAN AWAY FROM THAT!
RAN AWAY?
SO MANY SUFFER UNDER LODOVICA'S REIGN, ESPECIALLY WOMEN! ALL THOSE WHO DON'T ABIDE BY HER HOLY RULES GET PERSECUTED. SO MANY ARTISTS... BUT NORMAL PEOPLE TOO.
BUT YOU COULDN'T UNDERSTAND BECAUSE YOU'RE JUST A DOLL.
FRIDA OFFERS ASYLUM TO ALL REFUGEES HERE ON HER SPACE STATION.
YOU'RE SO LUCKY!
LUCKY?
SHE TAKES IN ALL KINDS OF PEOPLE, EMPLOYING THEM ON HER TV SHOWS, USING LODOVICA'S NAME AS A MASK TO HIDE BEHIND.
IN FACT, SHE EVEN USES THE PAPESS'S MONEY TO HELP THE VERY PEOPLE WHO ARE RUNNING FROM HER. IT'S PURE GENIUS!
I GUESS I MISJUDGED HER THEN!
BELIEVE ME, THIS IS THE BEST PLACE TO BE. ESPECIALLY IN THESE TRAGIC TIMES.
WHY ARE THEY TRAGIC? WHAT'S GOING ON?
WHERE DO YOU LIVE, MY DEAR? DON'T YOU WATCH TELEVISION?

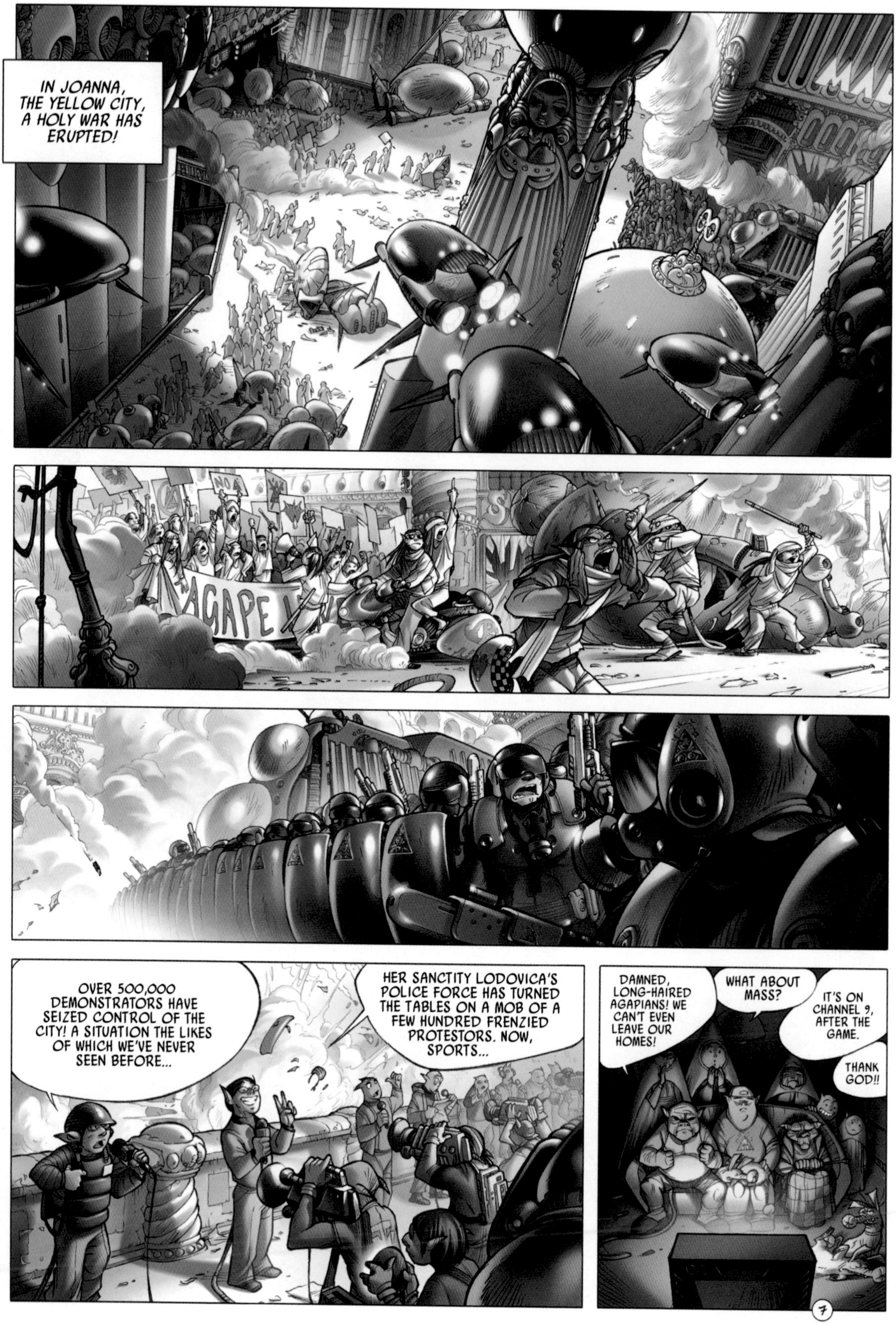
IN JOANNA, THE YELLOW CITY, A HOLY WAR HAS ERUPTED!
AGAPE
OVER 500,000 DEMONSTRATORS HAVE SEIZED CONTROL OF THE CITY! A SITUATION THE LIKES OF WHICH WE'VE NEVER SEEN BEFORE...
HER SANCTITY LODOVICA'S POLICE FORCE HAS TURNED THE TABLES ON A MOB OF A FEW HUNDRED FRENZIED PROTESTORS. NOW, SPORTS...
DAMNED, LONG-HAIRED AGAPIANS! WE CAN'T EVEN LEAVE OUR HOMES!
WHAT ABOUT MASS?
IT'S ON CHANNEL 9, AFTER THE GAME.
THANK GOD!!

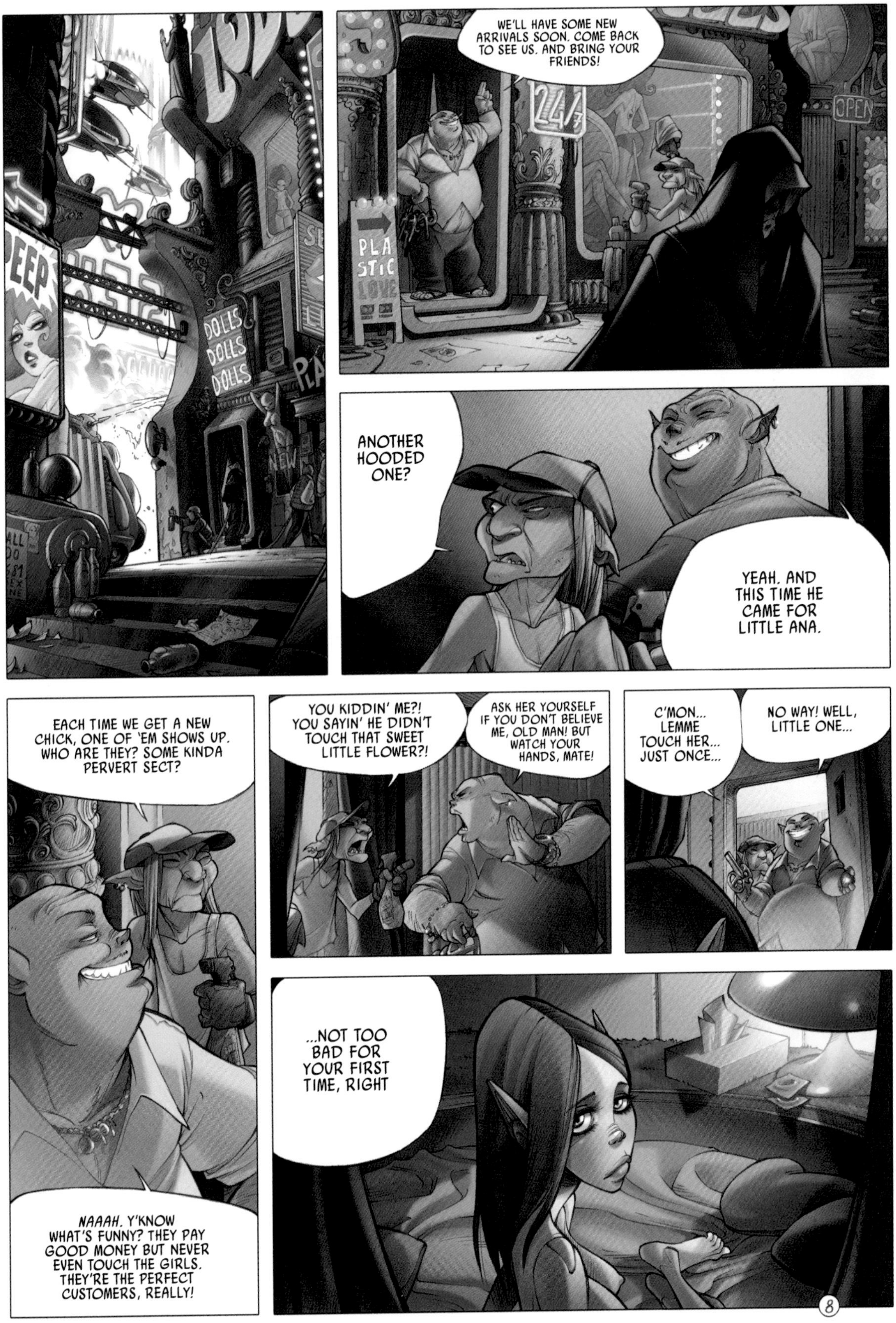

PEEP
DOLLS
DOLLS
DOLLS
NEW
WE'LL HAVE SOME NEW ARRIVALS SOON. COME BACK TO SEE US. AND BRING YOUR FRIENDS!
24/7
OPEN
PLA STIC LOVE
ANOTHER HOODED ONE?
YEAH. AND THIS TIME HE CAME FOR LITTLE ANA.
EACH TIME WE GET A NEW CHICK, ONE OF 'EM SHOWS UP. WHO ARE THEY? SOME KINDA PERVERT SECT?
NAAAH. Y'KNOW WHAT'S FUNNY? THEY PAY GOOD MONEY BUT NEVER EVEN TOUCH THE GIRLS. THEY'RE THE PERFECT CUSTOMERS, REALLY!
YOU KIDDIN' ME?! YOU SAYIN' HE DIDN'T TOUCH THAT SWEET LITTLE FLOWER?!
ASK HER YOURSELF IF YOU DON'T BELIEVE ME, OLD MAN! BUT WATCH YOUR HANDS, MATE!
C'MON... LEMME TOUCH HER... JUST ONCE...
NO WAY! WELL, LITTLE ONE...
...NOT TOO BAD FOR YOUR FIRST TIME, RIGHT

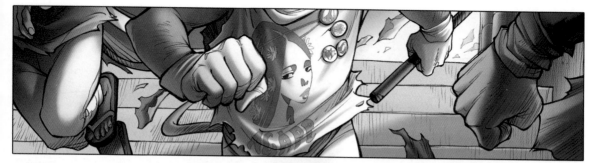

SCREW YOU, YOU SLAVES OF LODOVICA! HA HAAA!!

HEY, YOU LODOVICAN GOON! YOU MADE A BIG MISTAKE PASSIN' THROUGH HERE, YOU KNOW THAT?!

FORGIVE ME, YOUR HOLINESS!

WHAT'S WITH YOU? YOU SEE A GHOST?

ALMOST...HE WAS A "SEEKER"! ONE OF THE SUPREME BISHOPS OF OUR BELOVED AN' HOLY AGAPE!

THEY'RE NOT HERE TO SIMPLY STIR UP THE CROWD'S NOSTALGIC FERVOR. THEIR PRESENCE MEANS SOMETHING BIG'S GONNA GO DOWN SOON.

WE MIGHT NOT GET OUT OF THIS ALIVE. YOU'LL SEE! I CAN FEEL IT...

I CAN FEEL IT RIGHT HERE.

MUST BE SOMETHING YOU ATE.

DAMN DRIVER! WHY IS IT TAKING SO LONG? WE SHOULD BE BACK AT THE PALACE ALREADY!

WE HAD TO TAKE A DETOUR. THE MAIN ROUTE WAS BLOCKED BY DEMONSTRATORS.

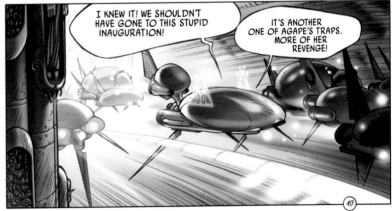

I KNEW IT! WE SHOULDN'T HAVE GONE TO THIS STUPID INAUGURATION!

IT'S ANOTHER ONE OF AGAPE'S TRAPS. MORE OF HER REVENGE!

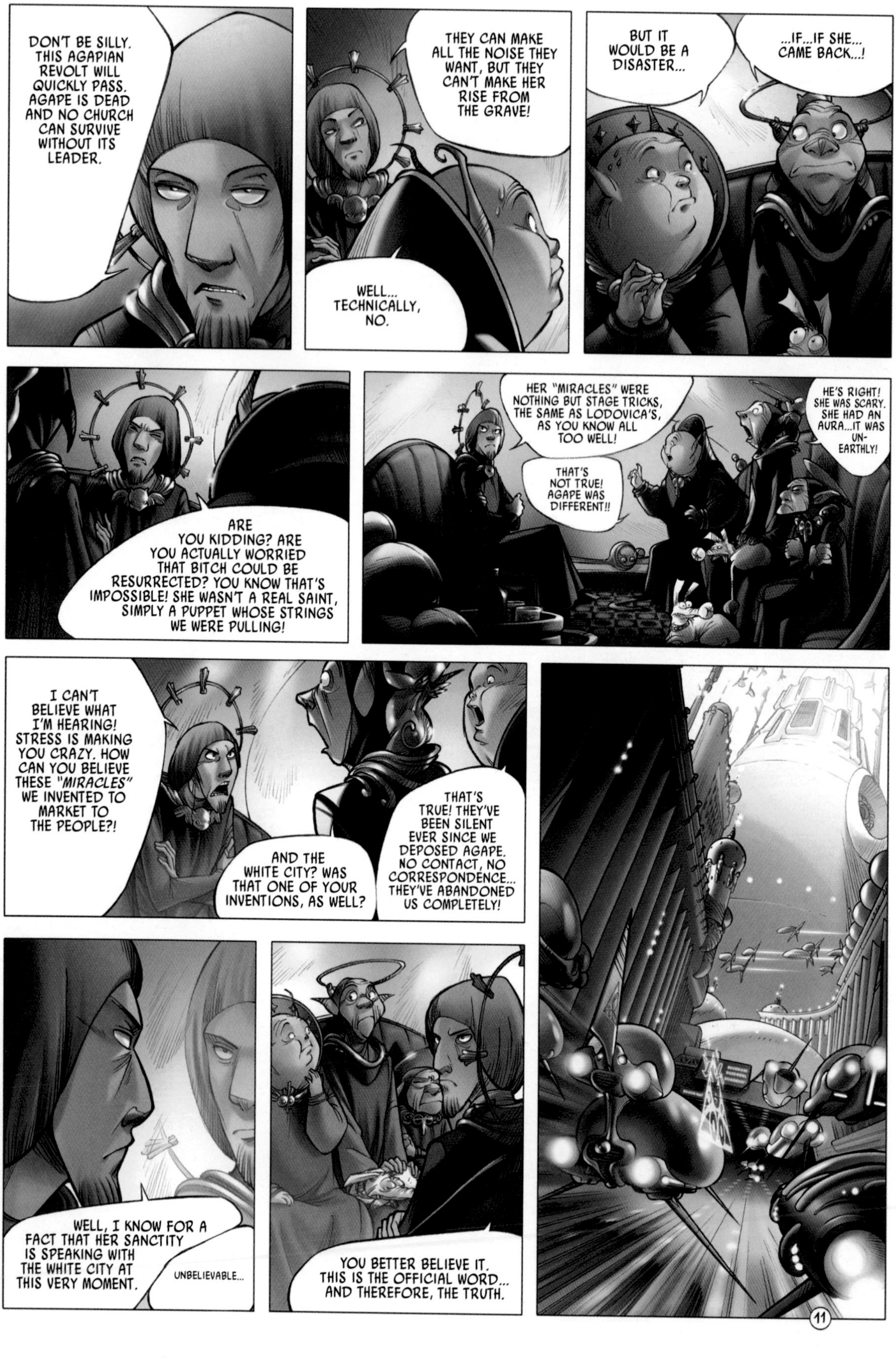
DON'T BE SILLY. THIS AGAPIAN REVOLT WILL QUICKLY PASS. AGAPE IS DEAD AND NO CHURCH CAN SURVIVE WITHOUT ITS LEADER.
THEY CAN MAKE ALL THE NOISE THEY WANT, BUT THEY CAN'T MAKE HER RISE FROM THE GRAVE!
WELL... TECHNICALLY, NO.
BUT IT WOULD BE A DISASTER...
...IF...IF SHE... CAME BACK...!
ARE YOU KIDDING? ARE YOU ACTUALLY WORRIED THAT BITCH COULD BE RESURRECTED? YOU KNOW THAT'S IMPOSSIBLE! SHE WASN'T A REAL SAINT, SIMPLY A PUPPET WHOSE STRINGS WE WERE PULLING!
HER "MIRACLES" WERE NOTHING BUT STAGE TRICKS, THE SAME AS LODOVICA'S, AS YOU KNOW ALL TOO WELL!
THAT'S NOT TRUE! AGAPE WAS DIFFERENT!!
HE'S RIGHT! SHE WAS SCARY. SHE HAD AN AURA...IT WAS UN-EARTHLY!
I CAN'T BELIEVE WHAT I'M HEARING! STRESS IS MAKING YOU CRAZY. HOW CAN YOU BELIEVE THESE "MIRACLES" WE INVENTED TO MARKET TO THE PEOPLE?!
AND THE WHITE CITY? WAS THAT ONE OF YOUR INVENTIONS, AS WELL?
THAT'S TRUE! THEY'VE BEEN SILENT EVER SINCE WE DEPOSED AGAPE. NO CONTACT, NO CORRESPONDENCE... THEY'VE ABANDONED US COMPLETELY!
WELL, I KNOW FOR A FACT THAT HER SANCTITY IS SPEAKING WITH THE WHITE CITY AT THIS VERY MOMENT.
UNBELIEVABLE...
YOU BETTER BELIEVE IT. THIS IS THE OFFICIAL WORD... AND THEREFORE, THE TRUTH.

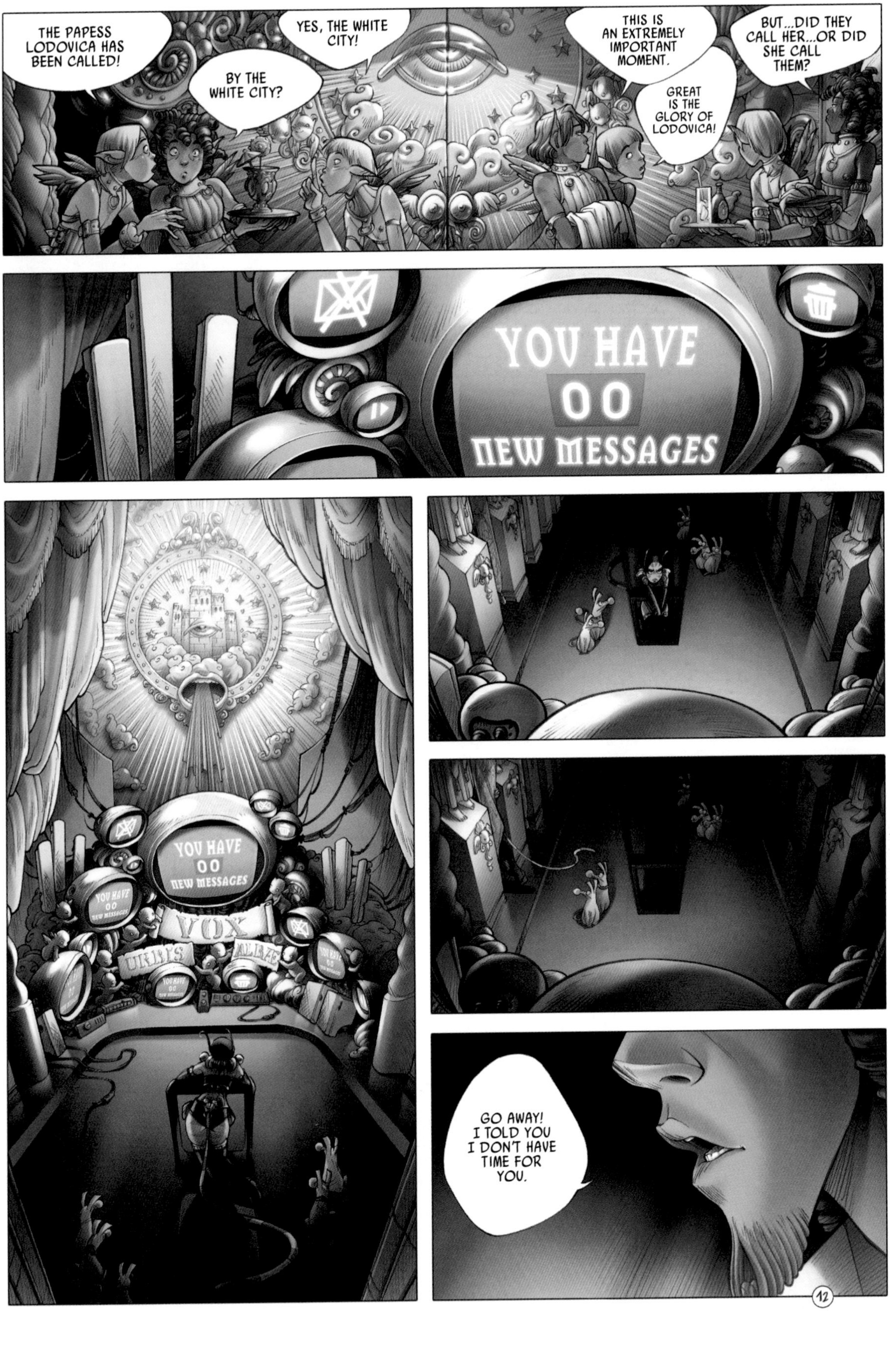
THE PAPESS LODOVICA HAS BEEN CALLED!
BY THE WHITE CITY?
YES, THE WHITE CITY!
THIS IS AN EXTREMELY IMPORTANT MOMENT.
GREAT IS THE GLORY OF LODOVICA!
BUT...DID THEY CALL HER...OR DID SHE CALL THEM?
YOU HAVE 00 NEW MESSAGES
YOU HAVE 00 NEW MESSAGES
VOX
URBIS
ALBAE
GO AWAY! I TOLD YOU I DON'T HAVE TIME FOR YOU.
12

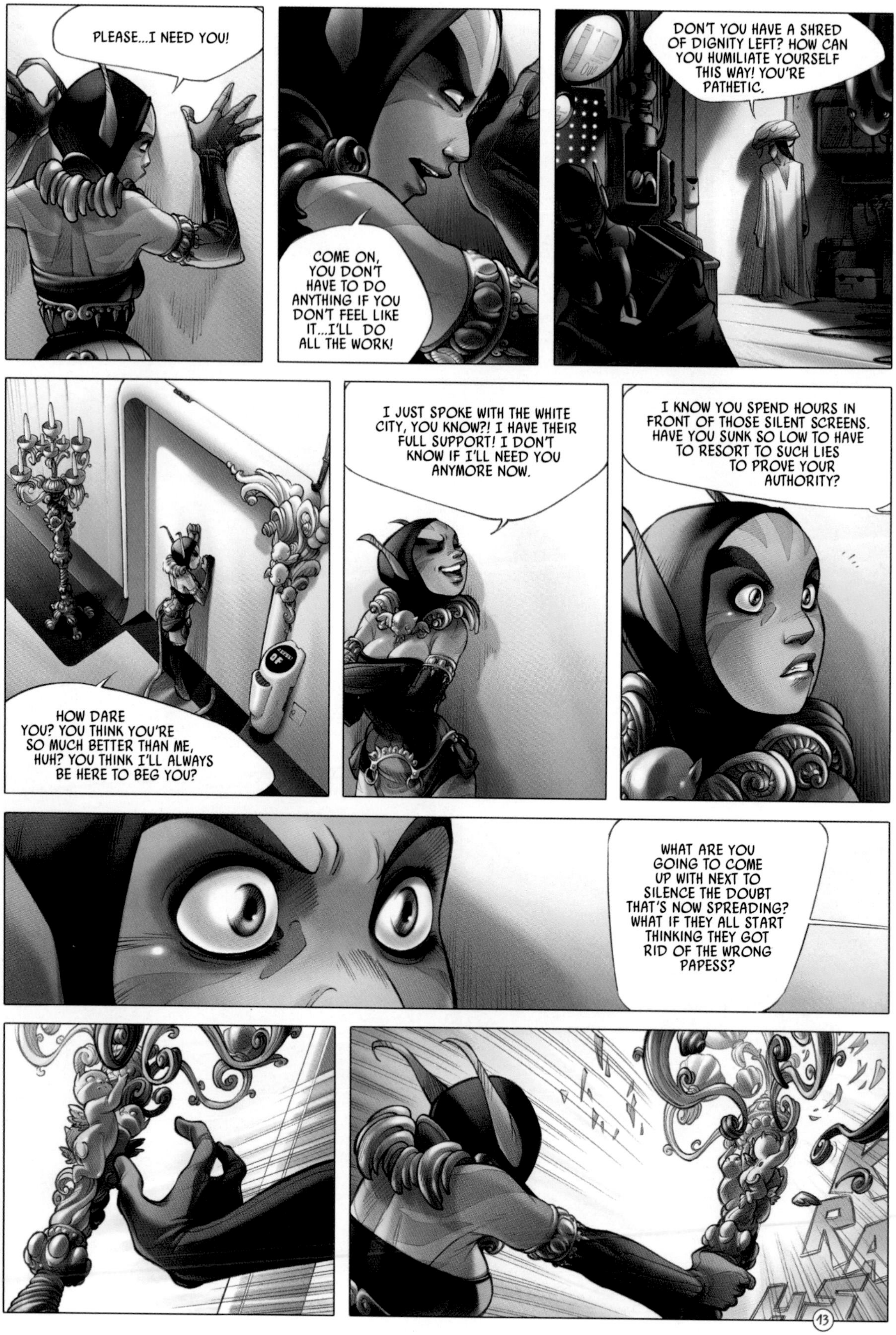
PLEASE...I NEED YOU!
COME ON, YOU DON'T HAVE TO DO ANYTHING IF YOU DON'T FEEL LIKE IT...I'LL DO ALL THE WORK!
DON'T YOU HAVE A SHRED OF DIGNITY LEFT? HOW CAN YOU HUMILIATE YOURSELF THIS WAY! YOU'RE PATHETIC.
HOW DARE YOU? YOU THINK YOU'RE SO MUCH BETTER THAN ME, HUH? YOU THINK I'LL ALWAYS BE HERE TO BEG YOU?
I JUST SPOKE WITH THE WHITE CITY, YOU KNOW?! I HAVE THEIR FULL SUPPORT! I DON'T KNOW IF I'LL NEED YOU ANYMORE NOW.
I KNOW YOU SPEND HOURS IN FRONT OF THOSE SILENT SCREENS. HAVE YOU SUNK SO LOW TO HAVE TO RESORT TO SUCH LIES TO PROVE YOUR AUTHORITY?
WHAT ARE YOU GOING TO COME UP WITH NEXT TO SILENCE THE DOUBT THAT'S NOW SPREADING? WHAT IF THEY ALL START THINKING THEY GOT RID OF THE WRONG PAPESS?

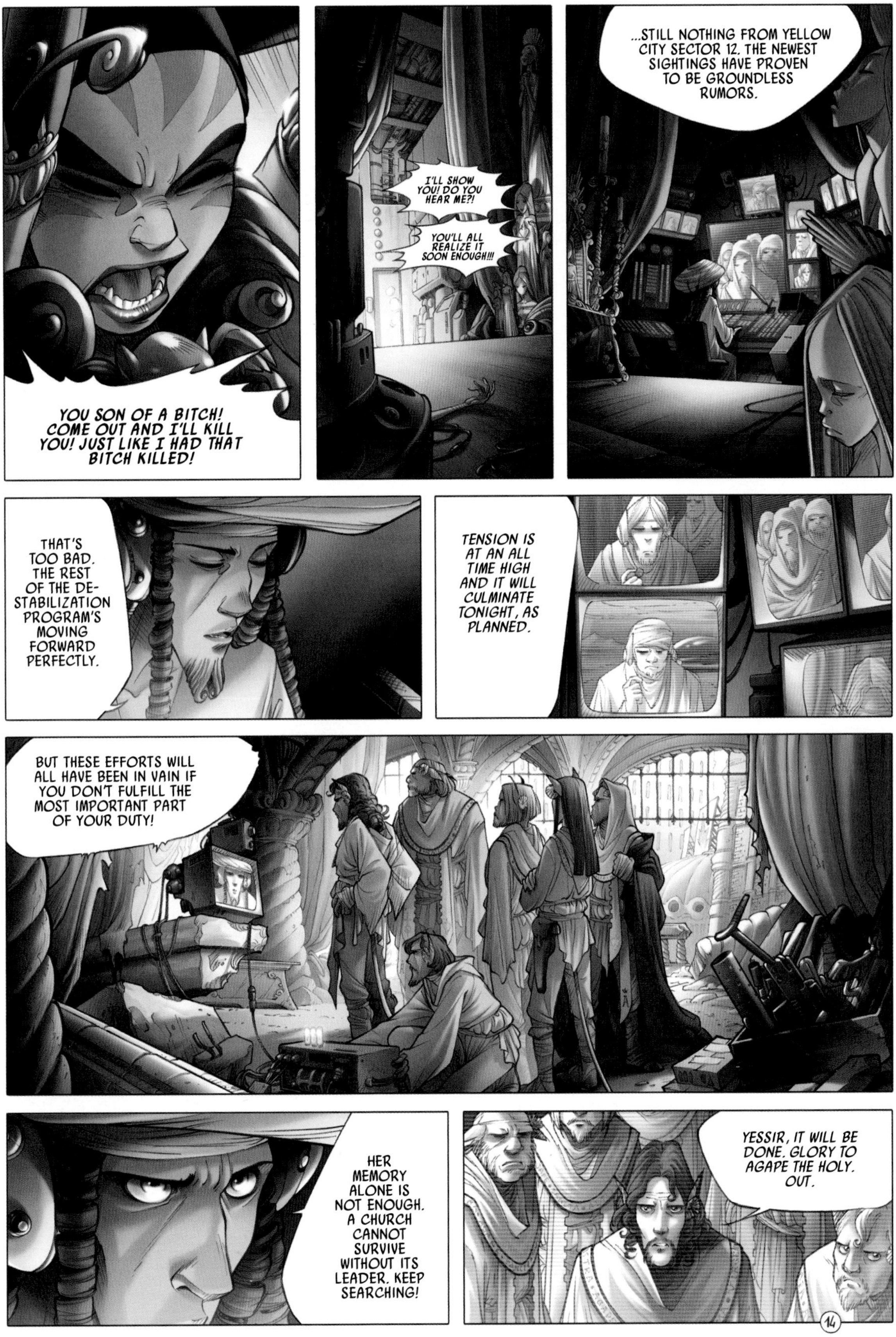
YOU SON OF A BITCH! COME OUT AND I'LL KILL YOU! JUST LIKE I HAD THAT BITCH KILLED!
I'LL SHOW YOU! DO YOU HEAR ME?!
YOU'LL ALL REALIZE IT SOON ENOUGH!!!
...STILL NOTHING FROM YELLOW CITY SECTOR 12. THE NEWEST SIGHTINGS HAVE PROVEN TO BE GROUNDLESS RUMORS.
THAT'S TOO BAD. THE REST OF THE DE-STABILIZATION PROGRAM'S MOVING FORWARD PERFECTLY.
TENSION IS AT AN ALL TIME HIGH AND IT WILL CULMINATE TONIGHT, AS PLANNED.
BUT THESE EFFORTS WILL ALL HAVE BEEN IN VAIN IF YOU DON'T FULFILL THE MOST IMPORTANT PART OF YOUR DUTY!
HER MEMORY ALONE IS NOT ENOUGH. A CHURCH CANNOT SURVIVE WITHOUT ITS LEADER. KEEP SEARCHING!
YESSIR, IT WILL BE DONE. GLORY TO AGAPE THE HOLY. OUT.

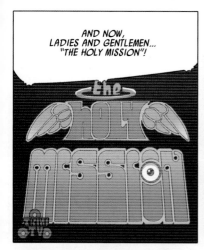

AND NOW, LADIES AND GENTLEMEN... "THE HOLY MISSION"!

BROADCASTING LIVE FROM GATAMAIGRE ORBITAL STATION STUDIO 5...

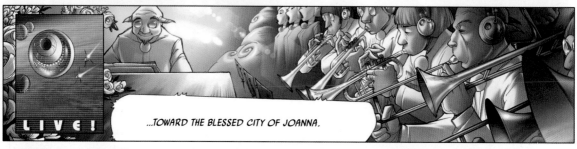

...TOWARD THE BLESSED CITY OF JOANNA.

WE STILL HAVE A LITTLE TIME BEFORE YOU GO ON THE AIR. IN THE MEANTIME, READ THE QUESTIONS YOU'LL BE ASKED. YOUR ANSWERS ARE HIGHLIGHTED IN RED.

ARE YOU GOING TO SHOVE YOUR HANDS UP OUR ASSES AND MAKE US DANCE LIKE PUPPETS, TOO?

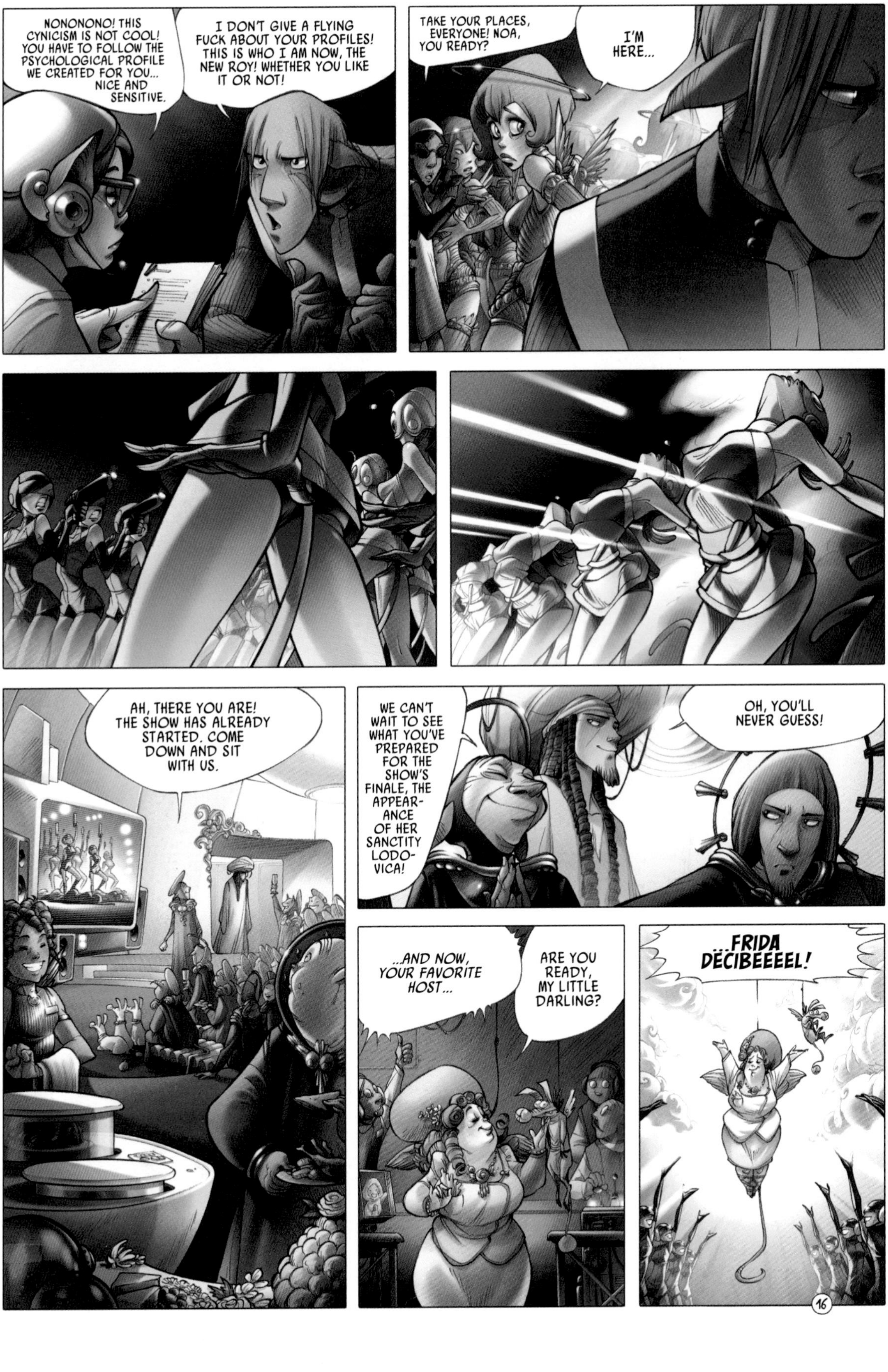
NONONONO! THIS CYNICISM IS NOT COOL! YOU HAVE TO FOLLOW THE PSYCHOLOGICAL PROFILE WE CREATED FOR YOU... NICE AND SENSITIVE.
I DON'T GIVE A FLYING FUCK ABOUT YOUR PROFILES! THIS IS WHO I AM NOW, THE NEW ROY! WHETHER YOU LIKE IT OR NOT!
TAKE YOUR PLACES, EVERYONE! NOA, YOU READY?
I'M HERE...
AH, THERE YOU ARE! THE SHOW HAS ALREADY STARTED. COME DOWN AND SIT WITH US.
WE CAN'T WAIT TO SEE WHAT YOU'VE PREPARED FOR THE SHOW'S FINALE, THE APPEARANCE OF HER SANCTITY LODOVICA!
OH, YOU'LL NEVER GUESS!
...AND NOW, YOUR FAVORITE HOST...
ARE YOU READY, MY LITTLE DARLING?
...FRIDA DECIBEEEEL!

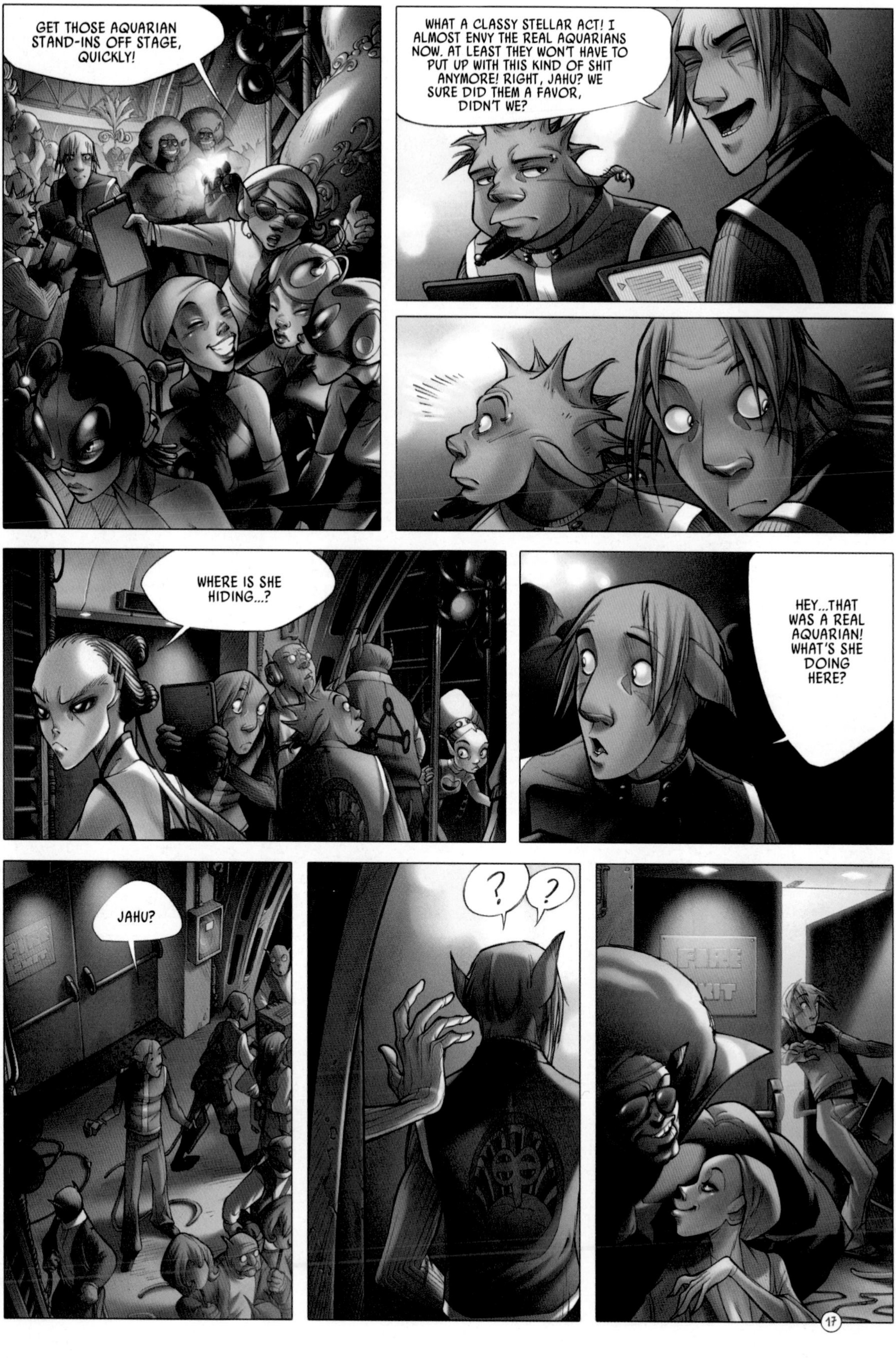
GET THOSE AQUARIAN STAND-INS OFF STAGE, QUICKLY!
WHAT A CLASSY STELLAR ACT! I ALMOST ENVY THE REAL AQUARIANS NOW. AT LEAST THEY WON'T HAVE TO PUT UP WITH THIS KIND OF SHIT ANYMORE! RIGHT, JAHU? WE SURE DID THEM A FAVOR, DIDN'T WE?
WHERE IS SHE HIDING...?
HEY...THAT WAS A REAL AQUARIAN! WHAT'S SHE DOING HERE?
JAHU?
?
?

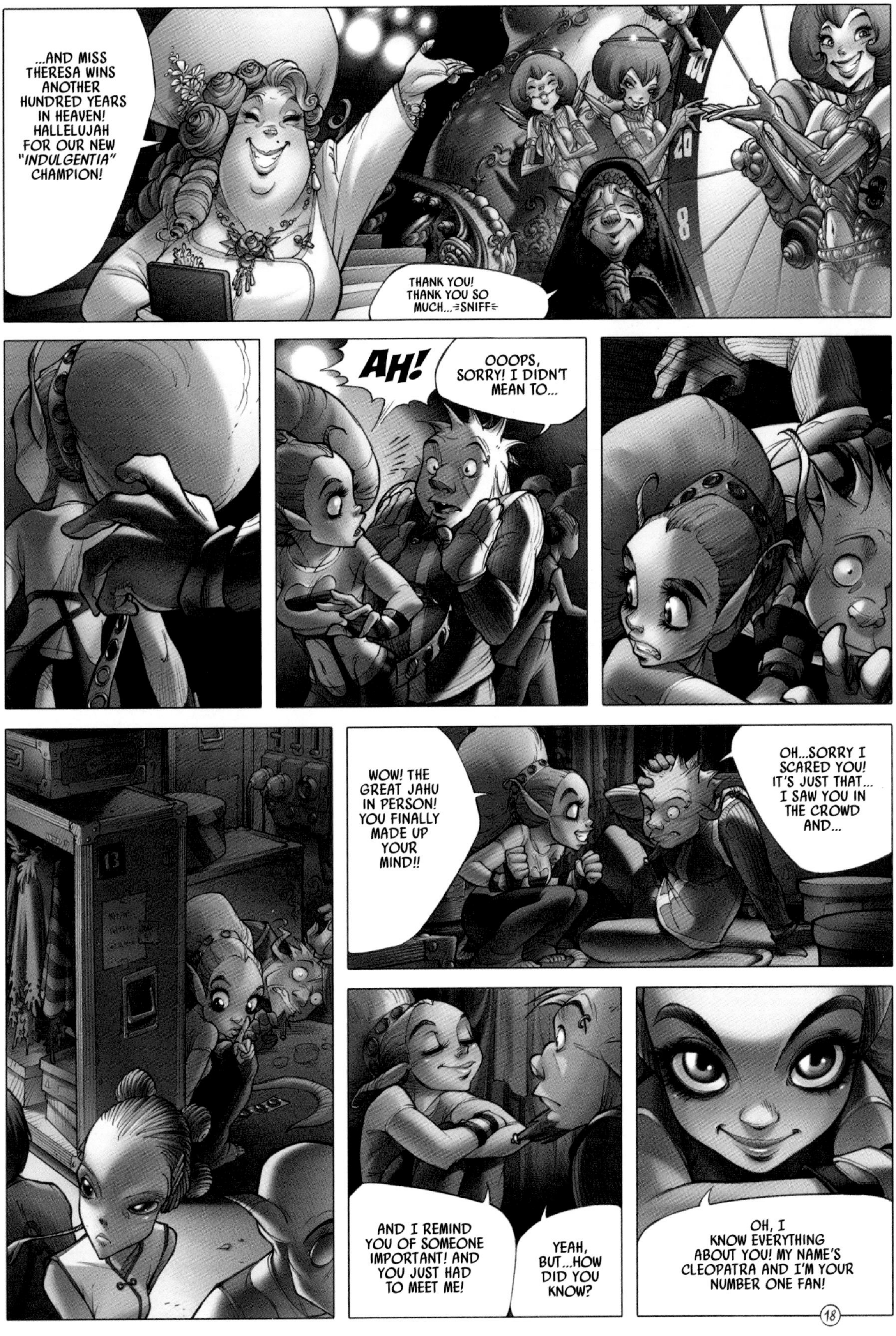
...AND MISS THERESA WINS ANOTHER HUNDRED YEARS IN HEAVEN! HALLELUJAH FOR OUR NEW "INDULGENTIA" CHAMPION!
THANK YOU! THANK YOU SO MUCH... ≡SNIFF≡
AH!
OOOPS, SORRY! I DIDN'T MEAN TO...
WOW! THE GREAT JAHU IN PERSON! YOU FINALLY MADE UP YOUR MIND!!
OH...SORRY I SCARED YOU! IT'S JUST THAT... I SAW YOU IN THE CROWD AND...
AND I REMIND YOU OF SOMEONE IMPORTANT! AND YOU JUST HAD TO MEET ME!
YEAH, BUT...HOW DID YOU KNOW?
OH, I KNOW EVERYTHING ABOUT YOU! MY NAME'S CLEOPATRA AND I'M YOUR NUMBER ONE FAN!

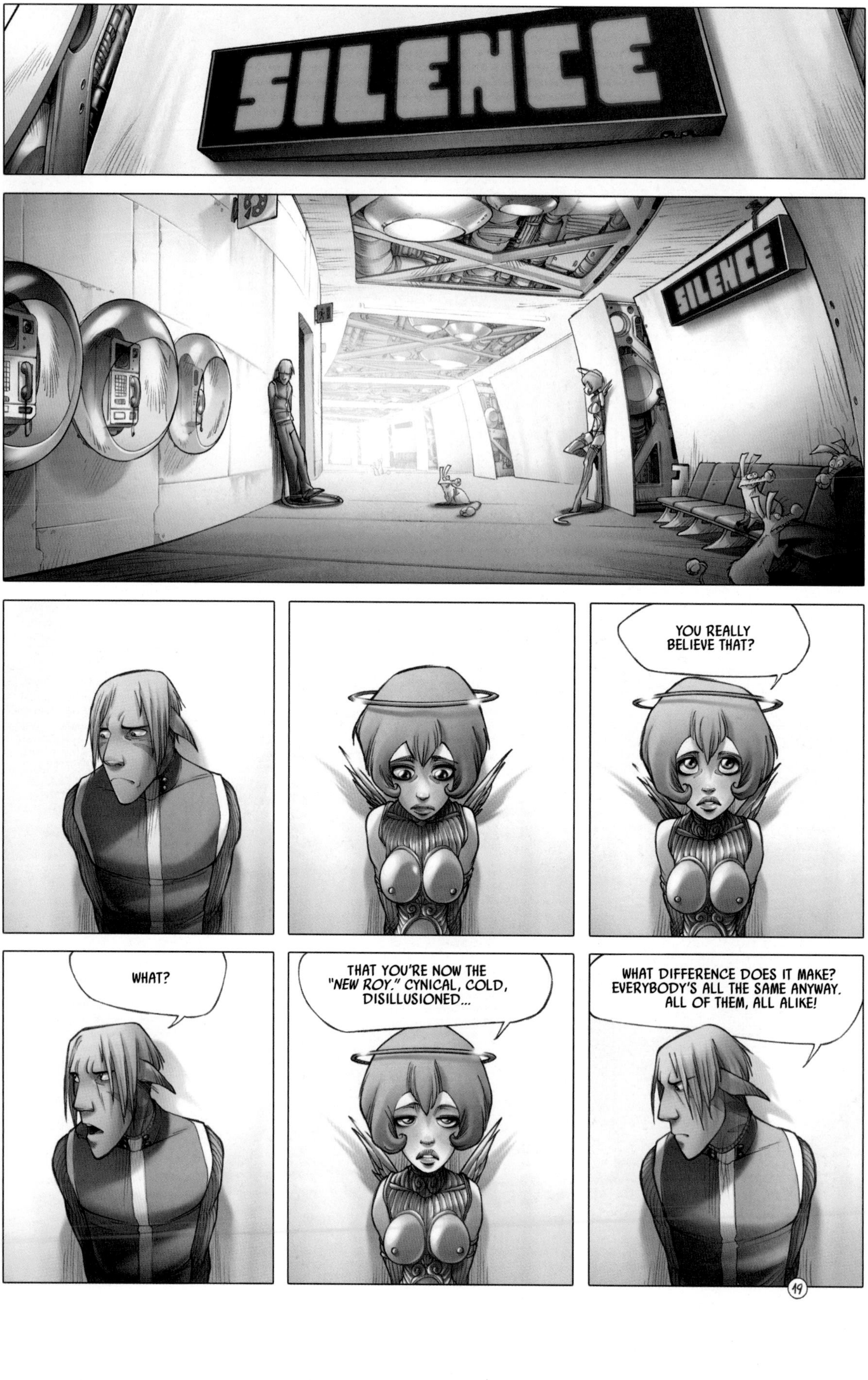
SILENCE
SILENCE
YOU REALLY BELIEVE THAT?
WHAT?
THAT YOU'RE NOW THE "NEW ROY." CYNICAL, COLD, DISILLUSIONED...
WHAT DIFFERENCE DOES IT MAKE? EVERYBODY'S ALL THE SAME ANYWAY. ALL OF THEM, ALL ALIKE!

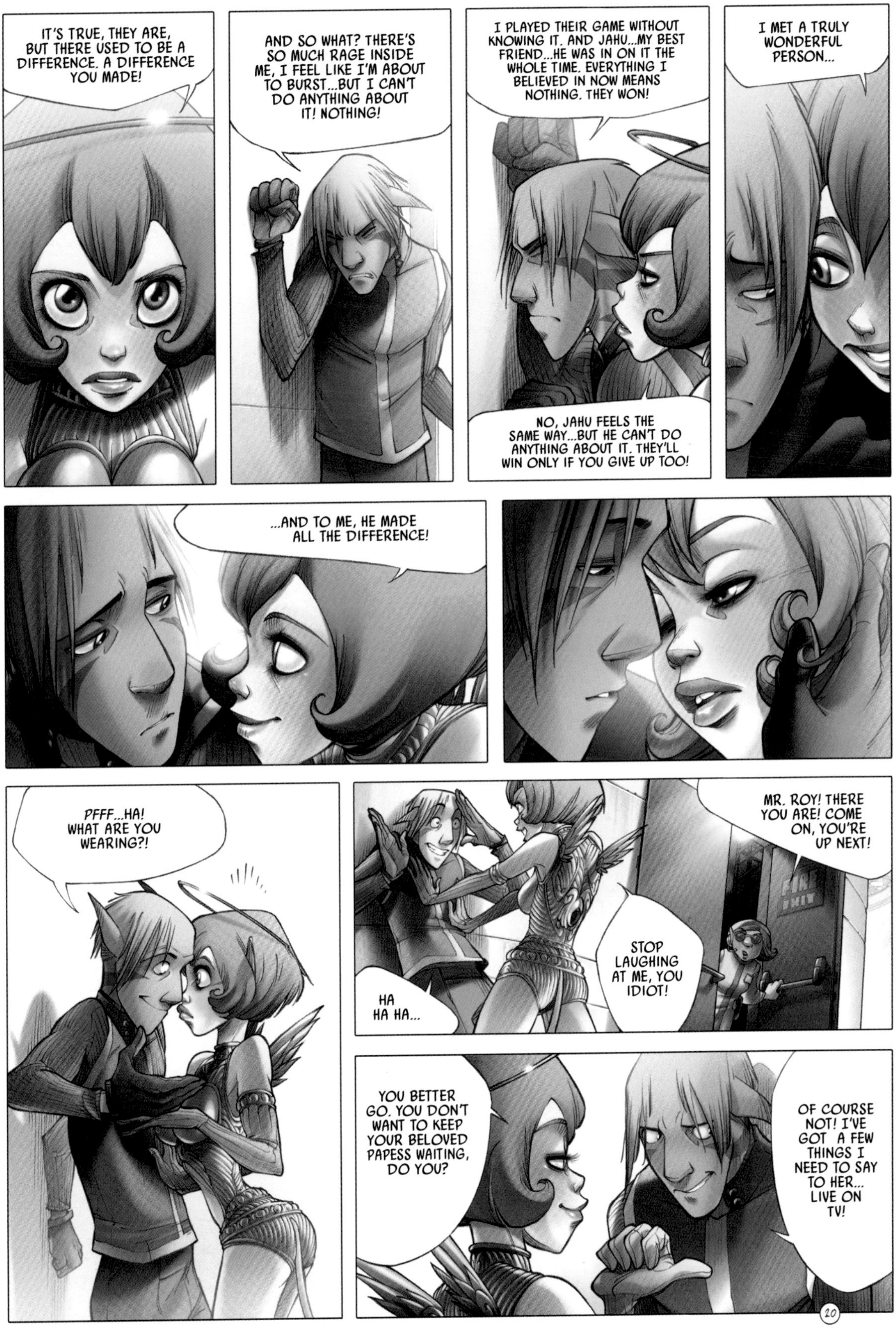
IT'S TRUE, THEY ARE, BUT THERE USED TO BE A DIFFERENCE. A DIFFERENCE YOU MADE!
AND SO WHAT? THERE'S SO MUCH RAGE INSIDE ME, I FEEL LIKE I'M ABOUT TO BURST...BUT I CAN'T DO ANYTHING ABOUT IT! NOTHING!
I PLAYED THEIR GAME WITHOUT KNOWING IT. AND JAHU...MY BEST FRIEND...HE WAS IN ON IT THE WHOLE TIME. EVERYTHING I BELIEVED IN NOW MEANS NOTHING. THEY WON!
NO, JAHU FEELS THE SAME WAY...BUT HE CAN'T DO ANYTHING ABOUT IT. THEY'LL WIN ONLY IF YOU GIVE UP TOO!
I MET A TRULY WONDERFUL PERSON...
...AND TO ME, HE MADE ALL THE DIFFERENCE!
PFFF...HA! WHAT ARE YOU WEARING?!
HA HA HA...
STOP LAUGHING AT ME, YOU IDIOT!
MR. ROY! THERE YOU ARE! COME ON, YOU'RE UP NEXT!
FIRE EXIT
YOU BETTER GO. YOU DON'T WANT TO KEEP YOUR BELOVED PAPESS WAITING, DO YOU?
OF COURSE NOT! I'VE GOT A FEW THINGS I NEED TO SAY TO HER... LIVE ON TV!

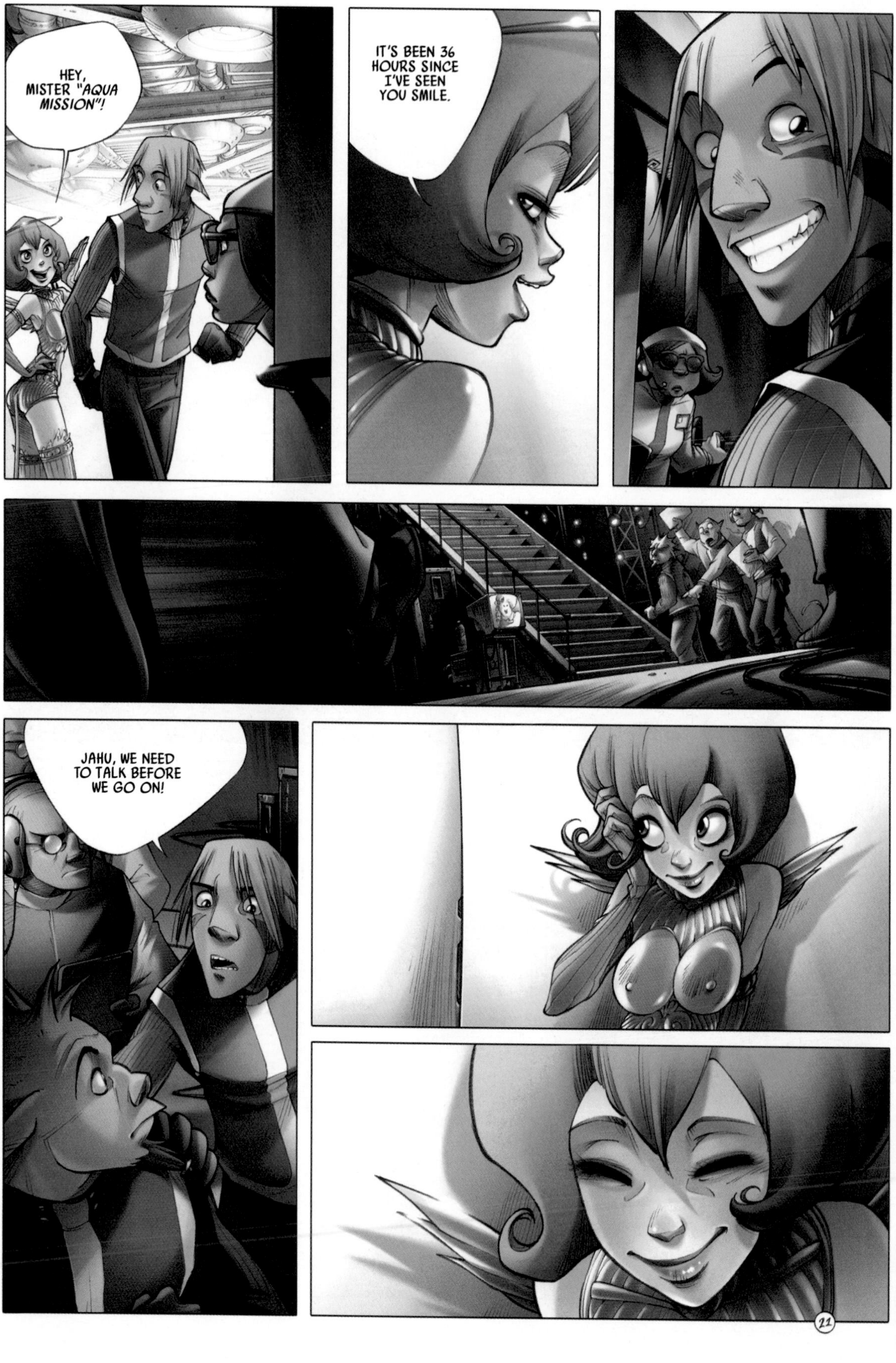
HEY, MISTER "AQUA MISSION"!
IT'S BEEN 36 HOURS SINCE I'VE SEEN YOU SMILE.
JAHU, WE NEED TO TALK BEFORE WE GO ON!

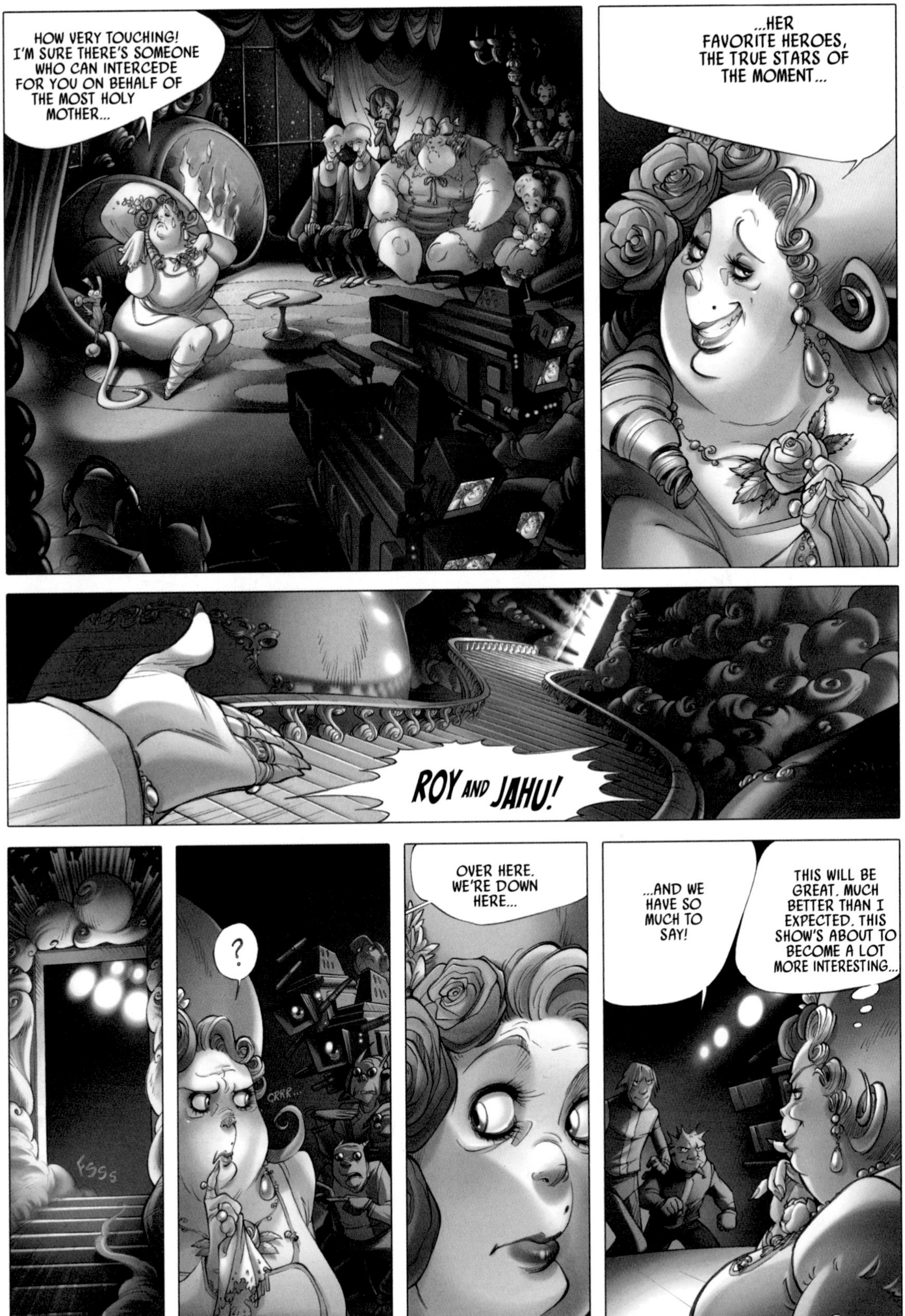
HOW VERY TOUCHING! I'M SURE THERE'S SOMEONE WHO CAN INTERCEDE FOR YOU ON BEHALF OF THE MOST HOLY MOTHER...
...HER FAVORITE HEROES, THE TRUE STARS OF THE MOMENT...
ROY AND JAHU!
FSSS
?
GRRR...
OVER HERE. WE'RE DOWN HERE...
...AND WE HAVE SO MUCH TO SAY!
THIS WILL BE GREAT. MUCH BETTER THAN I EXPECTED. THIS SHOW'S ABOUT TO BECOME A LOT MORE INTERESTING...

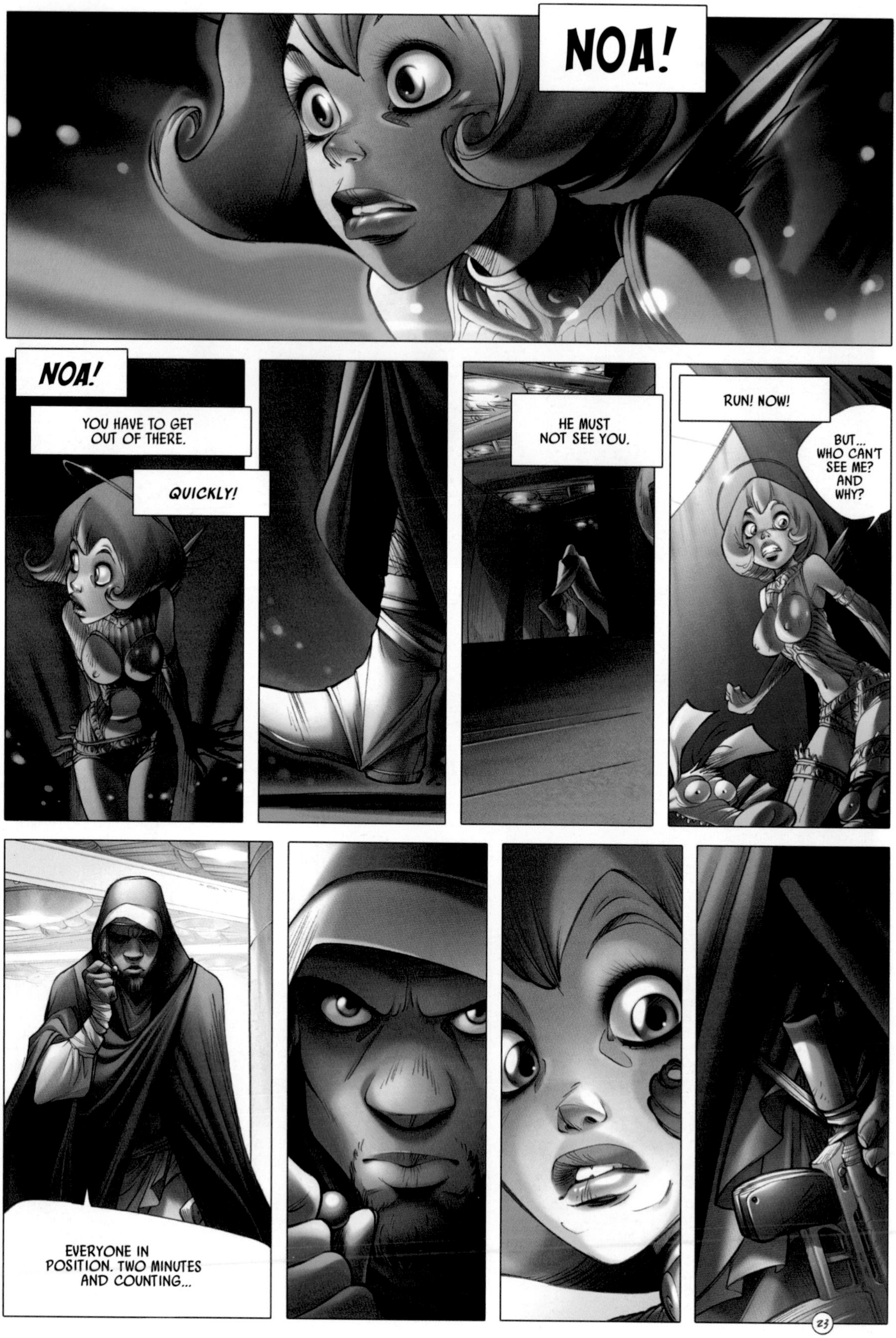
NOA!
NOA!
YOU HAVE TO GET
OUT OF THERE.
QUICKLY!
HE MUST
NOT SEE YOU.
RUN! NOW!
BUT...
WHO CAN'T
SEE ME?
AND
WHY?
EVERYONE IN
POSITION. TWO MINUTES
AND COUNTING...

HEY, YOU! STOP!

...BUT BEFORE WE HEAR WHAT THESE GENTLEMEN HAVE TO TELL US, LET'S TAKE A LOOK AT WHAT OUR HIDDEN CAMERAS ON THEIR SHIP PICKED UP!

YOU KNEW ABOUT THIS TOO?! AND YOU DIDN'T TELL ME?!

=SIGH=

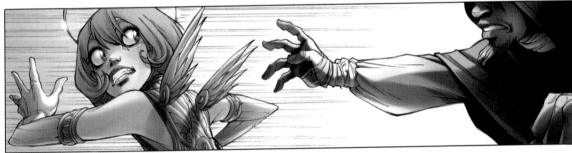

QUIET! WE'RE ON THE AIR!

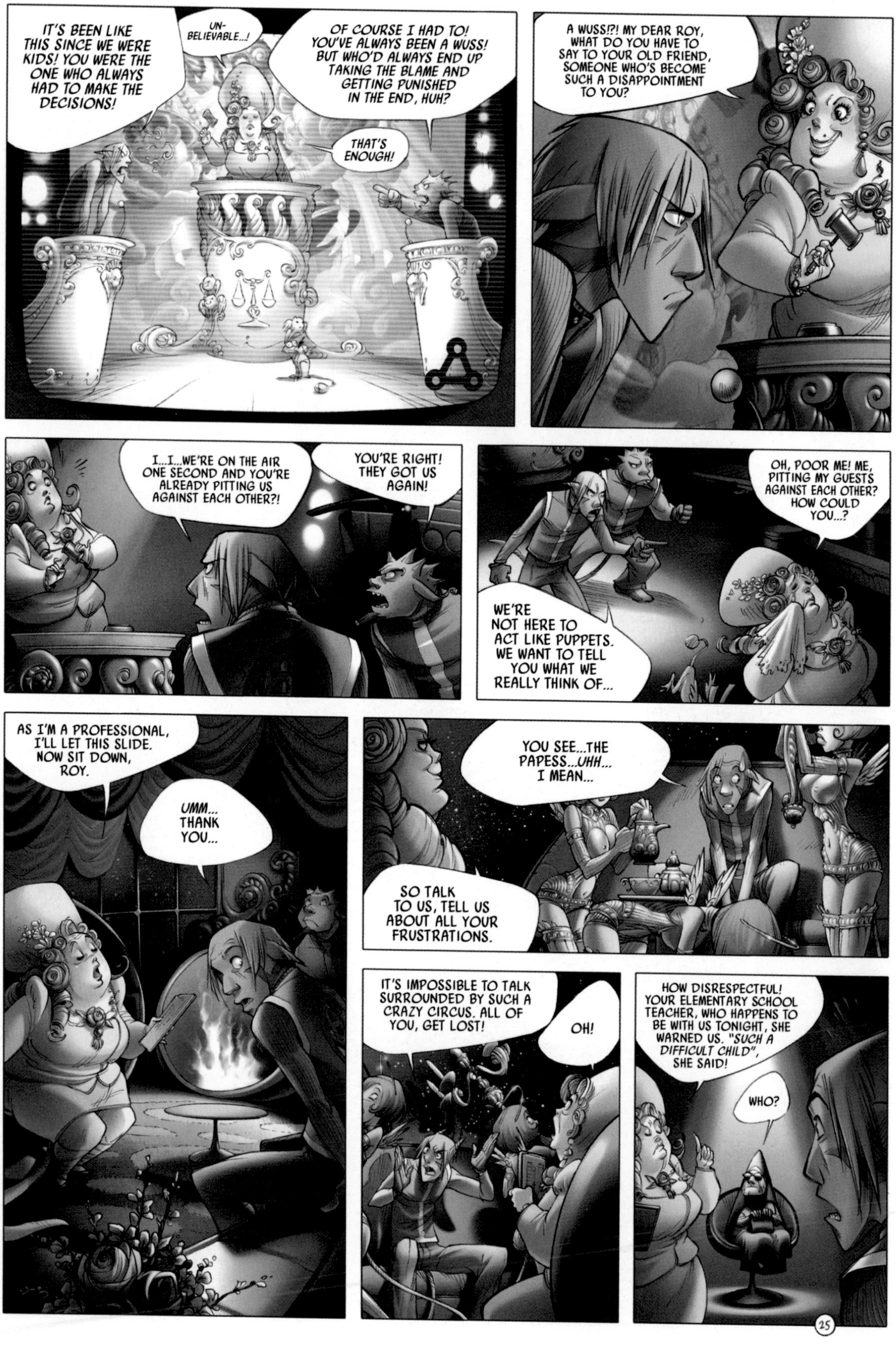
IT'S BEEN LIKE THIS SINCE WE WERE KIDS! YOU WERE THE ONE WHO ALWAYS HAD TO MAKE THE DECISIONS!
UN-BELIEVABLE...!
OF COURSE I HAD TO! YOU'VE ALWAYS BEEN A WUSS! BUT WHO'D ALWAYS END UP TAKING THE BLAME AND GETTING PUNISHED IN THE END, HUH?
THAT'S ENOUGH!
A WUSS!?! MY DEAR ROY, WHAT DO YOU HAVE TO SAY TO YOUR OLD FRIEND, SOMEONE WHO'S BECOME SUCH A DISAPPOINTMENT TO YOU?
I...I...WE'RE ON THE AIR ONE SECOND AND YOU'RE ALREADY PITTING US AGAINST EACH OTHER?!
YOU'RE RIGHT! THEY GOT US AGAIN!
OH, POOR ME! ME, PITTING MY GUESTS AGAINST EACH OTHER? HOW COULD YOU...?
WE'RE NOT HERE TO ACT LIKE PUPPETS. WE WANT TO TELL YOU WHAT WE REALLY THINK OF...
AS I'M A PROFESSIONAL, I'LL LET THIS SLIDE. NOW SIT DOWN, ROY.
UMM... THANK YOU...
YOU SEE...THE PAPESS...UHH... I MEAN...
SO TALK TO US, TELL US ABOUT ALL YOUR FRUSTRATIONS.
IT'S IMPOSSIBLE TO TALK SURROUNDED BY SUCH A CRAZY CIRCUS. ALL OF YOU, GET LOST!
OH!
HOW DISRESPECTFUL! YOUR ELEMENTARY SCHOOL TEACHER, WHO HAPPENS TO BE WITH US TONIGHT, SHE WARNED US. "SUCH A DIFFICULT CHILD", SHE SAID!
WHO?

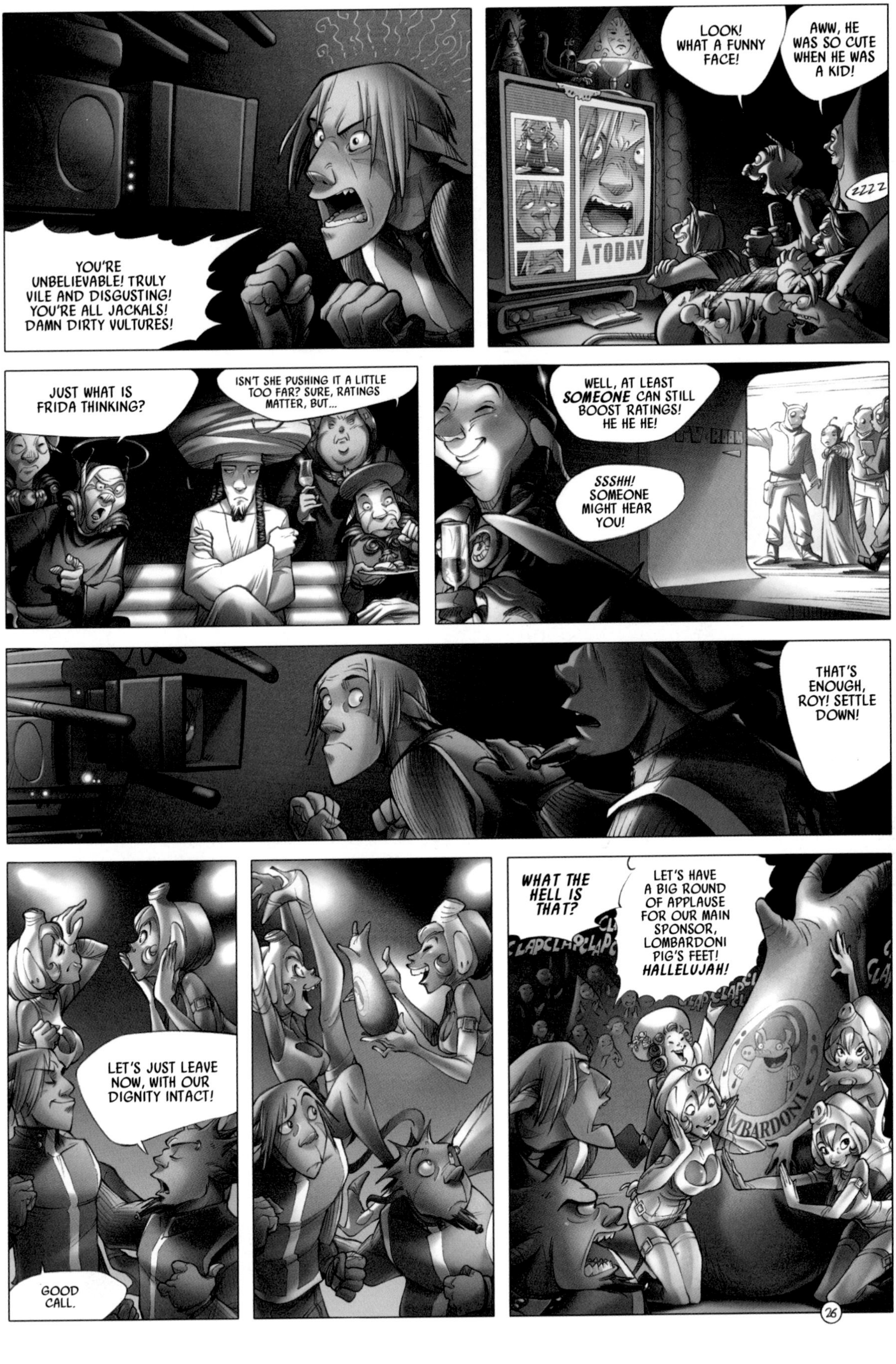
YOU'RE UNBELIEVABLE! TRULY VILE AND DISGUSTING! YOU'RE ALL JACKALS! DAMN DIRTY VULTURES!
TODAY
LOOK! WHAT A FUNNY FACE!
AWW, HE WAS SO CUTE WHEN HE WAS A KID!
ZZZZ
JUST WHAT IS FRIDA THINKING?
ISN'T SHE PUSHING IT A LITTLE TOO FAR? SURE, RATINGS MATTER, BUT...
WELL, AT LEAST SOMEONE CAN STILL BOOST RATINGS! HE HE HE!
SSSHH! SOMEONE MIGHT HEAR YOU!
THAT'S ENOUGH, ROY! SETTLE DOWN!
LET'S JUST LEAVE NOW, WITH OUR DIGNITY INTACT!
GOOD CALL.
WHAT THE HELL IS THAT?
LET'S HAVE A BIG ROUND OF APPLAUSE FOR OUR MAIN SPONSOR, LOMBARDONI PIG'S FEET! HALLELUJAH!
CLAPCLAPCLAPC
MBARDONI

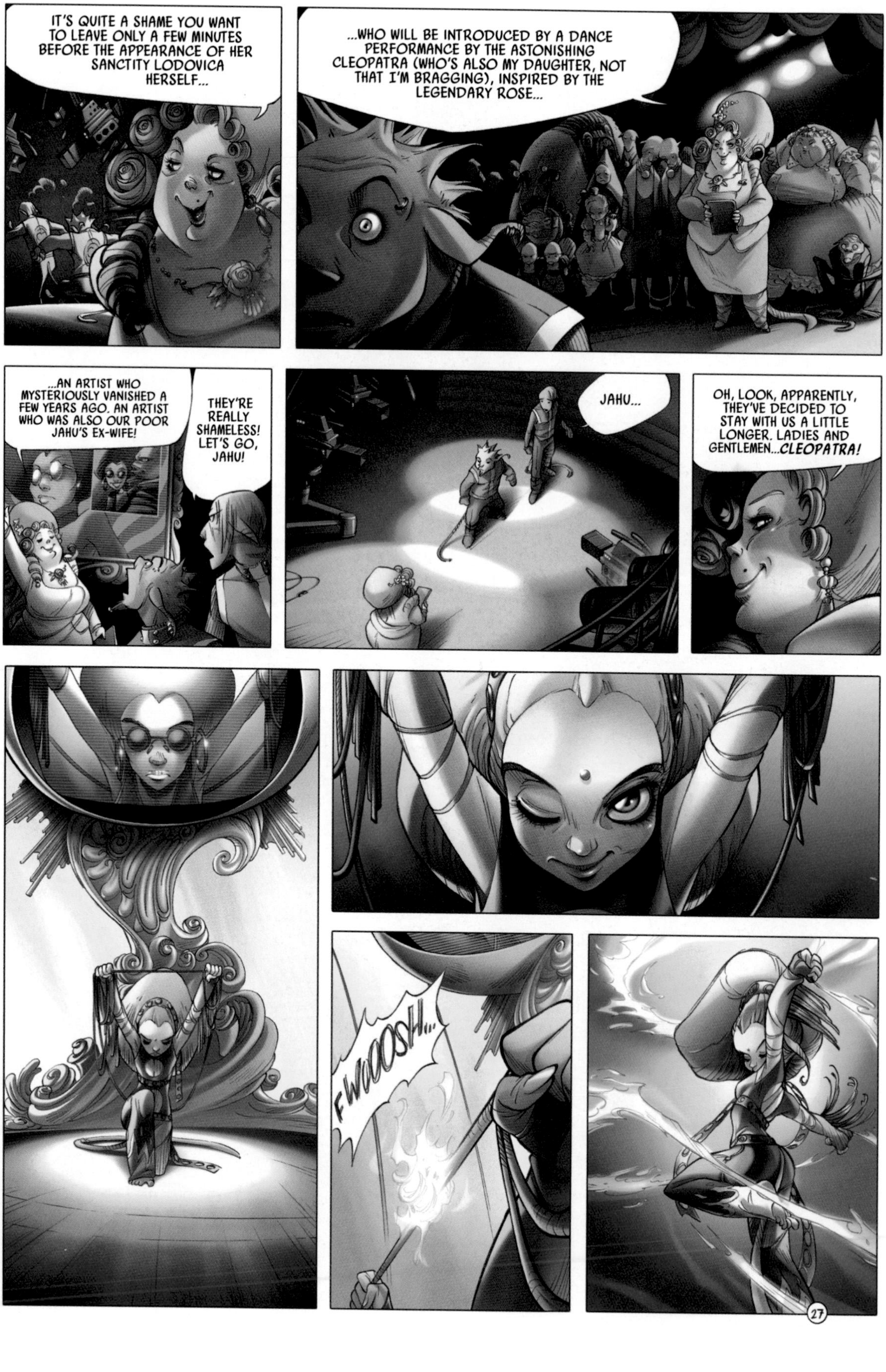
IT'S QUITE A SHAME YOU WANT TO LEAVE ONLY A FEW MINUTES BEFORE THE APPEARANCE OF HER SANCTITY LODOVICA HERSELF...
...WHO WILL BE INTRODUCED BY A DANCE PERFORMANCE BY THE ASTONISHING CLEOPATRA (WHO'S ALSO MY DAUGHTER, NOT THAT I'M BRAGGING), INSPIRED BY THE LEGENDARY ROSE...
...AN ARTIST WHO MYSTERIOUSLY VANISHED A FEW YEARS AGO. AN ARTIST WHO WAS ALSO OUR POOR JAHU'S EX-WIFE!
THEY'RE REALLY SHAMELESS! LET'S GO, JAHU!
JAHU...
OH, LOOK, APPARENTLY, THEY'VE DECIDED TO STAY WITH US A LITTLE LONGER. LADIES AND GENTLEMEN...*CLEOPATRA!*
FWOOOSH...

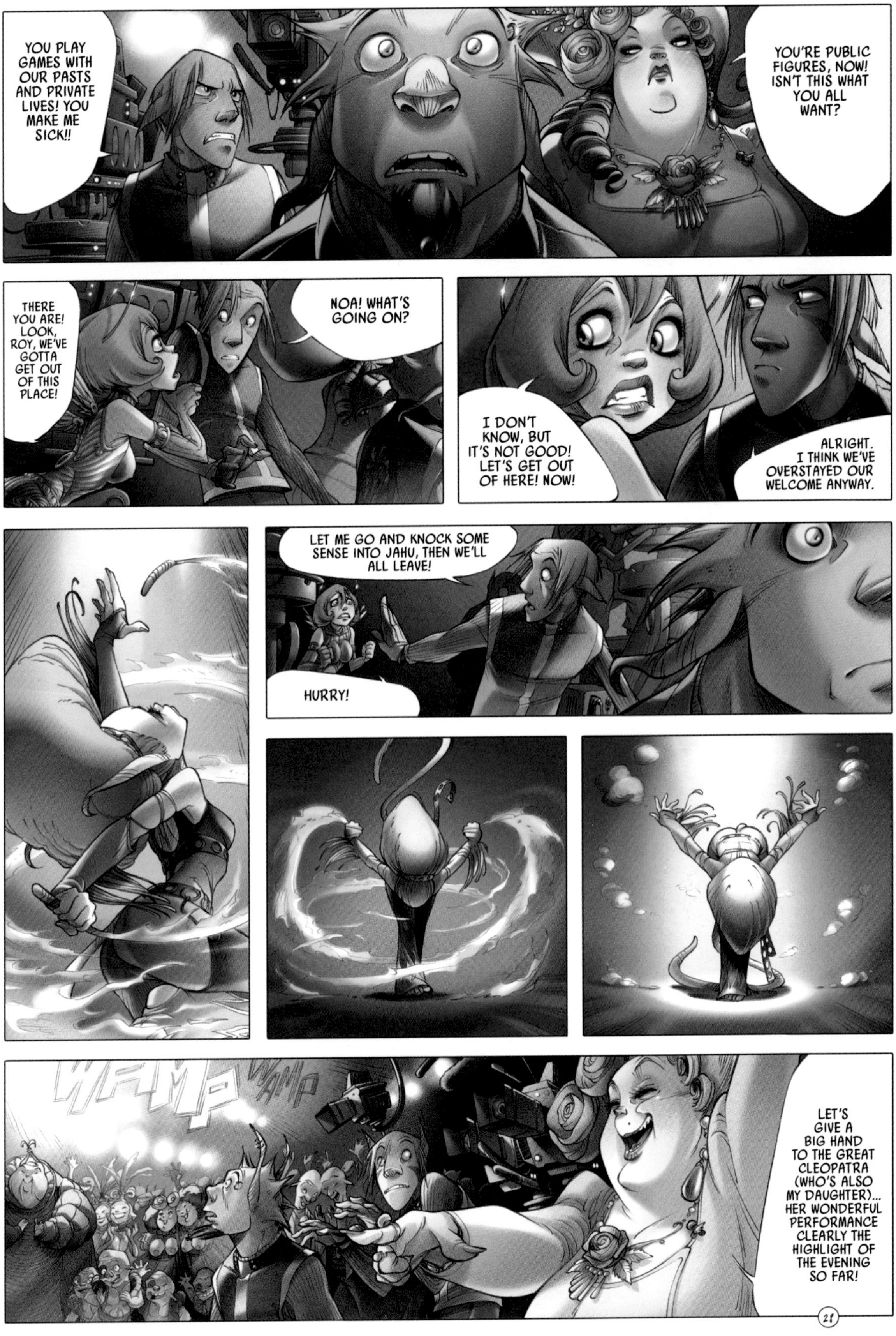
YOU PLAY GAMES WITH OUR PASTS AND PRIVATE LIVES! YOU MAKE ME SICK!!
YOU'RE PUBLIC FIGURES, NOW! ISN'T THIS WHAT YOU ALL WANT?
THERE YOU ARE! LOOK, ROY, WE'VE GOTTA GET OUT OF THIS PLACE!
NOA! WHAT'S GOING ON?
I DON'T KNOW, BUT IT'S NOT GOOD! LET'S GET OUT OF HERE! NOW!
ALRIGHT. I THINK WE'VE OVERSTAYED OUR WELCOME ANYWAY.
LET ME GO AND KNOCK SOME SENSE INTO JAHU, THEN WE'LL ALL LEAVE!
HURRY!
WAMP
WAMP
LET'S GIVE A BIG HAND TO THE GREAT CLEOPATRA (WHO'S ALSO MY DAUGHTER)... HER WONDERFUL PERFORMANCE CLEARLY THE HIGHLIGHT OF THE EVENING SO FAR!

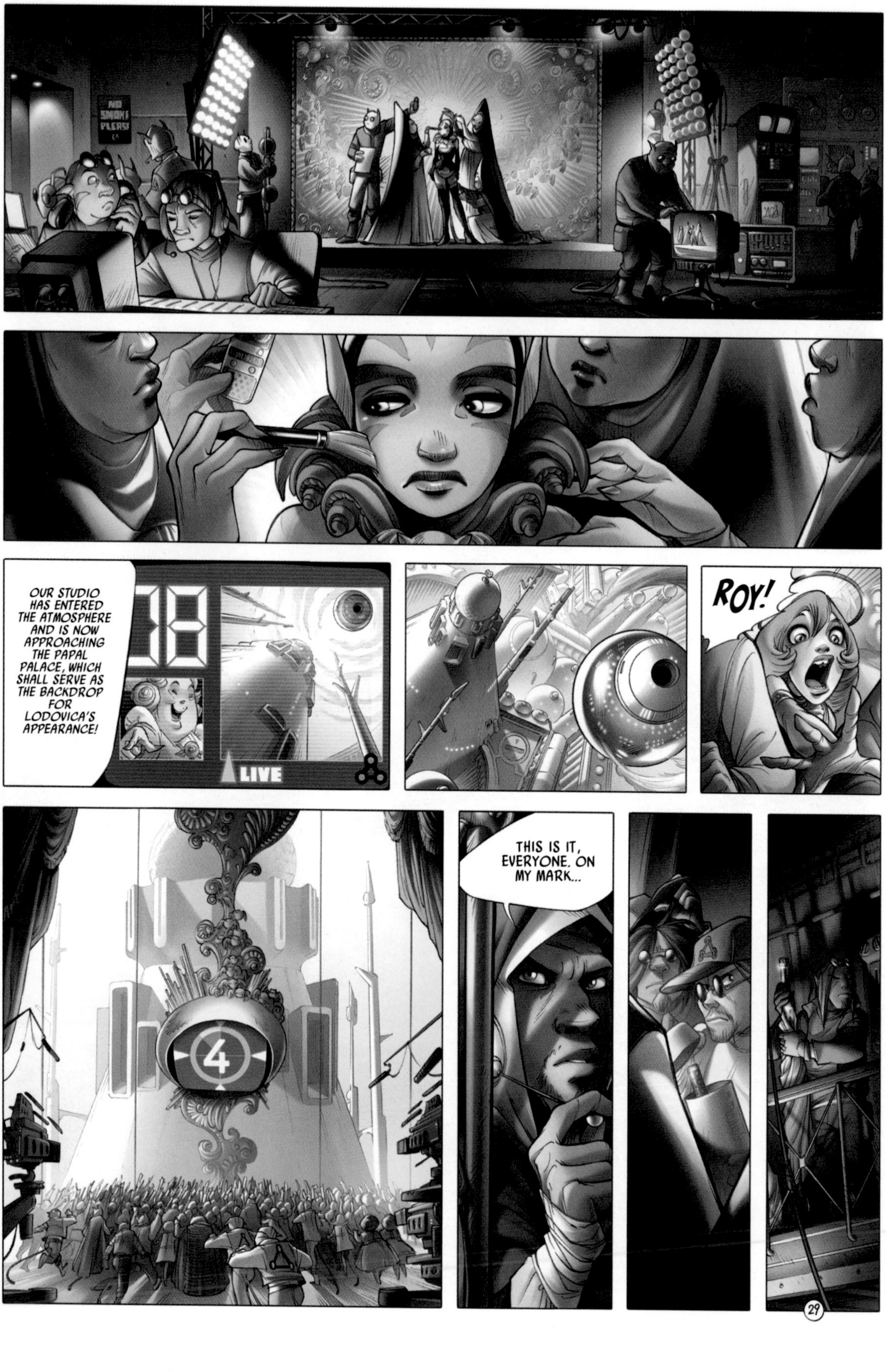
OUR STUDIO HAS ENTERED THE ATMOSPHERE AND IS NOW APPROACHING THE PAPAL PALACE, WHICH SHALL SERVE AS THE BACKDROP FOR LODOVICA'S APPEARANCE!
LIVE
ROY!
THIS IS IT, EVERYONE. ON MY MARK...

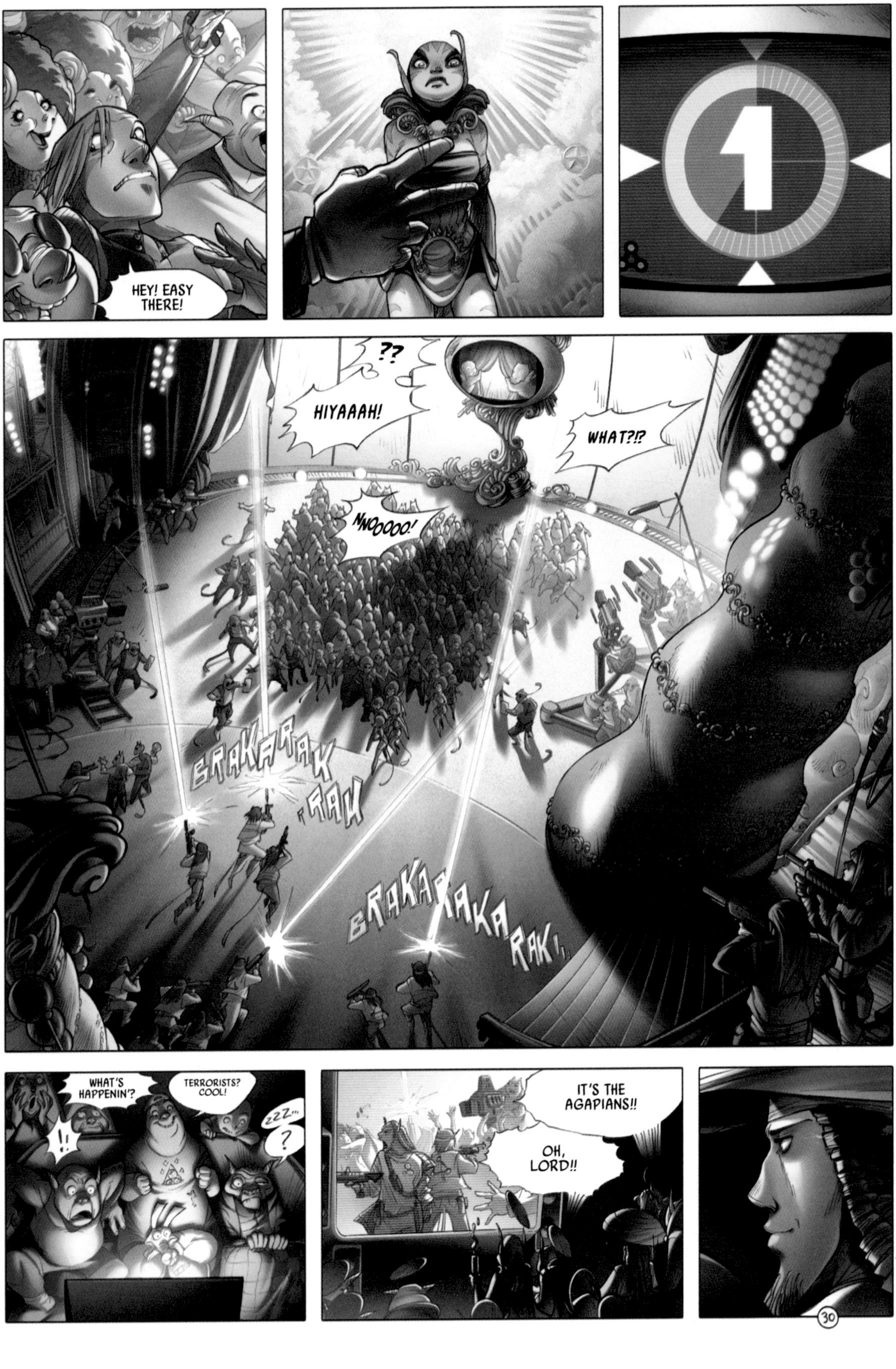
HEY! EASY THERE!
??
HIYAAAH!
WHAT?!?
NNOOOOO!
BRAKARAK RAK
BRAKARAKAKARAK
WHAT'S HAPPENIN'?
TERRORISTS? COOL!
!!
ZZZ...
?
IT'S THE AGAPIANS!!
OH, LORD!!

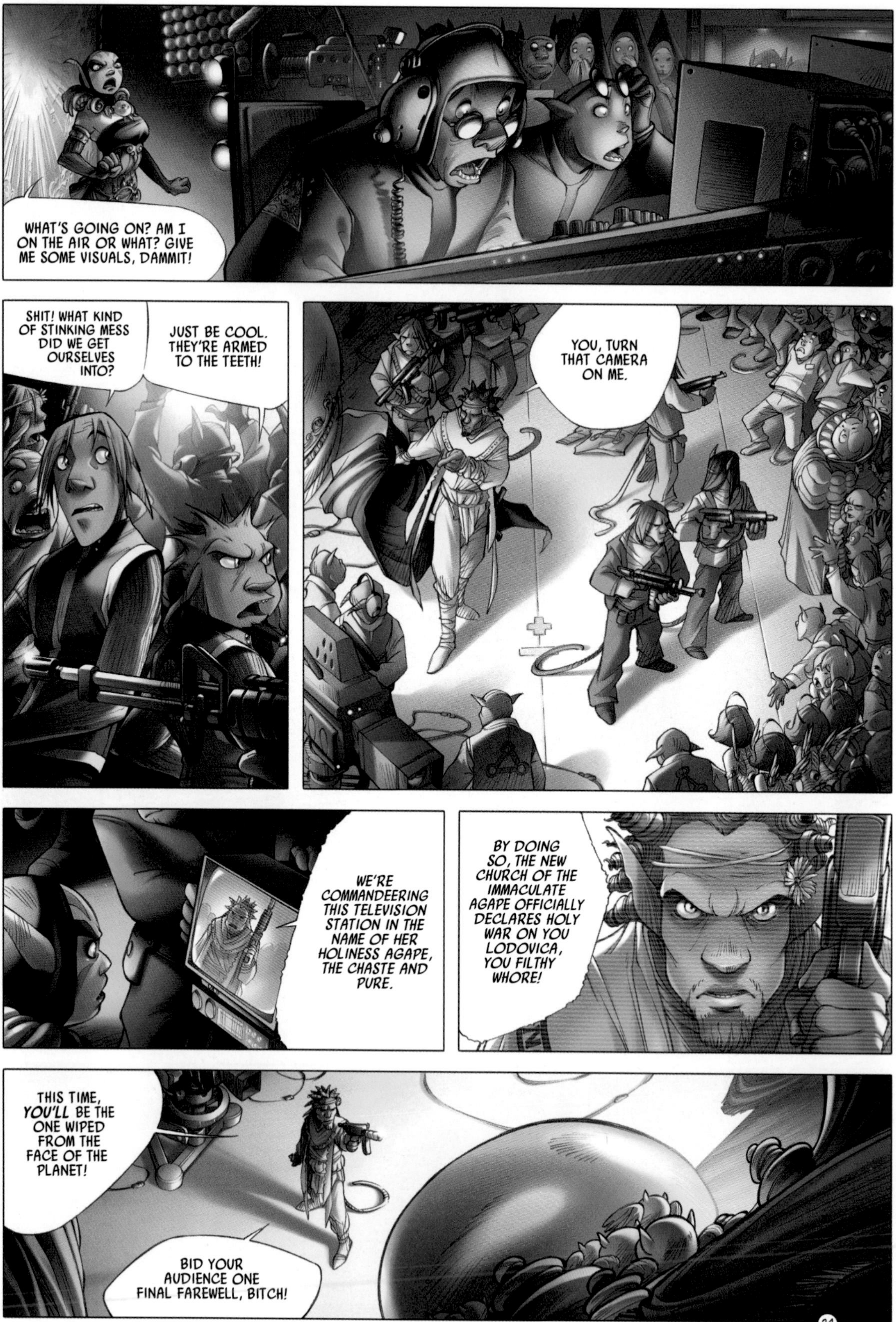
WHAT'S GOING ON? AM I ON THE AIR OR WHAT? GIVE ME SOME VISUALS, DAMMIT!
SHIT! WHAT KIND OF STINKING MESS DID WE GET OURSELVES INTO?
JUST BE COOL. THEY'RE ARMED TO THE TEETH!
YOU, TURN THAT CAMERA ON ME.
WE'RE COMMANDEERING THIS TELEVISION STATION IN THE NAME OF HER HOLINESS AGAPE, THE CHASTE AND PURE.
BY DOING SO, THE NEW CHURCH OF THE IMMACULATE AGAPE OFFICIALLY DECLARES HOLY WAR ON YOU LODOVICA, YOU FILTHY WHORE!
THIS TIME, *YOU'LL* BE THE ONE WIPED FROM THE FACE OF THE PLANET!
BID YOUR AUDIENCE ONE FINAL FAREWELL, BITCH!

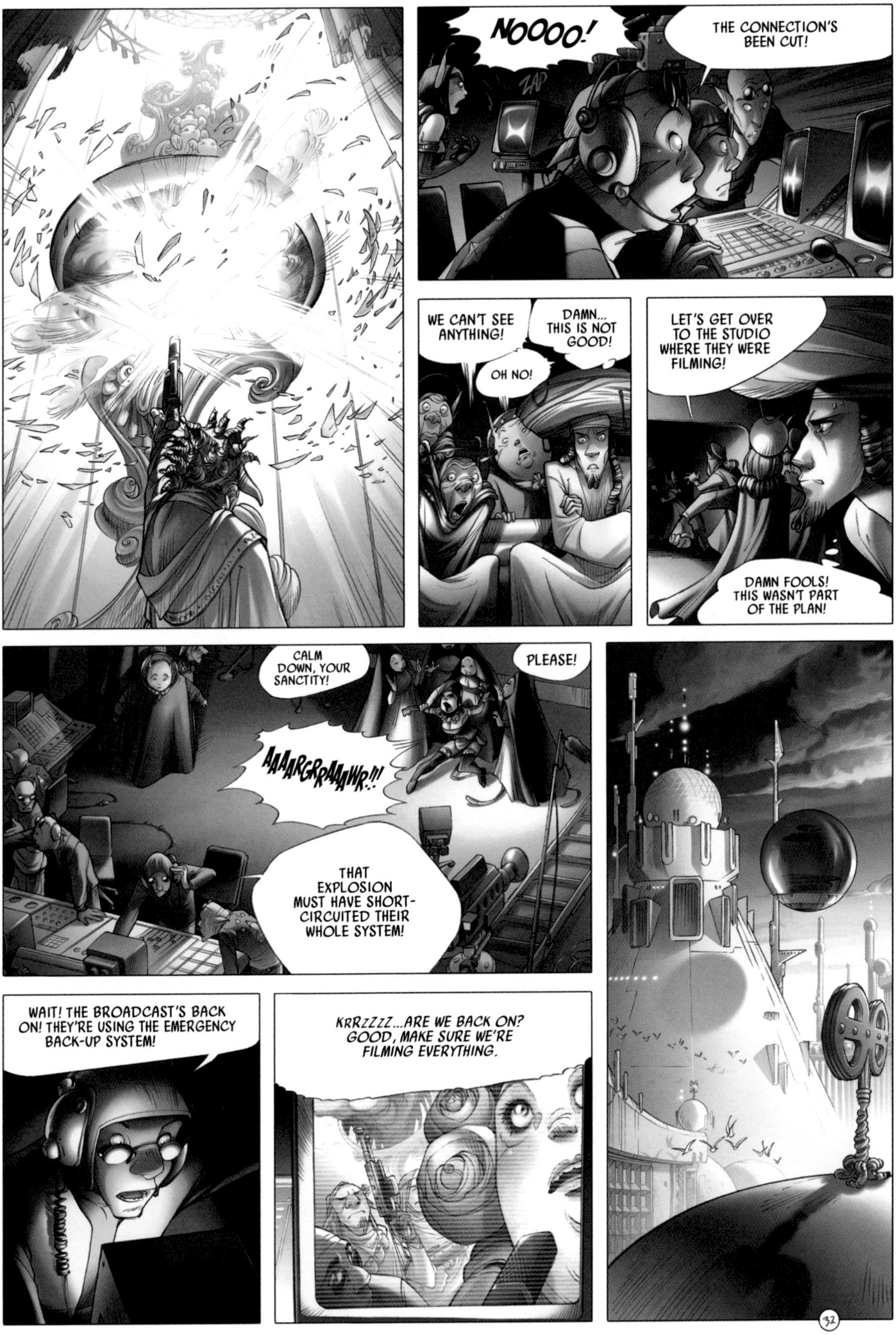
NOOOO!
ZAP
THE CONNECTION'S BEEN CUT!
WE CAN'T SEE ANYTHING!
DAMN... THIS IS NOT GOOD!
OH NO!
LET'S GET OVER TO THE STUDIO WHERE THEY WERE FILMING!
DAMN FOOLS! THIS WASN'T PART OF THE PLAN!
CALM DOWN, YOUR SANCTITY!
PLEASE!
AAAARGRRAAAWR!!!
THAT EXPLOSION MUST HAVE SHORT-CIRCUITED THEIR WHOLE SYSTEM!
WAIT! THE BROADCAST'S BACK ON! THEY'RE USING THE EMERGENCY BACK-UP SYSTEM!
KRRZZZZ...ARE WE BACK ON? GOOD, MAKE SURE WE'RE FILMING EVERYTHING.

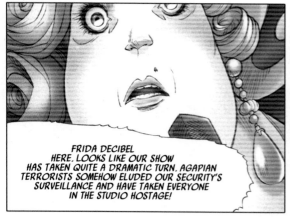

FRIDA DECIBEL HERE. LOOKS LIKE OUR SHOW HAS QUITE A DRAMATIC TURN. AGAPIAN TERRORISTS SOMEHOW ELUDED OUR SECURITY'S SURVEILLANCE AND HAVE TAKEN EVERYONE IN THE STUDIO HOSTAGE!

CAN YOU HEAR ME, LODOVICA? WE CHOSE THIS PATH OF VIOLENCE, EVEN THOUGH IT GOES AGAINST OUR BELIEFS, BECAUSE ONLY BY LOWERING OURSELVES TO YOUR LEVEL WILL WE MAKE YOU PEOPLE UNDERSTAND US.

YOU, WHO BROUGHT A PLANET OF BELIEVERS TO THEIR KNEES, WILL HAVE TO FORSAKE YOUR ARROGANCE, SATISFY OUR DEMANDS AND RESTORE ONE SINGLE TRUE FAITH.

UFF!

HEY!

...THAT SAME ARROGANCE EMBODIED BY YOUR SERVANTS HERE, THESE SO-CALLED HEROES!

THIS IS THE PEAK OF ABSURDITY.

YOU AND YOUR SPIRITUAL LEADERS, ALL DRESSED LIKE SLUTS, THE GLAMOUR AND OPULENCE OF YOUR PARADES, THOSE BLASPHEMOUS RITUALS HELD SOLELY FOR RATINGS...

...YOU, WHO HAVE DELIBERATELY FORGOTTEN...

...FORGOTTEN EVERYTHING YOU WERE MEANT TO REPRESENT, WILL NOW HAVE TO BOW DOWN...

...TO THE PURITY OF THE TRUE SPIRIT!

TRAITORS! BASTARDS!!

KRASH

POW

GET THE PAPAL DOCTORS, QUICKLY! SHE NEEDS A SEDATIVE!!

DON'T YOU DARE COME NEAR ME WITH THAT NEEDLE OR I'LL KILL YOU!!

IN ON ME NOW...

YOU'RE OUT OF YOUR MIND! HER SANCTITY LODOVICA WILL NEVER GIVE IN TO YOUR PATHETIC DEMANDS! HALLELUJAH!

BRAK

AARGH!!

OH MY GOD!!!

EEEK!

RUN! RUN!!

FREEZE! EVERYBODY CALM DOWN! NOBODY MOVE OR OTHERS WILL DIE!

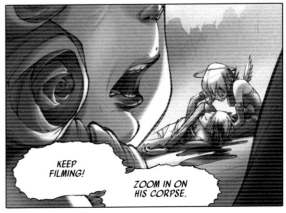

KEEP FILMING!

ZOOM IN ON HIS CORPSE.

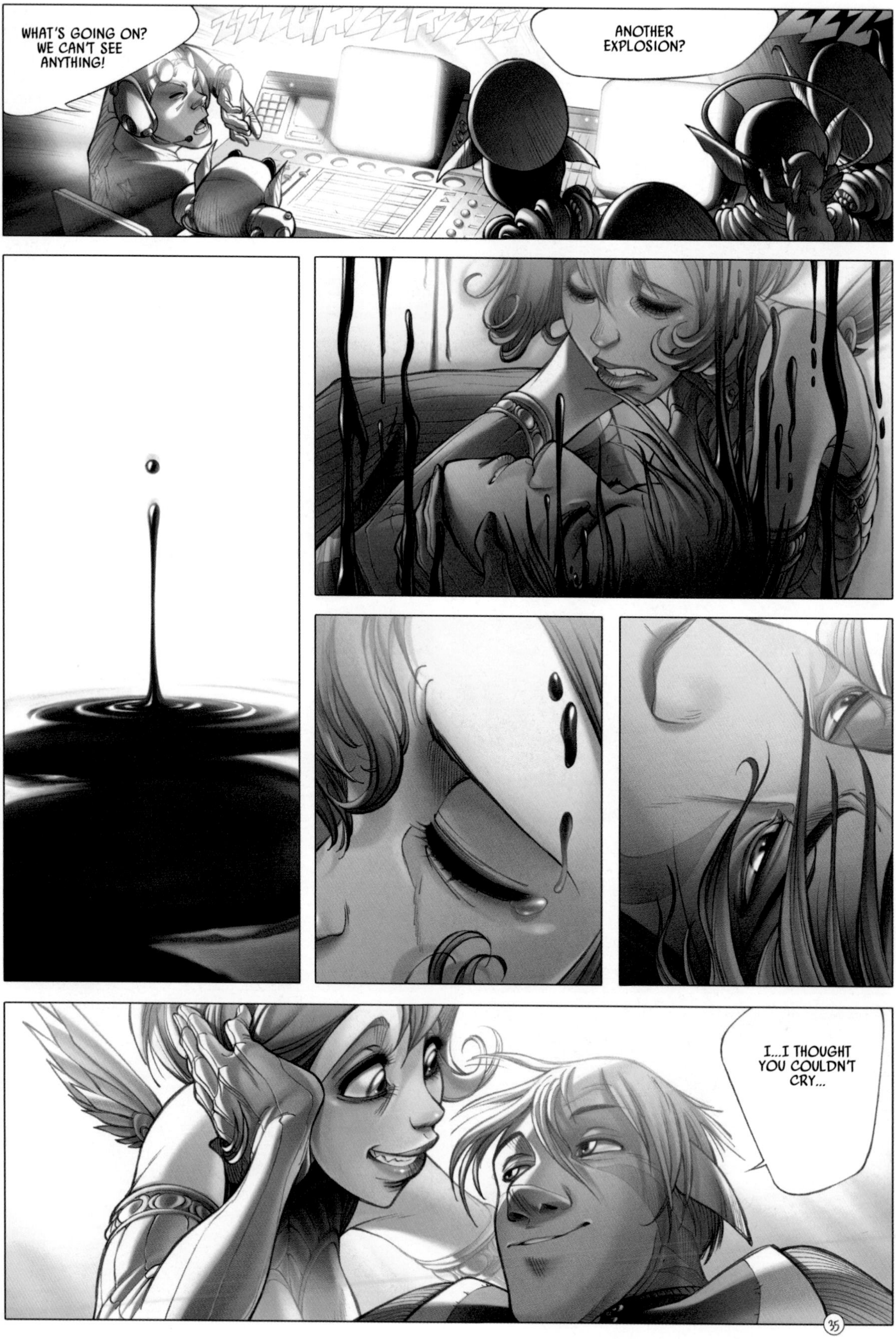
WHAT'S GOING ON? WE CAN'T SEE ANYTHING!
ANOTHER EXPLOSION?
I...I THOUGHT YOU COULDN'T CRY...

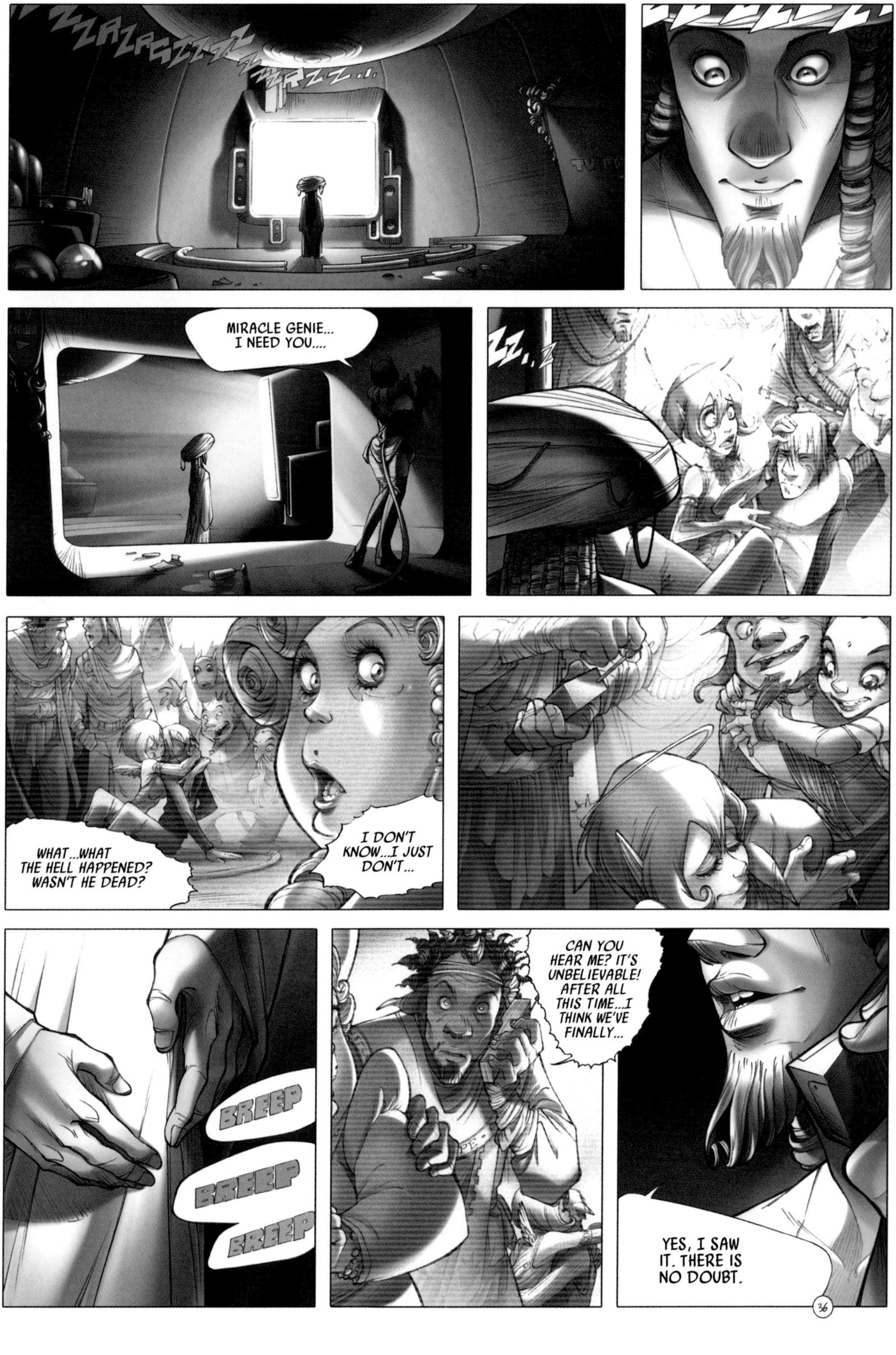
MIRACLE GENIE... I NEED YOU....
WHAT...WHAT THE HELL HAPPENED? WASN'T HE DEAD?
I DON'T KNOW...I JUST DON'T...
BREEP
BREEP
BREEP
CAN YOU HEAR ME? IT'S UNBELIEVABLE! AFTER ALL THIS TIME...I THINK WE'VE FINALLY...
YES, I SAW IT. THERE IS NO DOUBT.

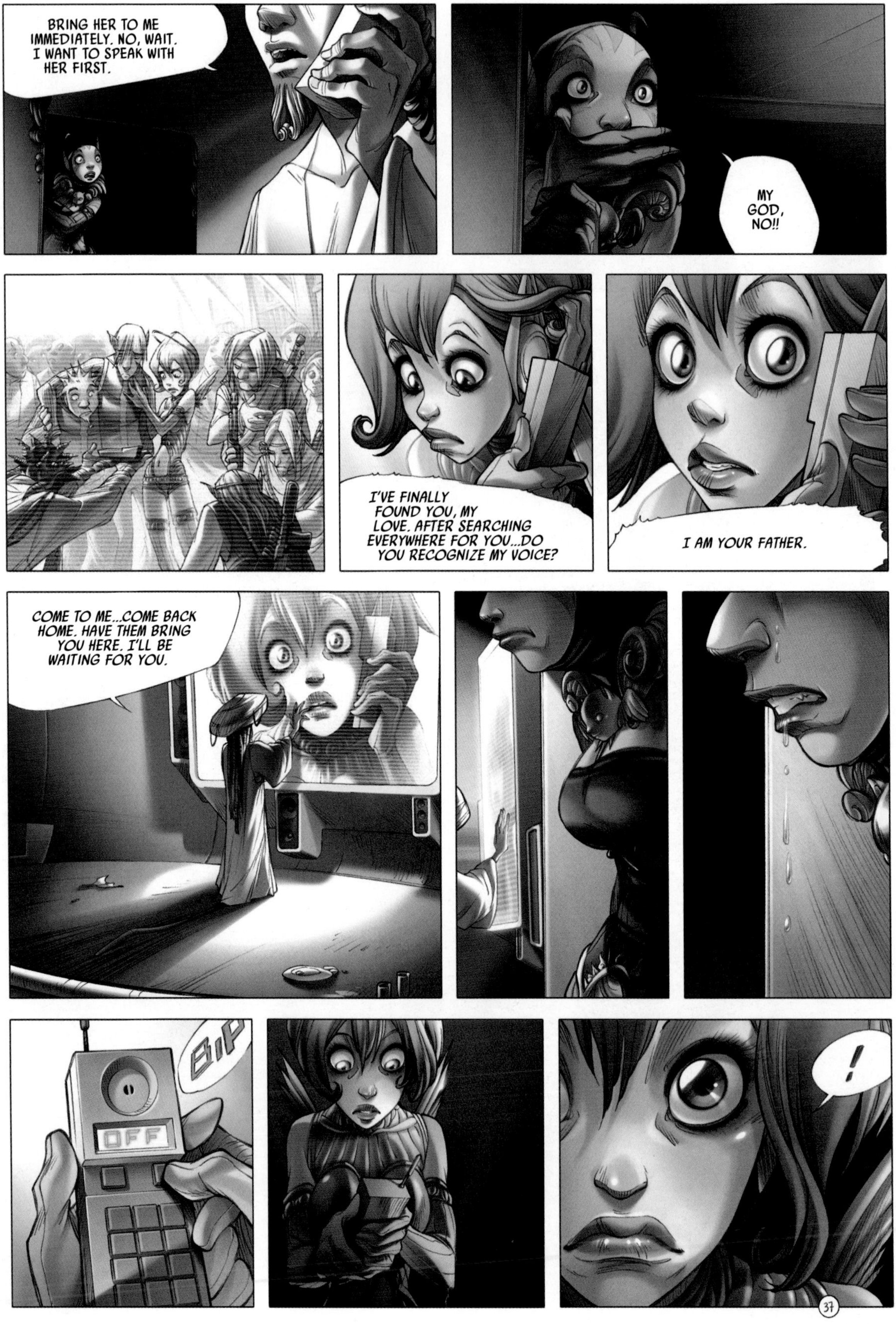
BRING HER TO ME IMMEDIATELY. NO, WAIT. I WANT TO SPEAK WITH HER FIRST.
MY GOD, NO!!
I'VE FINALLY FOUND YOU, MY LOVE. AFTER SEARCHING EVERYWHERE FOR YOU...DO YOU RECOGNIZE MY VOICE?
I AM YOUR FATHER.
COME TO ME...COME BACK HOME. HAVE THEM BRING YOU HERE. I'LL BE WAITING FOR YOU.
BIP
OFF
!

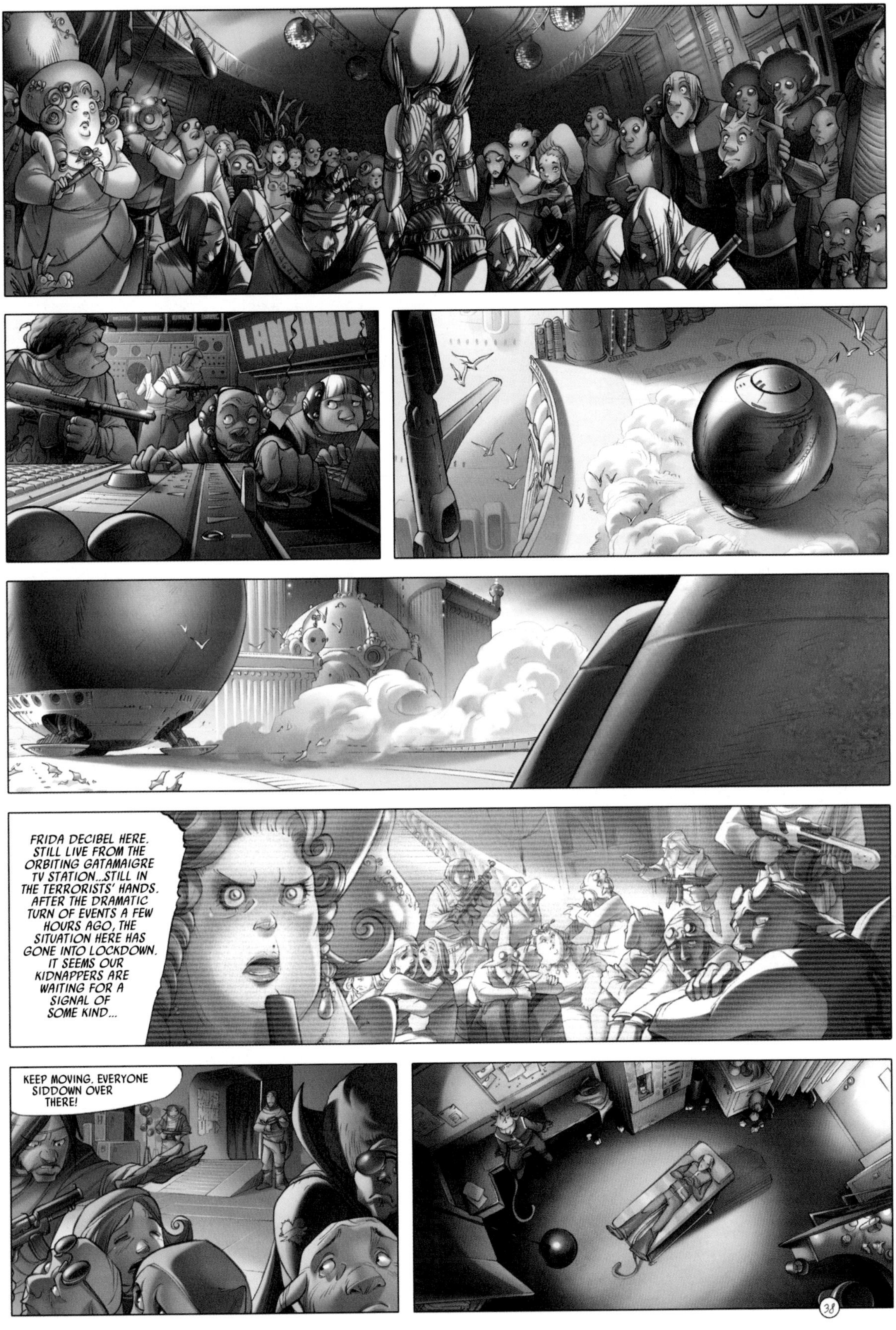
LANDING
FRIDA DECIBEL HERE. STILL LIVE FROM THE ORBITING GATAMAIGRE TV STATION...STILL IN THE TERRORISTS' HANDS. AFTER THE DRAMATIC TURN OF EVENTS A FEW HOURS AGO, THE SITUATION HERE HAS GONE INTO LOCKDOWN. IT SEEMS OUR KIDNAPPERS ARE WAITING FOR A SIGNAL OF SOME KIND...
KEEP MOVING. EVERYONE SIDDOWN OVER THERE!

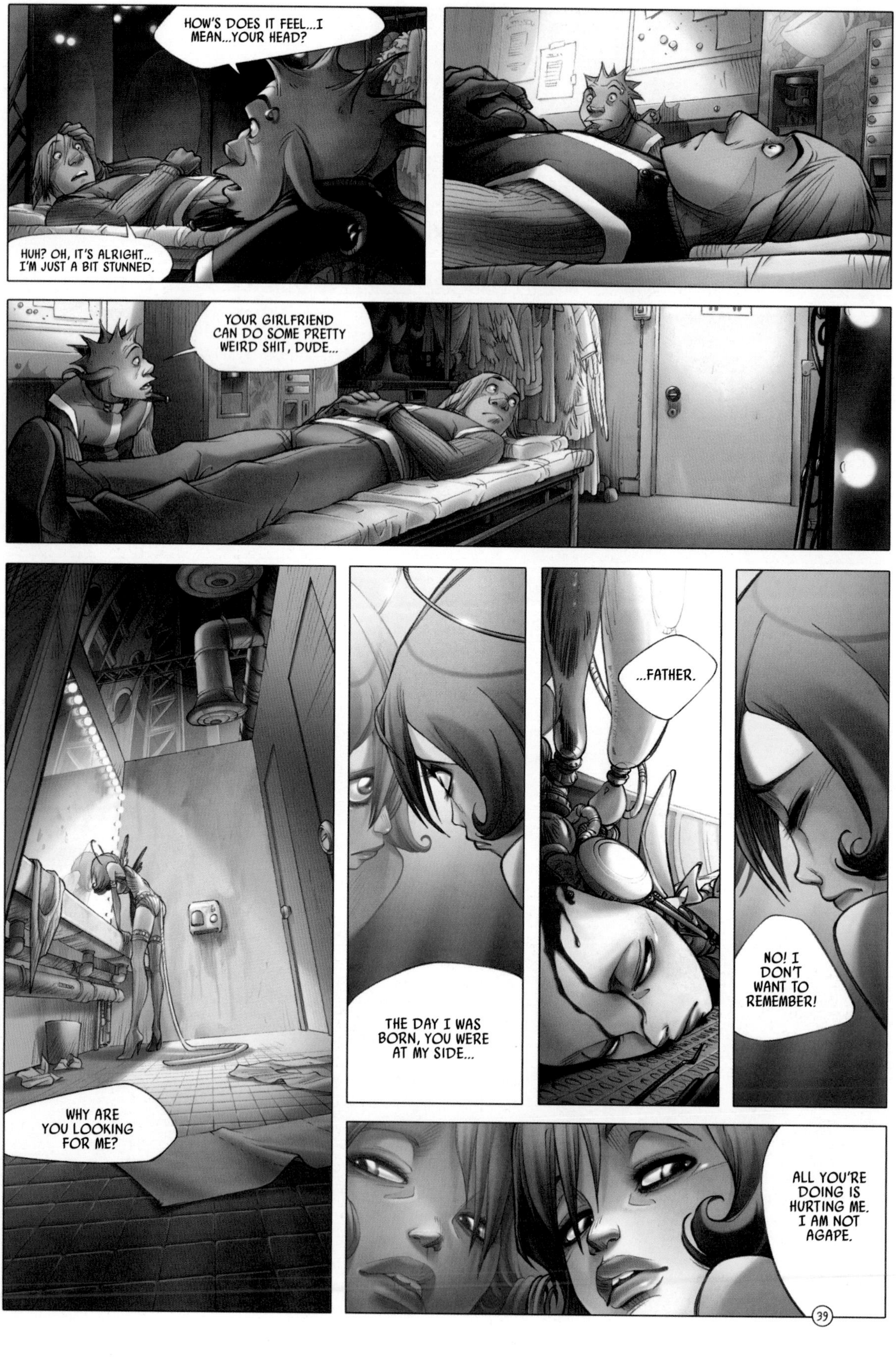
HOW'S DOES IT FEEL...I MEAN...YOUR HEAD?
HUH? OH, IT'S ALRIGHT... I'M JUST A BIT STUNNED.
YOUR GIRLFRIEND CAN DO SOME PRETTY WEIRD SHIT, DUDE...
WHY ARE YOU LOOKING FOR ME?
THE DAY I WAS BORN, YOU WERE AT MY SIDE...
...FATHER.
NO! I DON'T WANT TO REMEMBER!
ALL YOU'RE DOING IS HURTING ME. I AM NOT AGAPE.

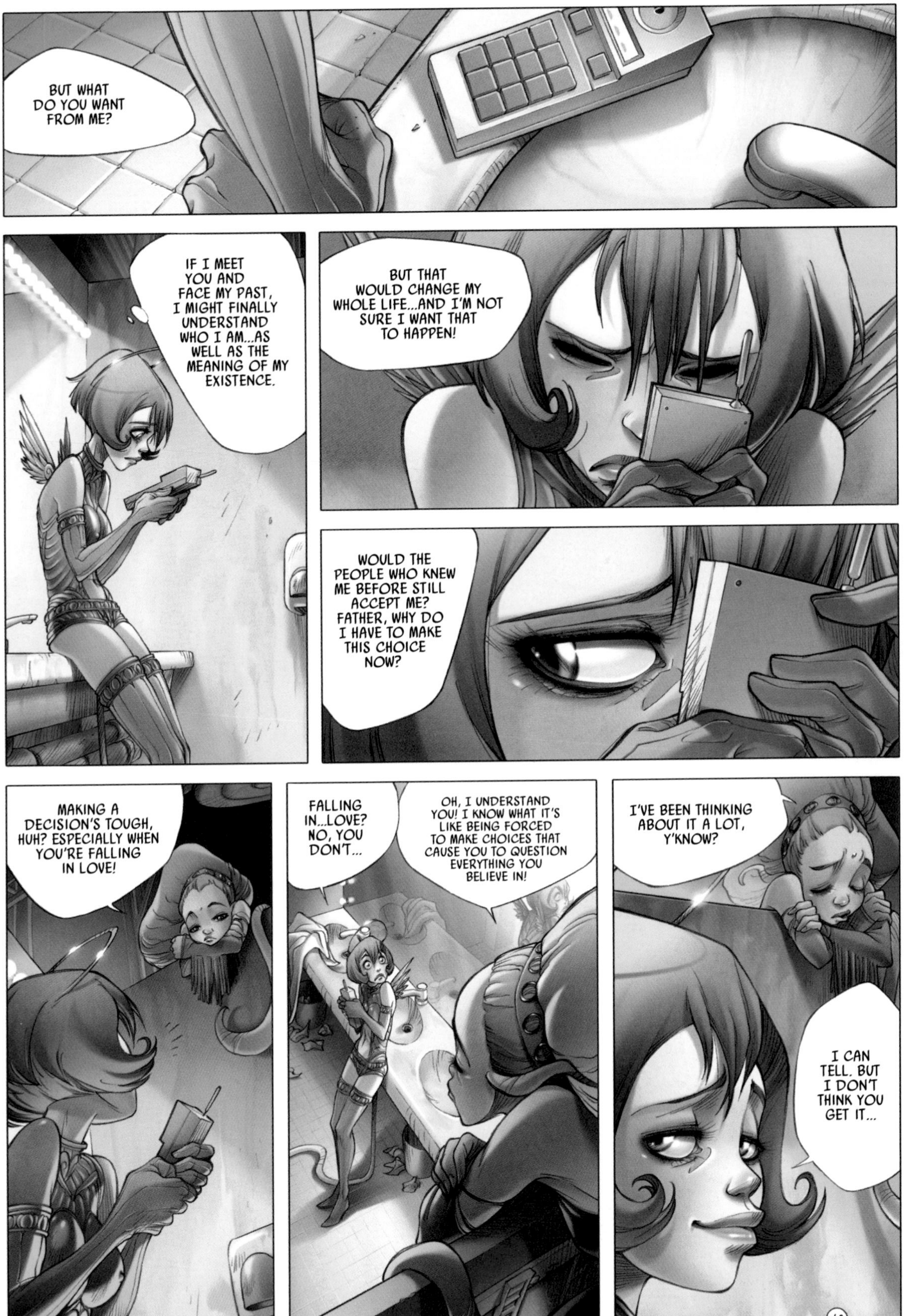
BUT WHAT DO YOU WANT FROM ME?
IF I MEET YOU AND FACE MY PAST, I MIGHT FINALLY UNDERSTAND WHO I AM...AS WELL AS THE MEANING OF MY EXISTENCE.
BUT THAT WOULD CHANGE MY WHOLE LIFE...AND I'M NOT SURE I WANT THAT TO HAPPEN!
WOULD THE PEOPLE WHO KNEW ME BEFORE STILL ACCEPT ME? FATHER, WHY DO I HAVE TO MAKE THIS CHOICE NOW?
MAKING A DECISION'S TOUGH, HUH? ESPECIALLY WHEN YOU'RE FALLING IN LOVE!
FALLING IN...LOVE? NO, YOU DON'T...
OH, I UNDERSTAND YOU! I KNOW WHAT IT'S LIKE BEING FORCED TO MAKE CHOICES THAT CAUSE YOU TO QUESTION EVERYTHING YOU BELIEVE IN!
I'VE BEEN THINKING ABOUT IT A LOT, Y'KNOW?
I CAN TELL. BUT I DON'T THINK YOU GET IT...

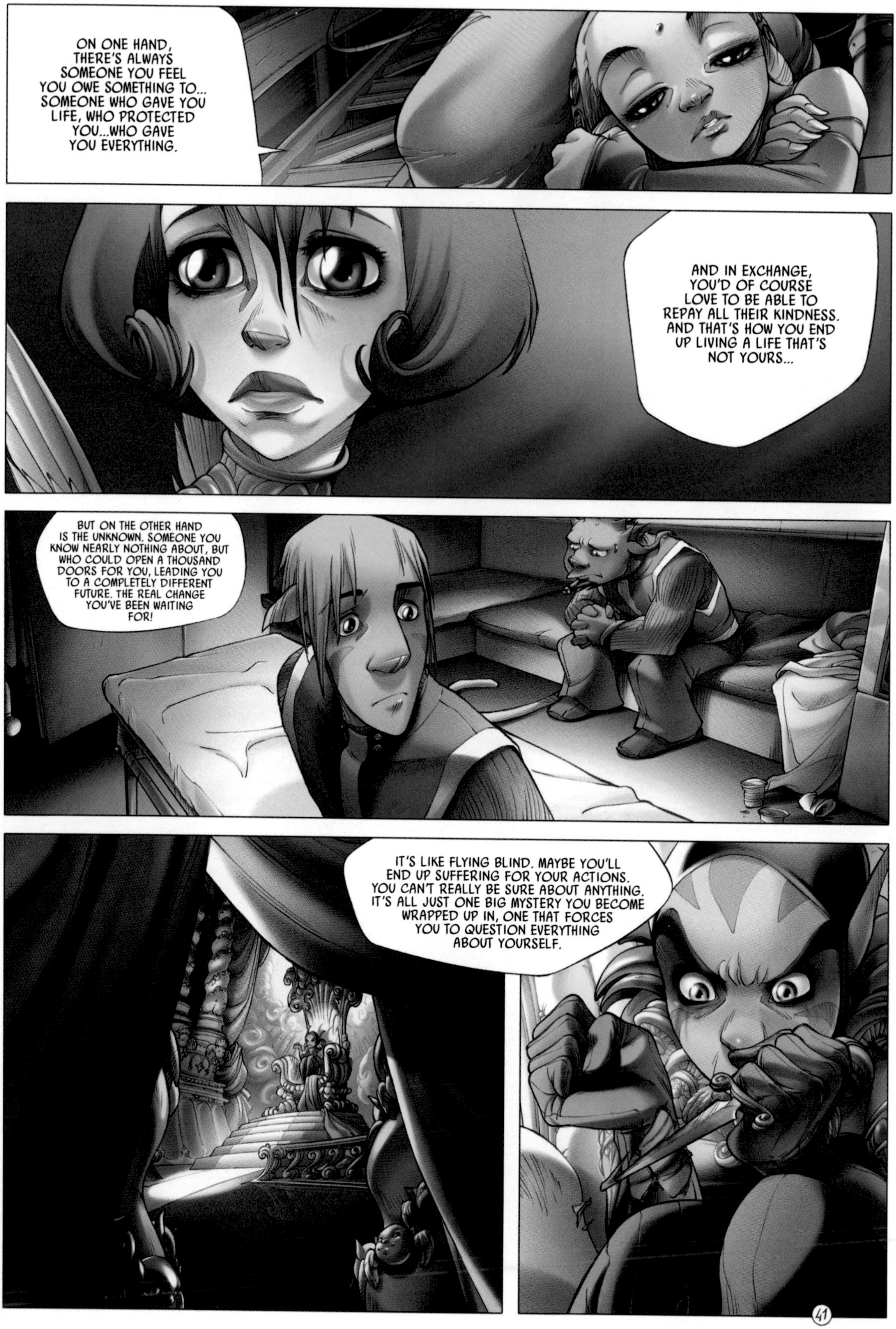
ON ONE HAND, THERE'S ALWAYS SOMEONE YOU FEEL YOU OWE SOMETHING TO... SOMEONE WHO GAVE YOU LIFE, WHO PROTECTED YOU...WHO GAVE YOU EVERYTHING.
AND IN EXCHANGE, YOU'D OF COURSE LOVE TO BE ABLE TO REPAY ALL THEIR KINDNESS. AND THAT'S HOW YOU END UP LIVING A LIFE THAT'S NOT YOURS...
BUT ON THE OTHER HAND IS THE UNKNOWN. SOMEONE YOU KNOW NEARLY NOTHING ABOUT, BUT WHO COULD OPEN A THOUSAND DOORS FOR YOU, LEADING YOU TO A COMPLETELY DIFFERENT FUTURE. THE REAL CHANGE YOU'VE BEEN WAITING FOR!
IT'S LIKE FLYING BLIND. MAYBE YOU'LL END UP SUFFERING FOR YOUR ACTIONS. YOU CAN'T REALLY BE SURE ABOUT ANYTHING. IT'S ALL JUST ONE BIG MYSTERY YOU BECOME WRAPPED UP IN, ONE THAT FORCES YOU TO QUESTION EVERYTHING ABOUT YOURSELF.

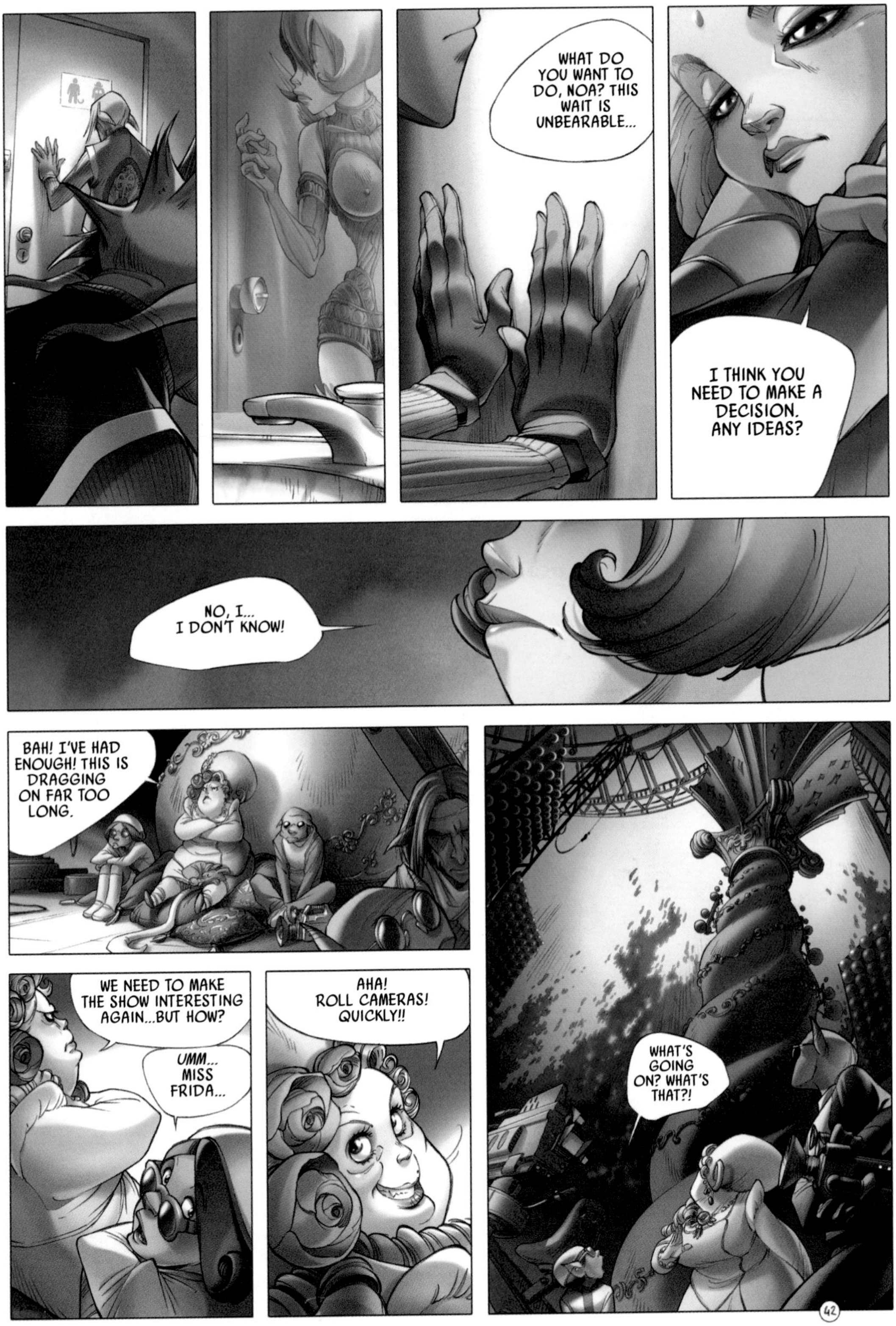
WHAT DO YOU WANT TO DO, NOA? THIS WAIT IS UNBEARABLE...
I THINK YOU NEED TO MAKE A DECISION. ANY IDEAS?
NO, I... I DON'T KNOW!
BAH! I'VE HAD ENOUGH! THIS IS DRAGGING ON FAR TOO LONG.
WE NEED TO MAKE THE SHOW INTERESTING AGAIN...BUT HOW?
UMM... MISS FRIDA...
AHA! ROLL CAMERAS! QUICKLY!!
WHAT'S GOING ON? WHAT'S THAT?!

NOA!

LISTEN TO US!

YOU MUST LEAVE!

IT'S TOO DANGEROUS.

LISTEN!

WE'VE WAITED LONG ENOUGH! THE GIRL MUST COME WITH US.

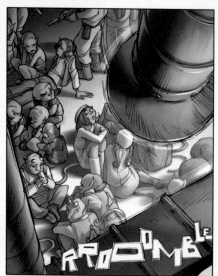

RROOMBLE

...AND IF I DON'T MOVE, WHAT'RE YOU GONNA DO ABOUT IT, HUH? YOU GONNA KILL ME AGAIN?

WE'RE COMING!

NOA!

TO TAKE YOU AWAY!

RRRROODLBR RRROOCORR R...

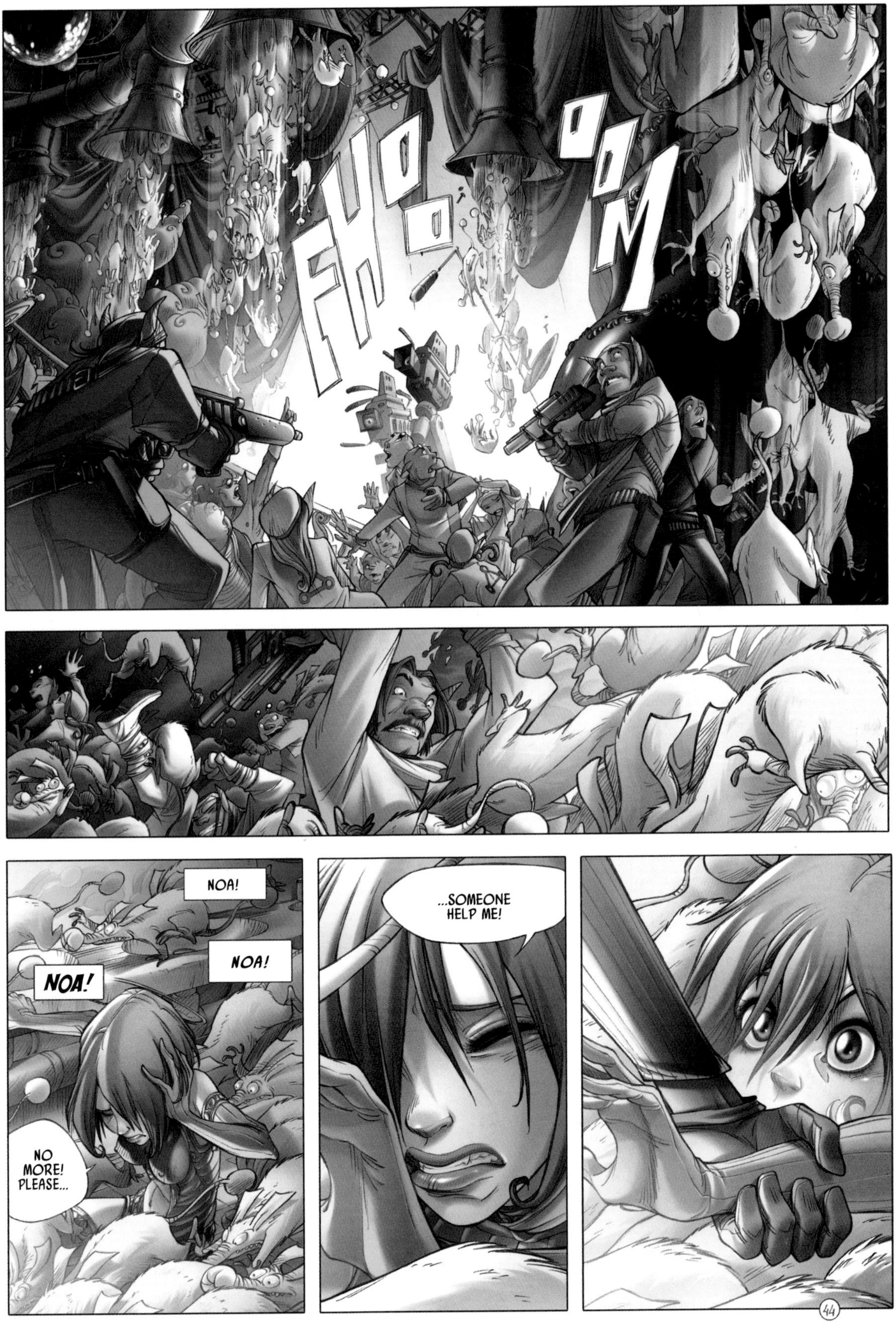
FHOOOOOM
NOA!
NOA!
NOA!
NO MORE! PLEASE...
...SOMEONE HELP ME!

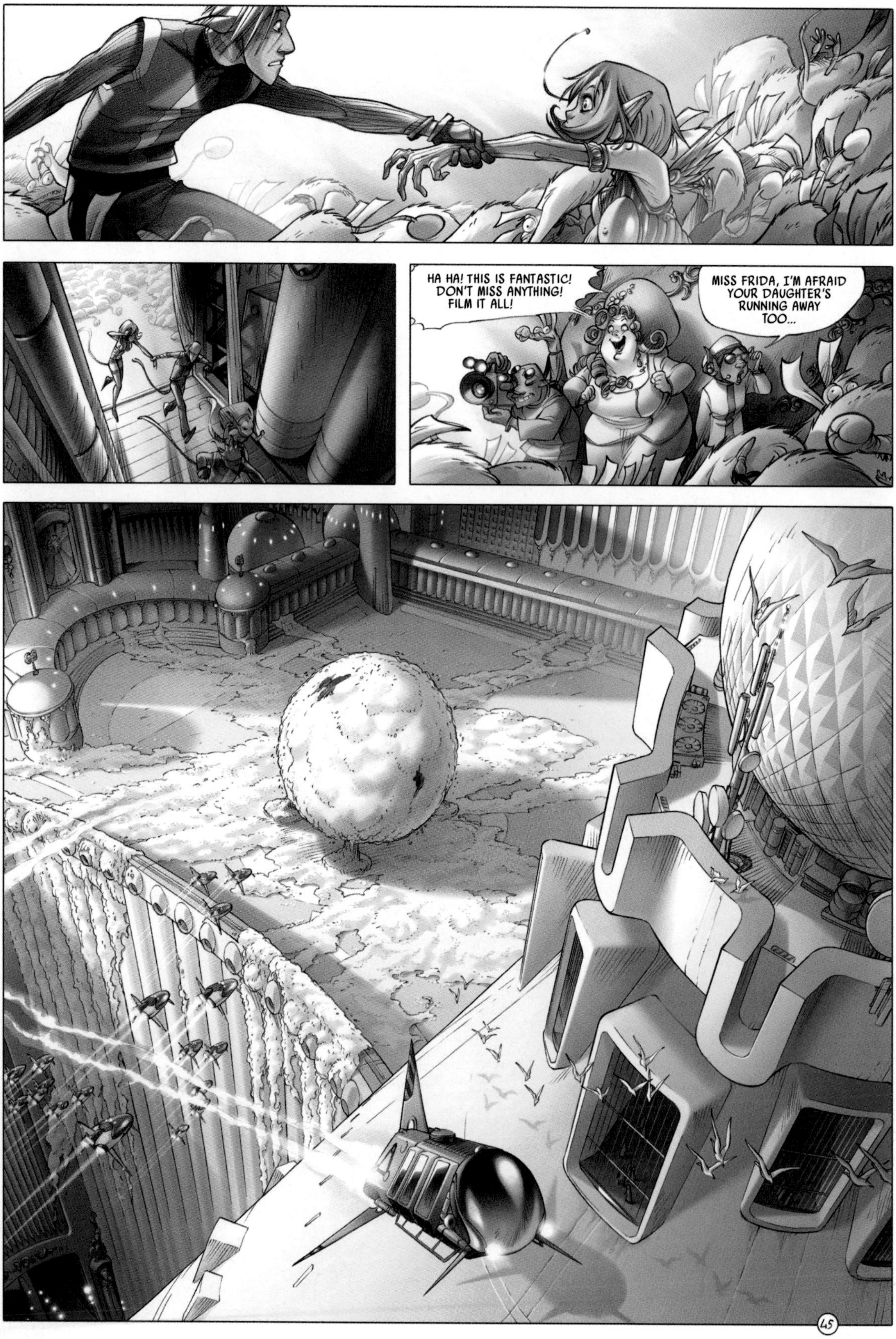
HA HA! THIS IS FANTASTIC! DON'T MISS ANYTHING! FILM IT ALL!
MISS FRIDA, I'M AFRAID YOUR DAUGHTER'S RUNNING AWAY TOO...

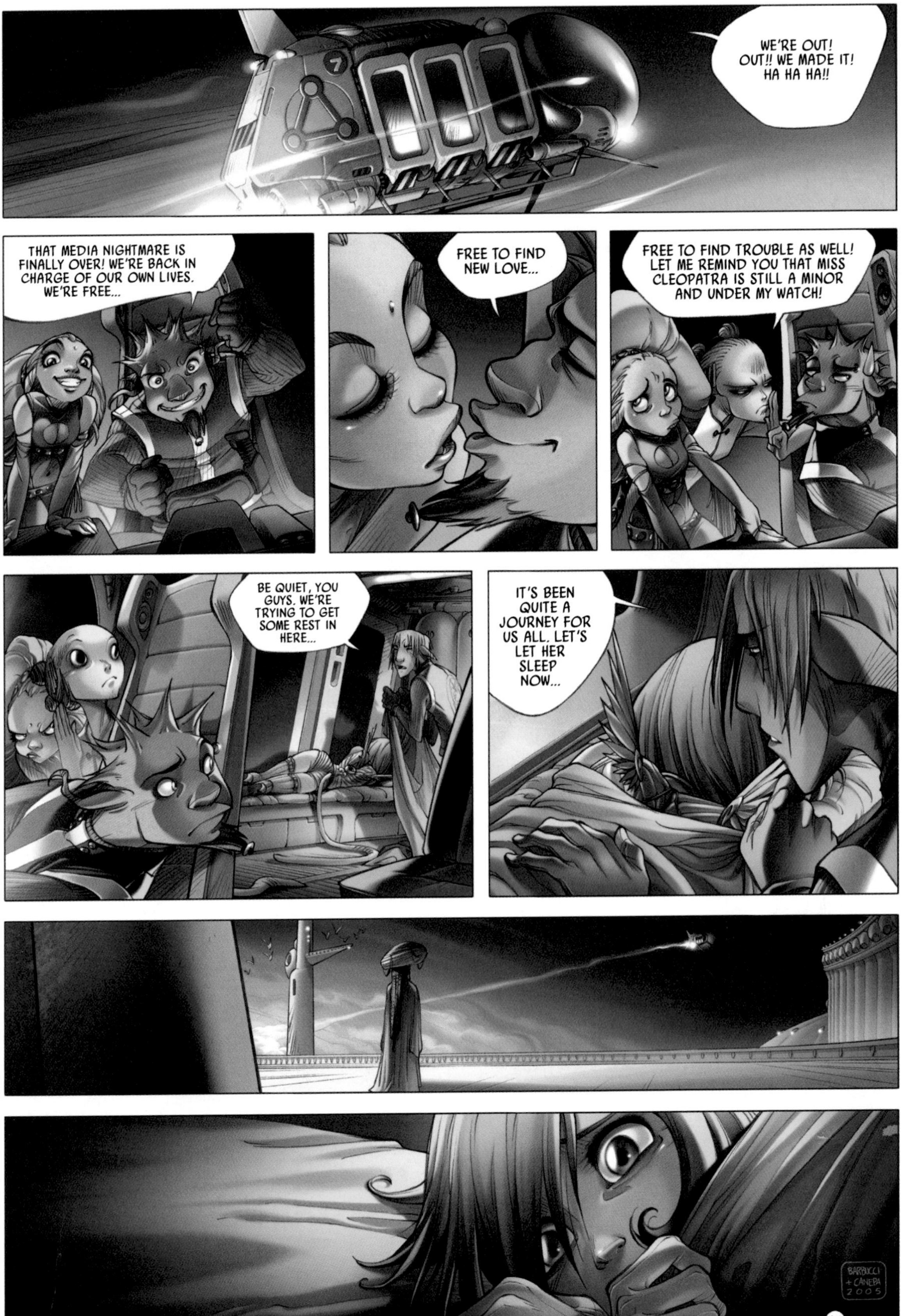
WE'RE OUT! OUT!! WE MADE IT! HA HA HA!!
THAT MEDIA NIGHTMARE IS FINALLY OVER! WE'RE BACK IN CHARGE OF OUR OWN LIVES. WE'RE FREE...
FREE TO FIND NEW LOVE...
FREE TO FIND TROUBLE AS WELL! LET ME REMIND YOU THAT MISS CLEOPATRA IS STILL A MINOR AND UNDER MY WATCH!
BE QUIET, YOU GUYS. WE'RE TRYING TO GET SOME REST IN HERE...
IT'S BEEN QUITE A JOURNEY FOR US ALL. LET'S LET HER SLEEP NOW...
BARBUCCI + CANEPA 2005

BARBARA CANEPA & ALESSANDRO BARBUCCI TALK SKY DOLL

dumb way out of life's distress for weak individuals, but also a personal search for truth. It's a true critique of our present day (and not just European) society with references to women's situation as a symbol and object—another problem of our daily life with the media. It is not by chance that our main character has the body of a model and large breasts, but also feels embarrassed by her physical richness. The story alternates from humorous and ironic to dramatic to some very realistic moments that fit the main theme of the book. We wanted to have a pop- and design-like feel to our work that comes straight from the '70s science fiction (like the famous *Barbarella*). The project was born many years ago as a comical series and stayed in our closet for many years, during which our characters "grew" and became more and more complex. That's how the story started tackling the more psychological and dramatic aspects of what is still a space opera.

Who are the main characters in the series?

AB+BC: There are many, and we are constantly adding more to the cast, but there are five main characters that fans should know. Noa, our heroine, is a Sky Doll—an android/doll created to satisfy her owner's every desire. As with every Doll, her mechanism runs out of 'battery' every 33 hours and the key needed to reload her is in the owner's custody. Since a Doll cannot recharge herself on her own, she always needs to belong to someone. But Noa is different. She dreams, she remembers (even her birth) and has extraordinary powers that are unimaginable!

The internationally acclaimed, award-winning bestseller **Sky Doll** makes its debut in English this May! The creative duo of Barbara Canepa and Alessandro Barbucci (the graphic creators of Disney's hit *W.I.T.C.H* and *Monster Allergies* series) share writing and art credits in presenting a gripping saga of one young android's quest to discover her own identity. We spoke with the famed creators to learn more about the series, debuting with **Sky Doll #1 (of 3)** in May 2008.

Let's start at the beginning. What's *Sky Doll* all about?

AB+BC: *Sky Doll* is a sci-fi saga that takes place on an imaginary world that shares a cultural environment similar to our Catholic and European society. The prime theme is the different forms religion can take: political means to manipulate the masses, a

Roy and Jahu are two young delegates of the diplomatic cabinet of Papess Lodovica. Roy is the 'good one,' the friendly and naive guy of the band. He finds Noa by chance, hidden on his spaceship, and he takes her as his protégé. Impossible to corrupt, he holds his principles high and is an idealist. He'll soon wake up from his slumber and will face reality thanks to Noa's arrival. Jahu is the more edgy and nervous of the pair. His past is stained by many dirty deeds that weigh on his conscience. He's looking for comfort and redemption through religion and is a fanatical, zealot-like believer. He'll also realize many things about himself and Lodovica's media power thanks to our heroine Noa. Papess Lodovica is the spirit guide of Planet Papathea, where our characters are born. Sister of Agape, second empowered Papess, she gained power on the Spiritual and Temporal Reigns thanks to her sister's mysterious death. Greedy and power-hungry, Lodovica lives to erase every trace of her sister and expand her religion throughout the universe, reaching out to the more distant planets. Agape, the Second Papess, represented the spiritual side of the Papathean religion. Since she died, her power grew thanks to the hidden Covens that want to overthrow the power of Lodovica. In all of this, one figure stands out: the Miraclemaker, the mind behind all the power plays of the whole planet. Agape was also renowned for her miraculous powers beyond her planet's galaxy.

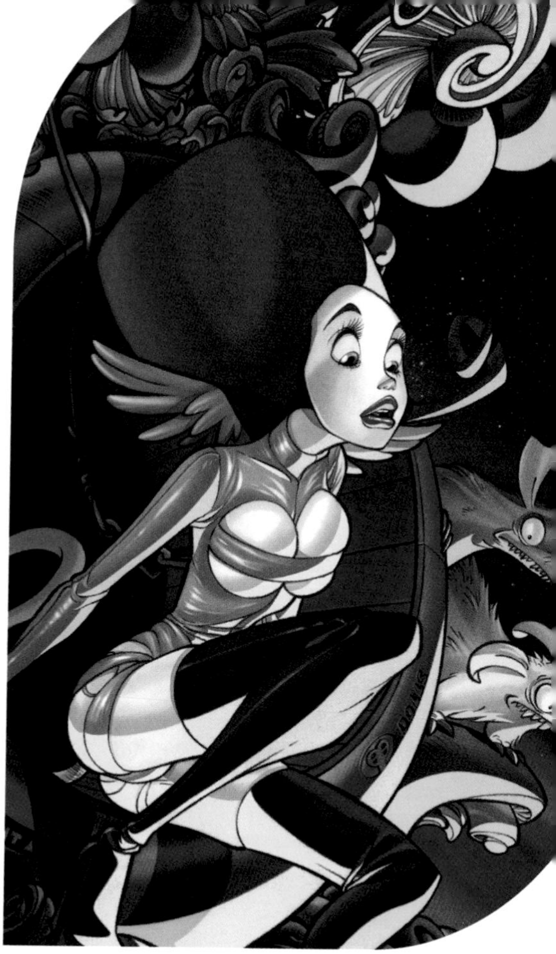

So, for those fans not familiar with Soleil and *Sky Doll,* what else would you like them to know about the series?

AB+BC: *Sky Doll* is the offspring of our long and varied professional—and personal even more so—mix of experiences. Readers around the world know us for a style that mixes manga, European and American comics in a natural way, with stories full of irony that always have depth. We think we are lucky to have the ability to communicate with people coming from very different cultural backgrounds. And we hope this can last for as long as possible!

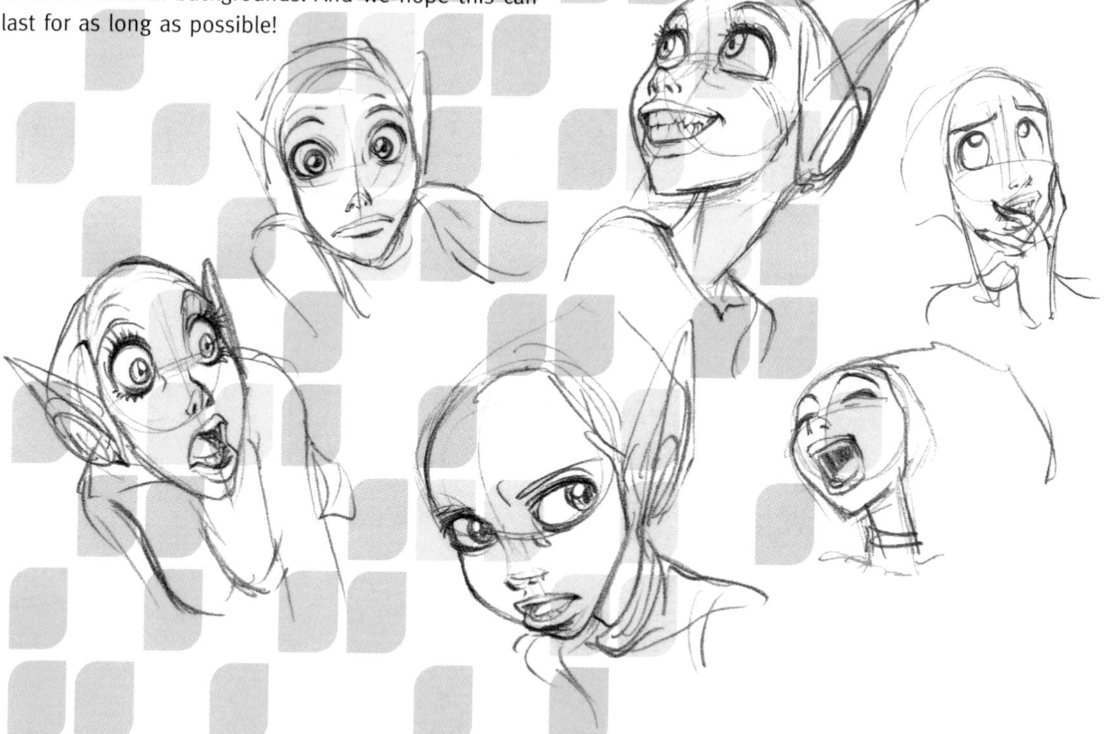